DOING BY LEARNING:

The Business Capstone Experience of a Real World, Work-based Project

Dr. Don Haggerty, M.A.T., M.B.A., Ed.D.
Calm Waters Press, South Burlington, Vermont

Calm Waters Press
203 Brand Farm Drive
South Burlington, VT 05403
www.mydoingbylearning.com

Published in the United States of America by Calm Waters Press

Haggerty, Donald
Doing by Learning: The Business Capstone Experience of a Real World, Work-based Project – 1ST edition

ISBN Print: 978-1-7357690-2-8

Book cover design by Jack Bigelow
Illustrations by Don Haggerty
Interior typesetting by The Illustrated Author Design Services

BRIEF CONTENTS

TABLE OF CONTENTS

You, the Business Graduate
- Congratulations on your Business Degree
- What You Learned
- The World of Business Competencies
- Summarizing the Competencies
- Using the Areas of Management Practice
- Now What?
- Passion
- Career Development

Why a Business Capstone?
- Capstones in all Disciplines
- More than a Course
- Capstone Models
- Capstone Timelines
- The Positive Change Project

Why a Project for a Capstone?
- Business Curriculum Pedagogy
- Business and Management Education Options

Integration is Job #1
- The Competency of all Competencies
- The Integration Process
- Where to Begin

Four Case Studies
- CASE 1 – Inventory Management Improvement
- CASE 2 – New Generation Target Market for Lending Institution
- CASE 3 – Employee Training and Development for less turnover and better customer service
- CASE 4 – Merging of multiple non-profits into one organization

Doing by Learning?
The World of Inquiry
- Roots of Reflective Inquiry
- Inquiry
- Questions, Questions, Questions!
- Powerful Questions
- Building Questions
- How to Frame Better Questions
- Sample Questions to Ponder
- Deepening Questions

Dialogue
- Dialogue
- Why Dialogue?
- Benefits of Dialogue
- Practicing Dialogue
- Dialogue Summary

Appreciative Inquiry (AI)
- AI's Positive Core
- AI's Positive Questions
- Flipping the Question
- AI Process

Action Research
- Action Research Overview

Action Learning
- Action Learning Revisited
- Stages of Action Learning
- Action Learning Teams

Design Thinking
- A Model for Innovation
- Design Thinking Process

Capstone Change Project Principles
Four Case Studies
- CASE 1 – Inventory Management
- CASE 2 – New Generation Target Market for Lending Institution
- CASE 3 – Employee Training and Development for less turnover and better customer service
- CASE 4 – Merging of multiple non-profits into one organization

Project Planning in Action Research

Four Case Studies
- CASE 1 – Inventory Management
- CASE 2 – New Generation Target Market for Lending Institution
- CASE 3 – Employee Training and Development for less turnover and better customer service
- CASE 4 – Merging of multiple non-profits into one organization

Get Ready to Network
- Learning is a social experience!
- Owning the Topic
- Building your language

Building your Network
- Building your Network
- Collaboration
- Network Resources
- The Courage to Ask

Four Case Studies
- Network Resources
- CASE 1 – Inventory Management
- CASE 2 – New Generation Target Market for Lending Institution
- CASE 3 – Employee Training and Development for less turnover and better customer service
- CASE 4 – Merging of multiple non-profits into one organization

Looking for a Change
- The Stage is Set
- The Beginning
- Change Drivers (PESTLE)
- Choosing a Project

Refining the Change
- Triangulate an Idea
- A Change Project's Value
- Identifying a Need
- Scale of Change
- Scope of Change
- "Gotta Do It" Projects
- Projects with Purpose
- Value Chain
- Top Three Areas of Management Practice
- Time to Write Something
- Focus

Four Case Studies
- CASE 1 – Inventory Management

- Products, Services, Marketing and Sales (Customers, Markets, Sales and Marketing)
- Processes Improved or Added (Measurement and Process Improvement)
- Information Systems
- Organizational Impact and Change Management
- Leadership Capabilities and Requirements
- Economic Business Case
- Project Implementation
- Economic Modeling
- Reflections on Learning

Four Case Studies
- Case #1 – Inventory Management System Upgrade
- Case #2 – New Target Market for Lending Institution
- Case #3 – Employee Training and Development to decrease employee turnover and increase customer satisfaction
- Case #4 – Merging of four non-profits into one organization to gain economies of scale

Outlining the Final Report
- A Skeleton Starting Point
- Project Example #1: A new product line extension
- Project Example #2: A major change in processes
- Project Example #3: A major restructuring

Before Beginning Research
- Why Research?
- Build on Strengths and Principles
- Build a Plan
- Research Anxiety
- Practitioner-Researcher Role
- Action Research Overview
- Ethical Considerations

The World of Research for Business and Management
- "Business Research"
- "Management Research"
- Focus, Focus, Focus
- Putting Positivity into your Change Project
- Positive Questions
- Four Huge Sources of Research Data

Finding Data and Information
- Useful Data Sources
- Internal Data - Primary and Secondary
- Student Conducted Primary #1: Interviews and Group Interviews
- Student Conducted Primary #2: Surveys
- Student Conducted Primary #3: Direct Observation
- Secondary Research and Literature Review

Four Case Studies
- CASE 1 – Inventory Management
- CASE 2 – New Generation Target Market for Lending Institution
- CASE 3 – Employee Training and Development for less turnover and better customer service
- CASE 4 – Merging of multiple non-profits into one organization

- Your Research Process
- Field Notebook and Reflective Learning
- Organize Areas of Management Practice
- Strengths-Based and Appreciative Inquiry
- Scheduling
- Metrics of Change
- Document and Quantify
- Hard Data and Strategic (Soft) Data
- The Organizational Landscape
- Shifting Sands of Research
- Stakeholder Landscape
- Ethical Landscape
- Your Social-Emotional-Leadership Landscape
- Ongoing Data Collection and Analysis
- Visual Data Analysis
- Building the Narrative

Four Case Studies
- CASE 1 – Inventory Management
- CASE 2 – New Generation Target Market for Lending Institution
- CASE 3 – Employee Training and Development for less turnover and better customer service
- CASE 4 – Merging of multiple non-profits into one organization

- Creating Value
- Goal = Economic Value
- Mapping the Change

Current State Benefits and Costs
- Activities and Costs
- Guesstimates in Current Activities and Costs
- Financial Model of Current Situation
- Typical Capstone Project Activities, Benefits and Costs

Future State Benefits and Costs
- Measuring Change in Activities
- Errors of Omission vs. Commission
- Defining the Investment
- Budget and Multi-Year Models

- Investment Analysis
- Moving Numbers and Shaky Ground

Four Case Studies
- CASE 1 – Inventory Management
- CASE 2 – New Generation Target Market for Lending Institution
- CASE 3 – Employee Training and Development for less turnover and better customer service
- CASE 4 – Merging of multiple non-profits into one organization

Pre-Work
Phase 1 – Mentor Review Draft Report
- Establish Format
- Identify Changes
- Modifying your Outline
- Elevator Pitch
- Write "Proposed Opportunity" section
- Write "Research Completed" section
- Write Executive Summary (first half+/-)
- Write Primary Sections
- Begin ALL Sections
- Write Recommendations
- Complete Economic Model (Worksheet)
- Write Economic Value Section (Report Section)
- Schedule your Mentor Review and/or Input

Phase 2 – Serious Draft
- Integration's Last Word
- Tables, Charts, Appendices – What, Where and When?
- Write, Write, Write
- Take Time Off and Share

Phase 3 – Final Draft(s)
Presentation

Reflective Practice
- What are the Skills of Reflective Practice?
- Application of Reflective Practice

Your Toolbox for Reflective Practice
- Workplace Learning
- Dialogue
- Experiential Learning
- Action Learning
- Appreciative Inquiry
- Design Thinking

- Reflective Learning
- Nine Dimensions of Reflective Practice

Capstone Topics of Reflection

ACKNOWLEDGEMENTS

No book is a solo effort, and this one has certainly not been an exception. Much of the primary content was written while I was able to be on sabbatical for which I am indebted to Champlain College. I am also grateful for its support of my work in experiential learning of which writing this book is a milestone in my higher education career. My greatest indebtedness, however, goes to my wife, Susan, whose patience with my endless time at the keyboard and willingness to review and edit my work is truly boundless. Her knowledge of experiential learning and field-based curriculum from her own professional experience in working with Social Work college students always provides a perspective that has been invaluable.

While, like many authors, I do not have a team of graduate teaching assistants or co-writers, I was blessed with the input of my late sister-in-law, Sara Medina, whose professional writing and editing career was instrumental in adjusting my somewhat informal and anecdotal writing style to be more readable and logical! Her professional writing perspective was enhanced by my daughter, Sara Wilkins, whose commitment to experiential and self-directed learning is unparalleled and who was able to provide her insights and edits based on her own work as both a professional educator and her own MBA.

I certainly would not have ever begun to undertake this endeavor without the ongoing support of both students and faculty, too numerous to mention, who have supported my efforts in bringing work-based and experiential learning into the classrooms, whether they were face-to-face, online, undergraduate or at the graduate level. Special thanks, of course, goes to one former student, Jack Bigelow, who provided the cover design.

INTRODUCTION

Welcome to *The Business Capstone Experience*! As the *Doing by Learning* title suggests, a capstone in the field of Business provides the greatest amount of learning when it is truly a "field based" experience consisting of an actual project in a living, breathing organization. Because of that, the perspective of this book may be surprising to you because so much of it is about how to manage the ***total learning experience*** as a gateway to your success in the capstone project itself.

The book is based on my decades of full-time professional work experiences prior to entering higher education full time, followed by twenty years of full time teaching and administration in both face-to-face and online course and program development for both undergraduate and graduate student populations. This work is also deeply grounded in my own research in the areas of work-based and experiential learning. On the above foundation and in order to write this book, I reflected on and formally analyzed over five hundred case studies of both undergraduate (Business) and graduate (MBA) capstone projects that I have personally facilitated and mentored over the past decade. Since the book's initial draft I have had the opportunity to test its contents with several hundred undergraduate and graduate Business Capstone students and used their feedback as input to this "final" first edition.

In this research of primarily MBA capstone projects, student reflections and correspondence, I took a "strengths-based" approach to understanding *how the most successful students excelled in their work and thrived* in completing projects that, to them, were transformational. As you are probably aware from conversations with fellow students, the capstone requirement can all too easily be characterized by uncertainties and unforeseen challenges. In addition to reviewing student work projects through the strengths-based lens, I supplemented my analysis with approximately fifty interviews conducted with many of my most successful former capstone students to further explore and probe what, in their minds, drove their outstanding success. Secondary research was also rounded out with interviews of multiple faculty serving as program directors of graduate programs using a similar experientially-based capstone as the final curriculum requirement.

The intended audience of this book is both students and faculty who are faced with the task of doing, or assigning and facilitating a "work-based" or "client-based" capstone project as a final requirement in a typical curriculum in Business, Management and Leadership. This applies, of course, to the many sub-disciplines found within schools of Business such as Marketing, Finance, Entrepreneurship, Organizational Development, and others.

Because all Business related disciplines are typically taught within a more general Business curriculum, it is important, then, that your work demonstrate the relationship of your capstone project, however specific to your sub-discipline it may be, to multiple areas of Business. This "integration" of your total Business curriculum is a key driver in this book's recommended process. A Marketing project in developing a Digital Marketing plan, for example, will probably need to address multiple organizational impacts through Finance, Organizational

Development, Information Systems and Data Analytics, as a starting point.

The underlying learning process in applying all that students have learned is called *Integrated Reflective Practice* in which the three components that make up the learning model include:

- *The Capstone Project* itself (Action Research based)
- *Reflective Practice* (ongoing reflection about learning and personal transformation)
- *Areas of Management Practice* (Business course content and other learning experiences)

This book and learning process expands on the **Areas of Management Practice** component by aggregating virtually all courses found in any Business curriculum into ten areas of study, explained in detail in Chapter One and listed here:

1. *Alignment of Mission, Values and Strategy*
2. *Products, Services, Marketing and Sales*
3. *Processes Improved or Added*
4. *Information Systems*
5. *Organizational Impact and Change Management*
6. *Leadership Capabilities and Requirements*
7. *Economic Business Case*
8. *Project Implementation*
9. *Economic Modeling*
10. *Reflections on Learning*

In some ways, this book is highly prescriptive and is based on a very deliberate process that was developed in response to the need for a highly efficient method for students to identify, research, and develop a robust project in as little as eight weeks. Unlike the typical fifteen-week semester, such short terms, now typical in many online MBA and Management programs, do not leave much "slack" in the project timelines.

While the use of the various tools and models in this book may vary depending on the instructor's and curriculum requirements, the core tool done by my MBA students in their first week of class can be found in Chapter 10 – *Mapping a Change to Areas of Management Practice*. The process outlined of identifying a project and immediately reflecting on the relevance of your entire curriculum and all you have learned over several years compiled neatly into a matrix is the secret weapon of this book. Doing this early in the project provides guidance and keeps your project on track at a time when efficiency and avoiding getting sidetracked are keys to your success. This process provides the rationale for the book's title, *Doing by Learning* because even engaging in an Action Research project (*Doing*) really begins with a deliberate and reflective process (*Learning*) to set the stage for inquiry.

You might be asking yourself why this "matrix" activity suggested for early in the project is deferred until so late in the book. There are three reasons. First, because the capstone is such a major *experiential* project and deviates so strongly from much of the structure of other courses, the groundwork in the concepts and skills of experiential or "work-based" learning makes up many of the earlier chapters. This material, therefore, is provided under the assumption that most business students have not encountered this material in their course of study. Second, for those topics that students may have actually experienced in studying Business and that are instrumental to such a project are summarized and reiterated within the context of the Business Capstone to bring to light their relevance and usefulness in your project. Third, and perhaps as important as any, is the difficulty of having such a short timeline to complete a major project. Many of the early chapters may be best used before the actual beginning of your "course" and project start time. In a nutshell, you can greatly improve the quality of your capstone experience by simply starting early. This is really the bottom line to Chapter 5 – Project Planning that provides timelines for just how early you might begin to get yourself grounded in the industry and the nature of this learning experience.

This book strives to be inclusive. Topics such as Design Thinking, Experiential Learning, Action Learning or others may have been highlighted briefly in a course but only now need to be dusted off and brought front and center into your work processes. In many cases you may want to review such topics briefly but others, such as Appreciative Inquiry or Collective Leadership, may provide only a jumping off point to a perspective that may become a foundation of your whole study. While I recognize that there are an extraordinary number of models, processes and conceptual frameworks being presented I can honestly say that they are all either important for context and background, for formulating your learning processes or managing such a large project that is so open-ended compared to virtually all of your previous classes.

You should also be sensitive to my methodology of spreading out a topic among multiple chapters, as appropriate. The rationale is simple enough. First, the level of detail on such topics in any chapter matches your stage of project completion at that point. Second, reiterating a topic when it is relevant again is consistent with the cyclical nature of your learning process as you inquire, reflect, return to previous conclusions and topics and create new learning. A topic being explained in multiple locations is not a typo!

In writing such a book one of the first decisions is, of course, what the fundamental organizing structure would be and how it relates to both the key research findings while addressing the need for accessibility by you, the reader. Obviously, the chapter titles and topics convey my final decisions! That said, it is important to highlight now, before drilling into the details, the highlights, or meta-learnings about excellence in Business capstone projects. When all of my analysis was completed and before actually writing the individual chapters, I stepped back and went up 30,000 feet or so to look at the big picture. The principles below play out in multiple chapters and various ways but each one is, itself, an onion with multiple layers waiting to be peeled as you read, inquire, engage in your action research, test various hypotheses and reflect on your learning.

Capstone Change Project Principles

1. *Question and listen carefully.*
2. *Look for strengths and know that your questions ARE the beginning of change.*
3. *Be prepared to pivot and modify your research approach and to need additional data.*
4. *Engage others in a process of iterative change.*
5. *Be the leader of learning and positive change.*

Chapter Structure

As mentioned above, the first potential major work product (potentially an assignment) associated with your project (creating a project matrix) isn't presented until two thirds of the way through the book. This is intentional and reflects the paradox of such a large and experientially-based project. While it is extremely important to follow a very deliberate and structured process, it is also important to consider simultaneously all aspects of this project as described in the first nine chapters. Depending on how much time your situation allows, it is highly recommended that you take a very mindful approach to those nine chapters. I believe that you will benefit from beginning them early and reading them reflectively with the goal of identifying those specific models and concepts that will best support your own learning *before* jumping into your first actual class assignments.

Each chapter includes three components:

1. **Content** in the form of materials, concepts, frameworks and models designed to support both your process of developing your project and the reflective learning that comes from both the project itself, as well as your experience in doing it.
2. **Doing by Learning Activities** that can be used as self-checks and opportunities to apply the chapter's materials through active learning. These activities include a wide range of learning opportunities that may be used as informal self-assessments or as the basis for major assignments or class discussions.
3. **Four Case Studies** have been compiled from actual students' Business Capstone projects and presented over the course of the book at the end of each chapter with its presentation linked to that particular chapter and the Areas of Management Practice model.

   - **CASE 1 – Inventory Management Improvement** – This case study was chosen as an example of a business process improvement because such a change is applicable to the MBA Capstone goal of creating value in virtually any organization including a for-profit, non-profit, NGO or any level of government.
   - **CASE 2 – New Generation Target Market for Lending Institution** –This case study, in the area of banking and credit unions demonstrates the process of choosing a new target market and customer value proposition in order to grow the business of lending.
   - **CASE 3 – Employee Training and Development for less turnover and better customer service** – The area of improvement to some aspect of Human Resource Management is a frequent topic, especially when working in a governmental agency or any organization where "profit" can be difficult to define. Value, here, can be defined as better, happier and more engaged employees, all of which can be directly linked to lower employee turnover and even better customer relations.
   - **CASE 4 - Merging of multiple non-profits into one organization** – While this case study is about the merger of two complimentary non-profit organizations, the lessons and analysis would be highly appropriate for virtually any merger, acquisition, or new business growing within the context of an existing organization.

Chapter Overviews

While the general order of the book leads you through the total learning experience of completing the Business Capstone and includes many topics, such as the Mindset for Leadership or creating Visions of Success, they can certainly be taken in whatever order makes sense to you. The titles of these chapters reflect the key elements of success in researching, writing and presenting a Business capstone. As a tool to facilitate your self-directed learning journey, each chapter is summarized below.

Chapter 1 – You and a Business Capstone

This chapter sets the stage for your capstone experience by providing some context. It also launches you into the process of seeing just how much you have learned in your Business education and how that compares to the competencies used nationwide. Finally, you will see how what you have learned matches a comprehensive framework called "Areas of Management Practice" that helps you begin the critical process of integrating your education with your capstone project.

Chapter 2 – Learning Through and Building on Experience

If your capstone consists of a project done in the real world, then get ready for some serious learning. The challenge is that learning through project-based "field" work is very different from almost any of your previous learning experiences, including internships. This chapter provides you with a perspective on learning that makes you better prepared for what you are about to encounter in learning experientially.

Chapter 3 – A Mindset to Lead Learning

Virtually any project you choose, by definition, involves some type of change to the organization. What you may not be prepared for is the fact that your proposed change may begin as soon as you initiate your inquiry and share your thinking. You are really in two roles, that of a researcher and that of a facilitator of learning. Being comfortable with and assuming a learning mindset prepares you for your role as a thought leader who is leading a learning process.

Chapter 4 – Inquiry and Doing by Learning

Because much of your project is likely to be grounded in the processes of Action Research, using inquiry to design good questions is your bread and butter for learning. Taking a strengths-based perspective and using Appreciative Inquiry further refines the nature of your questions. This and other methods of inquiry that provide the backbone of your research process are included in this chapter.

Chapter 5 – Project Planning

The timelines of your academic term and the workplace are seldom completely aligned. Completing a self-directed, work-based project in a semester that may be as long as fifteen or as short as eight weeks is a challenge. It is complicated by the need to constantly pivot as you inquire, learn, refine your thinking and repeat the cycle – a cycle that can be less than linear! This chapter helps you to establish the big milestones and prioritize your precious time to reach the finish line with as little stress as possible.

Chapter 6 – Create a Vision of Success

Every organization of any repute has a mission statement, a vision of success and a plan for how to move forward. So, too, must you and your project! Your vision for a capstone has two distinct parts. The first is the personal vision that fuels your personal and professional development. The second, and distinct from the first, is the vison for a successful project. Both visions are examined in this chapter.

Chapter 7 – Building Your Collaborative Network

Even if your capstone project is an individual one (not team-based), you need to involve others in your project. While it might be ideal, your "Collaborative Network" doesn't need to be composed of experts in your project's area of inquiry. Others with any experience that may help to inform your topic can be included. Perhaps as important as expertise is *engagement* so find others who can give you time, feedback and, if nothing more than moral support, can help you through what will inevitably include challenging and perplexing times. The key point of this chapter is to build a network and, like swimming, never go alone!

Chapter 8 – The Positive Change Project

Choosing a project of the correct scale and scope is clearly important to your success. This chapter provides some things to consider as you engage with others to identify a need or a topic for your work. The chapter also sets the framework for choosing a project tropic that is "positive" and is directed toward opportunity in the future rather than more retrospective problem solving, alone. It also helps you to take a critical first step in linking your project to its key Areas of Management Practice, introduced in Chapter One, and put you on the road to fully integrating your Business education into the capstone project.

Chapter 9 – Leading Positive Change

This is a follow-up to Chapter 3, "Mindset to Lead Learning." At some point in your project you may cross the line from learning to managing a change. If your project has any chance of going forward, then you really need to be ready to "step up to the plate" and take a more assertive role in leading change. This chapter reviews some of the most usable leadership models and frameworks of leadership to support you in doing that.

Chapter 10 – Mapping a Change to Areas of Management Practice

This may be one of the most useful chapters in the book. Picking up on the *Areas of Management Practice* introduced in Chapter 1 and applied in Chapter 8, this chapter finishes the job. Here, you will map your learning to every aspect of your project and lay out a road map for your research and final work products. Despite being Chapter 10 in the book, the process is typically done as early as possible in the semester. This suggests that, as seen in Chapter 5, Project Planning, that many activities in earlier chapters are best accomplished before the start of your semester.

Chapter 11 -- Research for Positive Change

Work-based projects are typically not done in the same manner as experimental research. This chapter provides you with both the context and specific direction needed to be successful in a work-based project. This chapter links nicely to Chapter 4 on Inquiry when thinking about designing your Action Research and Appreciative Inquiry processes.

Chapter 12 – Ongoing Data Collection and Analysis

Once you have designed and launched your research processes (Chapter 11), you will quickly find yourself immersed in the project's "data" coming at you from all angles! This chapter is designed to help you in making sense of it all and managing your project without becoming overwhelmed, the goal being to constantly pull you forward in making progress towards the finish line at a time in the project when progress may be the least obvious to you.

Chapter 13 – Economic and Strategic Value

The topic of defining, measuring and, to the extent appropriate, monetizing the value of your proposed change is one of the most important parts of any Business Capstone. This chapter walks you through the process of designing metrics of success and translating those into your project's economic value.

Chapter 14 -- Creating a Report

Writing a report is both the beginning and end of your capstone experience. It is the beginning to your experience because it is always "top of mind" when you know that a capstone requirement is in your future. It is the end because, as you may see by now, so much of the work is done long before any final report gets written. This chapter provides a general sequence for tackling such a large writing endeavor that reduces, or hopefully avoids, any of that hand wringing, anxiety producing, wheel spinning unproductive time!

Chapter 15 – Reflect on Your Experience

Reflection during, and following, your experience is a skill in itself and can be challenging to initiate. This chapter lays out some guidelines to help you jump-start your reflections and to enhance your learning.

Best wishes in moving forward on what, I hope, will be the most transformational experience of your soon-to-be-completed degree in Business!

LIST OF *DOING BY LEARNING* ACTIVITIES

LIST OF FIGURES

LIST OF TABLES

LIST OF CASE STUDIES

Each of the four case studies (described in the Introduction) is distributed and included at the end of each chapter in order that each portion of their story match the content in any particular chapter. If reading all parts of a single case study is desirable, then the page numbers below can be used to identify all consecutive portions of each case study.

LIST OF CASE STUDIES (CONT'D)

CHAPTER 1
YOU AND A BUSINESS CAPSTONE

You, the Business Graduate

Congratulations on your Business Degree

So, you are almost there! If you are reading this book, then the odds are that you are no more than one semester or so from completing your undergraduate or graduate degree in Business, Management, Leadership or another discipline such as Healthcare Management or Social Work. In any of these disciplines and many others you will be called on to take responsibility for leadership, even if in an "entry level" position to launch your career. Whether you are taking responsibility for a project, changing to a new process or overseeing as little as one employee, you will be called on to use all of your skills that you have developed in your studies over the past few years. While this book uses the competencies that are typically found in programs associated with Business and Management, the process is highly applicable to any work-based project or learning experience, whether you are an employee, intern, or simply doing a project in an organization to fulfill your capstone requirements.

What You Learned

If you are like most students, your life has been extremely full while pursuing your degree. Most of the time just getting the reading and assignments completed on time and to your level of satisfaction is a full plate. Because "courses" still represent the primary structure for most schools, it does encourage a mindset, unfortunately, of short-term thinking and doing "what's next" to complete the course requirements. Many students describe this as being on a treadmill, without ever having the time to really reflect on or appreciate what they are learning. Finding time to expand your learning about a particular topic of interest is just a dream needing to be deferred until after graduation. That said, students regularly report that the capstone fulfills that dream because, for the first time in years, there is no "new" course material and the objective is to look back and apply what you have learned in some way.

So, what was it that you learned? While program structures may vary in specific majors under the umbrella of "Business," it can be safely said that there is more consistency than you think. In my own studies of Business and Management programs, I derived my own "model" that I call *Areas of Management Practice* for business, management and leadership. These ten buckets are broad and encompassing enough that they can be defined to fit virtually any organizational context and, therefore, have the ability to serve as an outline or filter to reviewing any business or management program. They are:

1. *Alignment of Mission, Values and Strategy*
2. *Products, Services, Marketing and Sales*
3. *Processes Improved or Added*
4. *Information Systems*
5. *Organizational Impact and Change Management*
6. *Leadership Capabilities and Requirements*
7. *Economic Business Case (rationale)*
8. *Project Implementation*
9. *Economic Modeling (quantitative model)*
10. *Reflections on Learning*

If you think back to your own program, using your transcript or a list of courses taken, you will probably find that each course fits into one or more of the above areas. You will probably also see that all of these Areas of Management Practice were addressed in your program. Go ahead and try it!

The World of Business Competencies

It is no accident, really, that your courses fit so neatly into my model. The world of undergraduate and graduate business education works hard to ensure a reasonable level of consistency in the learning outcomes that you have presumably mastered. Whether your courses were very traditional (quizzes, tests, big paper) or highly experiential (simulations, work-based projects) the *competencies* are generally very comparable. The difference is in how you get to those competencies.

So, where do these business competencies come from? In the U.S., and for many other nations' Business programs, the suggested competencies can be found in one of several accrediting agencies. Two widely used accrediting bodies are the AACSB (Association to Advance Collegiate Schools of Business) and the ACBSP (Accreditation Council for Business Schools and Programs). Both are recognized worldwide for their work to ensure that business degrees are meeting standards of rigor, professionalism and quality.

The competencies from both the AACSB and ACBSP are compared to the *Areas of Management Practice* model in the table below. Listed in the far-right column are some typical Business and Management courses that are found in many Business programs. While comparisons like this are never based on a perfect match for every competency, this does help you to see the range of skills that you have acquired, which of your courses are likely to have contributed, and how they fit into the overall picture of Business and Management education. Where do each of your courses fit into the right-hand column?

Table 1: Business Areas of Management Practice and Curriculum

Areas of Management Practice	AACSB Skills and Knowledge Areas (1)	ACBSP Common Professional Components (2)	Typical Courses in a Business Curriculum
Alignment with Mission/ Strategy	Ethics, Political, Legal and Regulatory, Social Responsibility, Social Context	Global Dimensions of Business, Business Policies	Business Strategy/Policy, Entrepreneurship
Products, Services, Marketing and Sales	Markets, Marketing and Distribution	Marketing	Marketing Consumer Behavior Digital Marketing Advertising Marketing Research
Processes Improved or Added	Systems and Processes, Production and Operations	Production and Operations Management, Quantitative Techniques, Statistics	Operations Management, Quantitative Analysis
Information Systems	Technological, Data Analytics, Data Management, Information Technology	Information Systems	Management Information Systems, Information Technology, Data Analytics
Organizational Impact and Change Management	Group and Individual Behaviors, Thinking Creatively, Interpersonal Relations and Teamwork	Organizational Behavior, Human Resource Management	Organizational Behavior, Organizational Development, Human Resource Management
Leadership Capabilities and Requirements	Evidence-Based Decision Making, Leading, Managing in Diverse Global Context, Analytical Thinking	Business Ethics, Management, Leadership	Leadership, Change Management, Innovation
Economic Business Case	Economic, Financial	Business Finance, Accounting, Economics	Financial Management, Economics (Micro and Macro), Accounting (Managerial and Financial)
Project Implementation Plan	Complexities of Decision Making, Application of Knowledge	Management	General Management, Project Management
Reflections on Learning	Integrating Knowledge across Fields, Reflective Thinking	Integrating Experience	Capstone Business Policy and Strategy

1. AACSB Competencies, General Skill Areas and General Business Knowledge Areas, 2018
2. ACBSP Undergraduate Common Professional Components and Curriculum Design in Graduate Programs, 2018

Summarizing the Competencies

Wow, so that's what you did with the past few years of your life! Another way to simplify and reflect on your studies and the skills you've developed is to bundle your studies into just a few buckets including:

- **Technical or Professional** Skills – Typical business disciplines (Accounting, Human Resource Management, Marketing, etc.) provide tools, techniques, processes and methodologies to manage many of organization's largest opportunities to apply your learning in a very direct way. Using Marketing Research techniques or Accounting procedures are two good examples.

- **Leadership** Skills – Generally beginning with at least one self-assessment of both your values/strengths and typical leadership competencies, these skills can be seen in how you, first, manage your own life (leading self) and then help to inspire others reach their potential (leading others).

- **Reflective Learning** Skills – Also frequently called meta-learning, critical thinking, inquiry, lifelong learning or "learning-to-learn" these skills are among the most important of your studies. While your work may take you far away from your "Business major" or "MBA Concentration" these *learning* skills will always be with you. The ability to be mindful about your work, step back and gain perspective, reframe problems and deepen your understanding is the learning counterpoint to "taking action." This is especially important in a learning environment that is less formal than an academic course, such as the workplace. In your work experiences that you have had to date, I am confident in saying that at least once you were asked to "figure it out" with no playbook and specific direction and a clean slate.

- **Applied Learning** Skills – While these begin with your more technical skills, they quickly require work-based inquiry and the ability to research and plan your projects or organizational change. In doing so, you will be applying your technical skills but very quickly adapting your academically built competencies to your organizational context. The ability to apply skills to a new context is something that only work experience (or to some extent, simulations) can provide.

- **Integration** Skills – The challenge of organizational success, in both for-profits and non-profits is that problems are complicated and multi-dimensional. Business opportunities require that a number of pieces all be in place and leaving any one of them out is the difference between flourishing and failing. Seeing the points of intersection and overlap is an expectation of any business program graduate. Like applied learning, however, it is difficult to learn in the classroom and requires persistence in identifying where a Marketing project that begins in, for example, the Sales/Marketing/Customers Area of Practice quickly requires skills in understanding implications for changes in Information Systems and Analysis, Human Resource policies, Organizational Development requirements or Strategic focus of the organization!

"Doing by Learning" activity

My Business Curriculum Competencies

1. Locate the program description for the Business Degree that you are about to complete and read it thoroughly.

2. Identify the program competencies that stand behind your program and match them to the generic areas listed in the table above. Are there any missing? Any program competencies for which

you can't find a place?
3.   Reflect on your personal development in each of your program competencies through both your courses as well as other learning experiences such as internships, etc.
4.   Reflect on any experiences outside of your program (work experiences, volunteer work, family and group activities, etc.) that have contributed to your development in the program and generic competencies.

Using the Areas of Management Practice

With an understanding of where your courses fit into the picture and align with the *Areas of Management Practice* and a bit of perspective on what you have learned and are still learning, the next step is to see how these can be used in a project, such as your capstone. When engaged in a work-based project of any kind, it is highly unlikely that you will be referring directly back to specific courses and textbooks. What you will do, however, is use the competencies and general frameworks of your courses which may lead you to using specific techniques, models, tools or concepts from those courses in each *Area of Management Practice*. Further, it is more than likely that you will begin with one of the areas and then move into most or eventually all as you explore the true scope of your project. This process begins simply enough by asking yourself the big questions about each *Area of Management Practice*. When you do this, there is virtually no area of business (or your project) that is not covered in this framework.

Think of it this way: the competencies that you learned in your courses exist because they respond to some basic questions about the organization that need to be understood. As an example, look below at the area of Products, Services, Marketing and Sales. Everything in this general area has to do with the customer needs (and generally, revenue) or, to simplify it, the Marketing side of the organization. One of the most important questions you need to understand for any opportunity is whether "customer data are used to support change or new products or services." Whether you ascribe to traditional large sample size market research or more anthropologic customer observation, the question remains the same because there is an enduring need to use customer data to inform decisions. So, too, are the remaining questions under that same *Area of Practice* and in others.

The Areas of Management Practice provide a framework that is consistent with virtually all business education programs such as yours, allowing you to see where your specific curriculum fits into this model while simultaneously allowing you to see some of the most important "big picture" questions you need to ask yourself when confronted with a new project, such as a work-based capstone project. Of course, all of these questions needn't be answered for every project, but many do and making clear decisions about where to focus your attention is the first step in successfully managing your capstone project.

1.   ***Alignment of Mission, Values and Strategy***
2.   ***Products, Services, Marketing and Sales***
3.   ***Processes Improved or Added***
4.   ***Information Systems***
5.   ***Organizational Impact and Change Management***
6.   ***Leadership Capabilities and Requirements***
7.   ***Economic Business Case***
8.   ***Project Implementation***

    9. Economic Modeling
    10. Reflections on Learning

Below are some suggested questions to launch your thinking about virtually any change in the workplace. They are specific enough to focus on a central part of the project or functional area but are broad enough to generate some high-level thinking about the nature of your opportunity for change.

1. **Alignment of Mission, Values and Strategy**

- What is of value to the organization or what values seem to be driving the organization in this project?
- How much of a gap is there between the espoused organizational core values and the actual values demonstrated by choices to be made?
- Will your change allow you to take on the tough ethical challenges or is there avoidance?
- Is decision making driven by a long-term perspective or is it consumed by short term thinking?
- Are the choices that are made consistent with organizational, personal and global values?

2. **Products, Services, Marketing and Sales**

- How is customer data used to support change or new products and services?
- Does an understanding of specific market segments provide guidance?
- To what extent are sales processes and feedback linked to our core business?
- How are new products and services truly innovative?

3. **Processes Improved or Added**

- How is success measured and communicated?
- How do metrics drive decisions, resource allocations and strategic choices?
- Are there feedback loops that generate improvements and are identified improvements implemented and measured?
- Is quality well understood?
- How are process improvement projects measured for performance?

4. **Information Systems**

- How is information used strategically and for data-driven decisions?
- Is innovation based on a culture of widely shared information?
- What systems exist to capture, analyze and share information?
- Is there an upward and cross-organizational flow of information?

5. **Organizational Impact and Change Management**

- Are people and organizational units open to learning and change based on input from all parts of their respective systems?
- Is there a spirit of mentorship, coaching and facilitation?
- How are people communicating and are they really listening to each other?
- Are organizational members trusted and empowered?
- Do organizational members trust senior management to identify and facilitate changes?

6. **Leadership Capabilities and Requirements**

- Is leadership capable of change consistent with new thinking?

- Is leadership development and mentorship part of the culture?
- Do organizational members trust senior management to identify and facilitate changes?

7. <u>Economic Business Case</u>

- What are the financial criteria used for measuring success?
- How are financial and economic resources allocated?
- Are resources sufficient to support the chosen strategy and growth?
- Are resources enough to meet short-term objectives?
- Does financial planning exist and, if so, does it have long term goals and how will the organization meet those goals?

8. <u>Project Implementation Plan</u>

- Does any plan take on the complexities of the project?
- Is planning consistent with other initiatives at the organization?
- Are best practices in Project Management applied to the extent possible?

9. <u>Economic Modeling</u>

- Does the model capture changes in revenues, costs or cost savings in all other areas of the organization?
- Are all benefits and positive changes quantified to the extent feasible?
- Are all costs and uses of resources accounted for to the extent feasible?
- Does the "model" express clearly the assumptions, benefits, costs and limitations of the analysis?
- Is the model transparent and honest in its assumptions and presentation of input and output?

10. <u>Reflections on Learning</u>

- To what extent are all Areas of Management Practice represented and is time given to learn them?
- Is there adequate reflection and time for effective learning?
- Are all aspects of the project and the organization included?
- How have you changed as a result of this project?
- What new perspectives on ethical behavior come out of the project?

"Doing by Learning" activity

Areas of Management Practice Introductory Questions

Think back to an organization and a project or organizational change that you have experienced. Quickly answer all of the above questions with the project in mind. Once done, review and reflect on your responses. What has this revealed about the organization and the project? What were the project's and the organization's strengths in moving the project forward? What could have been given more attention and why?

Now What?

If you are just finishing your Business degree and are like thousands of students I've known, then you've been so busy completing your coursework that taking time for career development hasn't been your focus. The good news is that the capstone may be your first real opportunity to begin a systematic process of building your own career. It is time to break free of the short-term thinking of "just getting through this course" or "just finishing this semester" on your way to "just getting my degree." Some of the most successful business students I've known typically take a longer-term perspective and view the capstone, in particular, as a huge opportunity to launch a new way of thinking about the "course."

In their recent book, *The Start Up of You*, Reid Hoffman and Ben Casnocha provide a roadmap on why and how you need to manage your career in today's environment. Their fundamental thesis is that we are all "works in progress" in which "each day presents an opportunity to learn more, do more and grow more in our lives and careers" (R. Hoffman and B. Casnocha, 2012, p. 22). I couldn't agree more that we are living in a fast-paced age in which lifetime employment at one or a few organizations is no longer part of career thinking.

This is an important thing for you to pause and consider now, early in your capstone experience, because the capstone provides a bright line in the sand between how you have approached previous "courses" in which learning may have been engaging but, from a pedagogical viewpoint, passive, and to begin now to adapt to a more active level of career management. Said another way, in most "courses" what you learn is assembled for you before you get there but in a capstone you need to be more entrepreneurial and create the curriculum from scratch, more in the manner of work-based projects that are given to employees every day on-the-job! So, what does that mean for you and the capabilities you need to succeed? Hoffman and Casnocha describe a new entrepreneurially oriented career mind-set as permanent beta and present a case for the skills needed. These include:

- Developing your **competitive advantage** in the market by combining your **assets**, **aspirations** and market realities;
- Using **ABZ Planning** to formulate Plan A based on your competitive advantages, and then iterating and **adapting** that plan based on feedback and lessons learned (to plan "B" all the way up to "Z");
- Building real, lasting **relationships** and deploying these relationships into a powerful **professional network**;
- Finding and creating **opportunities** for yourself by tapping **networks,** being **resourceful** and staying in **motion**;
- Accurately appraising and taking on **intelligent risk** as you pursue professional opportunities; and
- Tapping **network intelligence** from the people you know for the insight that allows you to find better opportunities and make better career decisions (Hoffman and Casnocha, 2012, p. 23).

It may be a bit challenging at the early stages of your capstone to see the relevance of how these skills fit your capstone, and that's the point. Whether you realize it or not you are in a transitional state in which these skills may have almost no relevance to your success in an academic program but are *critical* once you launch a career. Taken as a whole, they point to a mindset of managing your learning in a way that you haven't needed to before now. Most importantly, it is about being responsive to what you learn along the way and entrepreneurial about anything connected to your career.

Adapting is all about the pivot! Hoffman and Casnocha state that "Pivoting isn't throwing a dart on the map and going there. It's changing direction or changing your path to get somewhere based on what you've learned along the way." (Hoffman and Casnocha, 2012, p.68 see second reference in book). This entrepreneurial attitude is both a key to your capstone and to launching your active career management. Successful "careers" are seldom built on a single linear path. Instead, just as a successful entrepreneur is working tirelessly on the "plan," success often comes from "adaptions and iterations" (Hoffman and Casnocha, 2012, p. 23).

*Think about at least one person whose career you consider to be successful. This doesn't necessarily mean that your choice is a CEO or business owner but someone who is successful according to what measures they have chosen to apply to their life. If you can, schedule a time when that person can share his or her story and, in particular, how he or she managed to simultaneously be driven by a **singular focus** and open to **adaptive and entrepreneurial behavior** as they made positive choices and decisions. You may be surprised to learn how these seemingly contradictory forces helped them to shape their lives!*

Passion

Career development and the process of career management needs to be married, of course, to your passion. In discussions with other professors about student success, there is probably no word that comes up with greater frequency. Ask any successful entrepreneur how he or she made it through the inevitable bleak times when money was running out or customers showed no interest in their product and some form of the word passion will surface!

Another valuable perspective comes from Angela Duckworth's highly acclaimed book *Grit: The Power of Passion and Perseverance*, in which she clearly demonstrates that our ability to persevere is largely driven by having passion for what we are doing. This is amazingly consistent with our own research on successful capstone students who routinely reported that the greatest difficulty in a capstone project was in needing to "push through" discouraging moments. What got them through? The single biggest factor, by far, was having a passion for the topic they were exploring. Duckworth's research on passion led to her development of several broad questions to ask yourself in searching for a passion (Duckworth, 2016, p. 115). They are:

- Where does my mind wander?
- What do I really care about?

- What matters most to me?
- How do I enjoy spending my time?
- In contrast: What do I find absolutely unbearable?

If these are difficult in your immediate situation, she suggests reflecting back to your teen years, because those are times when "vocational interests commonly sprout." She then suggests taking an approach that would fit nicely with the entrepreneurial mindset described earlier by building off of any clues brought out in answering these questions and to build from there. Her advice is directly relevant to the early stages of your capstone project, because you need to start somewhere, and trying out a concept is how to begin the process of building a passion one step at a time.

Yes, this is hard work, some of the most difficult work involved in a capstone project because, again, this learning is self-directed and not outlined in a syllabus. The "self" in "self-directed" requires strong motivation to succeed when failure seems all too likely, and passion is the fuel that feeds the flame. While critical, identifying your passion can be challenging, and it certainly requires some commitment. Henri Juntilla in *Find Your Passion, 25 Questions You Must Ask Yourself* (2013) provides a comprehensive framework to help you through the journey and is an excellent resource. He is quick to point out that "Living a passionate life doesn't happen overnight. It's hard work, and it's not as glamorous as people make it out to be...but it's worth doing because once you gain momentum, your life will change." (Juntilla, 2013, p. 73).

So, you ask, what types of questions should I begin with? Given the wide range of meanings that passion has for all of us and the challenge in meeting any theoretical "expectations," Juntilla smartly begins with basic and obvious reflective questions such as "How do you define passion?" and "How will you know when you're living a passionate life?" These are a great starting point for self-reflection and for reconciling your own starting point. From there, the book (process) asks you to work through areas of your life that are most likely to influence your choice of passion such as Personality (Myers-Briggs), Your Strengths, and Personal Interests and Behaviors, all of which are extremely important in understanding your "passion." There is a strong compatibility between Duckworth's and Juntilla's work. Juntilla's small but powerful book walks you through multiple dimensions of self-reflection and may spark clarity of passion through the act of self-discovery that Duckworth is advocating.

"Doing by Learning" activity

Finding your Passion(s)

Stop and take the time to reflect on your passion. Begin with the questions proposed by Angela Duckworth and other resources as required. When you identify an area of interest (and you will, I am confident), think about what opportunities there might be to engage in that area of interest and begin the search for a capstone opportunity. Build on a positive interest and do something to test your level of interest or to unveil associated areas of potential interest and build from there.

Career Development

The career opportunity before you in your capstone cannot be overemphasized. It isn't about applying for jobs but engaging in the network through inquiry and dialogue. Whether your interests are in working for a large organization, small/family business, non-profit or becoming an entrepreneur, this course has the potential to be life changing and course setting. For one, unlike traditional courses in which you work independently or in teams, the capstone is socially open ended, and part of your learning is about how to learn with and through others without the structure of a classroom. Your capstone is a perfect way to engage or, at the very least, simulate, the types of relationships that are necessary to develop as you manage to build your career. One way to think about the capstone is that it is not a dress rehearsal but rather is the beginning of your lifelong network.

Burnett and Evans in their self-help guide to career and life management, *Designing Your Life: How to Build a Well-Lived, Joyful Life* (2016), describe the network as the "hidden job market that's only open to people who are already connected into the web of professional relationships in which the job resides."

While it may be difficult to penetrate this web as an outsider and typical "job seeker," it is possible to crack into it as what they call a "sincerely interested inquirer." This is *exactly* what you, as a capstone student, need to leverage, since you are given, essentially, a free ticket to engage in dialogue that opens doors. Use this ticket to begin your journey now even if the capstone project choices available to you right now seem loosely or not connected to where you see yourself in the future.

When you complete the capstone, you will have a story to share that points to your ability to build and learn independently -- which is what makes you part of the larger team of successful leaders! A case could be made for the fact that the way in which you manage your capstone experience is more important than the topic itself, since the active learning habits you build and your level of passion are two of the most important attributes that will be carried forward into any career path.

Why a Business Capstone?

Capstones in all Disciplines

Capstones are not unique to business degrees or to higher education and can vary widely in their design, depending on the academic discipline. Capstones are increasingly popular, especially in an educational environment focused on career preparation, such as business. Regardless of the major or curriculum, capstones fulfill what their name suggests, a finishing piece placed at the summit of other building blocks. Consider, for example, degree programs in Literature, Sciences or the Fine Arts, and just imagine how each of those disciplines might offer a comprehensive and culminating experience for soon-to-be graduates!

In a discussion on the history of capstones in all disciplines and, in particular, reviewing the current trends in capstones, Hauhart and Grahe (2015. p. 5), in *Designing and Teaching Undergraduate Capstone Courses*, list two points: capstones are more generally discipline-specific (as opposed to general education) and these capstones are generally research-based. Heinscheid et al., in their study of capstone course structures, *Professing the Disciplines: An Analysis of Senior Seminars and Capstone Courses* (2000), reported that most (70.3%) are discipline specific. This was also confirmed in a national study of capstone experiences in which it was reported that capstones were 84.7% discipline-based, with interdisciplinary courses at 12.9% (Padget and Kilgo, 2012). Both studies found numerous alternatives making up the small difference. These include traditional classroom-based courses, internship experiences and comprehensive exams (Hauhart and Grahe (2015. p. 45). At the highest level, according to Kerka in *Capstone Experiences in Career and Technical Education* (2001), capstone learning, regardless of discipline, takes place through "culminating experiences in which students synthesize subject-matter knowledge they have acquired, integrate across cross-disciplinary knowledge, and connect theory and application in preparation for entry into a career."

More than a Course

One of the greatest differences between a capstone and all of your previous courses is the multiple levels of learning that can be achieved at the Cognitive, Affective and Psychomotor levels. You have been experiencing these different levels of learning by design in all of your education so far. The Cognitive level, which is probably the most familiar in most of your curriculum, will be addressed in the capstone through the recall and application of knowledge that you acquired in your previous courses. The Affective level, which is achieved by learning about the values, attitudes, beliefs and other contextual variables seen in the chosen workplace, is difficult to build into your previous courses except indirectly through case studies and possibly simulations. Internships or real work experiences, even if part time, provide the most notable opportunities for affective learning.

Finally, Psychomotor learning is developed by engaging in the physical production of deliverables and presentation of the work consistent with the professional standards of the workplace (Moore, 2017). Many business courses work hard at this level of learning by asking you to replicate professional work in the form of business plans, marketing plans, audit reports, research papers, human resource plans and more. When creating such "work products," you are really achieving many important professional competencies such as contextual competence, adaptability, persistence, leadership, ethical decision-making and others that are normally not available in either a traditional classroom or an online course.

Capstone Models

Capstones also follow several models or structures, depending not only on the discipline but on the philosophy of your school and department. Here are some of the most widely used models:

- **Course** – Taking a final course, with several very specific prerequisites, may be focused on the discipline of a single major, such as business, by examining a single problem or by students producing work as individuals working in small teams. It may also be a course that looks broadly at the discipline in an attempt to touch multiple topics in order to bring a sense of connection among them that may be difficult to do through individual courses. Course-based capstones, of course, are still classroom or online learning.
- **Experiential Project** – Capstones can be designed to be part of an internship or other work-based experience. A typical one might ask the student to work independently or in teams to solve a "client" or "organizational" challenge through problem solving or to design an innovative utilization of an emerging opportunity. For non-traditional undergraduate students and part-time graduate students this presents a unique opportunity to do a project in your own workplace that is outside the scope of your usual assignments and provides a new learning

experience in a location that you already know well. It is easy to see how this supports the development of the more affective and contextual learning.

- **Independent Study** – Students doing an independent study are given the freedom to select a topic of interest and to research and report on it, generally with the oversight of a faculty advisor. The obvious strength of this capstone design is that the level of flexibility works extremely well for true "research" in academic disciplines in everything from art history to natural sciences and supports cognitive learning but, if focused on a work-based deliverable, can also be very experiential for affective learning.

- **Senior Seminars** – Small, discussion-based seminars are frequently used as a culminating experience in several disciplines. The advantage of these is that a number of current topics can be addressed and, given the nature of dialogue and inquiry, can quickly and effectively be integrative by reframing topics and viewing them through multiple lenses. In business studies, for example, case studies and outside readings can be successfully integrated and used to leverage themes of ethical decision-making or organizational values in a very reflective way. Because of this, seminars can be very effective in facilitating deep learning that results in both affective as well as cognitive development.

- **Internships** – Internships can be used with the obvious justification that getting "in the field" or doing "hands on learning" in a real organization, provides some much needed affective and contextual learning to supplement the more cognitively-oriented traditional courses. That said, internships need to be managed to ensure that the learning is more than just spending time doing routine or menial work and that it truly becomes a "capstone" experience that brings a new and higher-level perspective to your business studies. When done well, an internship is virtually indistinguishable from an "Experiential" capstone that may or may not have a project associated with the internship experience itself.

- **Comprehensive Case Study or Exam** – Rather than the use of multiple case studies or other learning experiences designed to test your knowledge across disciplines, a single "event" can be used. In a comprehensive exam, a selected set of previous courses or curricula will be identified in advance to manage the scope of the inevitable review needing to be done in preparation for the exam. If using a single case study, then a set of broad questions may be provided to ensure a level of consistency and the ability to assess the learning.

- **Portfolio** – Developing a portfolio of your student projects and artifacts is an excellent way to end any academic program. Because portfolios are frequently supported by a written reflection that integrates the learning, it can be a valuable way to leverage years of pushing hard through courses with little time to reflect on relationships between courses and key deliverables. In many disciplines, such as the arts, a portfolio provides the added benefit of "pulling together" disparate projects into a single story of accomplishments as a valuable tool to launching a career. The portfolio is probably a combination of both cognitive and affective development, while also more focused on delivering a professional deliverable capable of being shared with prospective employers, clients and colleagues.

- **Client Consultancy** – This type of capstone is most frequently undertaken by teams for a corporate client, generally under the advisement of a faculty member. Student teams typically meet with a client on a regular basis and are given access to internal and proprietary data while performing research to solve a problem or develop an innovative opportunity. At the undergraduate level, this model works especially well with students who have previous experience in internships or other more experiential learning since a high level of independence and self-directedness is necessary. At the graduate level, this model works especially well for non-online (classroom-based) programs in which students can meet with the client and one another face-to-face. This model has all the affective, cognitive, contextual and professional deliverable types of learning embedded in the experience.

- **Reflective Journals** – These have a huge value to learning but have their greatest value, of course, when linked to some experience on which to be reflective. In many curricula that experience might include literature, journal articles, exposure to new concepts or artifacts, video/media or other interactions with community members or professionals in your field. Journals are done over some period of time, which can also vary from years to the span of a single course. When done over time or retrospectively about an extended period, they can provide both the cognitive and affective elements of a portfolio but without the professional deliverables. They can also easily be combined with another capstone structure such as an experiential or internship capstone to enhance the depth of learning and to capture the transformational aspects of the learning.

- **Integrative Course** – A single course, designed to "bring together" multiple courses and disciplines is, historically, one of the most widely used capstone experiences because it is easiest to manage and deliver to students. In Business, for example, a single course on Business Strategy and Policy is often used with case studies to touch on all aspects of business and management simultaneously through both written work and class discussions. For many business students this single class, while still primarily cognitive in nature, provides numerous "aha moments" of seeing, often for the first time, the relationships between areas of business and courses taken. It is also possible for this course to use reflective journals for students to link the course content to personal work or internship experiences and derive some affective learning despite the classroom focus.

- **Other Culminating Experiences** – While the above categories cover most of the available capstone design options, the sky is the limit for how these may be combined or linked to other experiences, as well. Study abroad opportunities or other experientially based phenomena have the potential to deliver an unforgettable learning experience for students.

Capstone Timelines

While most capstones take place during a single semester, it deserves mention that many capstones may extend over more than one semester or even begin in other parts of the curriculum. Programs with such a design typically recognize that students benefit from building slowly and laying the groundwork for a major project long before the capstone is due for completion. Having more than one semester provides time to build a foundational knowledge of an industry or specific topic, create a network of colleagues and advisors to serve as a sounding board, conduct some preliminary research, do some baseline analyses, and even "test" possible design solutions. This leaves the final, or actual "capstone" semester for drawing together and completing research, proposing a final design and possibly beginning the implementation and/or monitoring/evaluation/testing.

The Positive Change Project

As seen above, the range of possible capstone projects is very wide, especially when one considers the multiple combinations of types combined with various timelines. The purpose of this book is to focus, primarily, on the Experiential Project as your capstone. I believe that this type of capstone presents students with some unique challenges, and that my own experience in working with students and subsequent research can provide guidance that can help other students, such as you, to be successful in an efficient and relatively low-stress way.

Underlying student success is another deeply held value behind this book—the "strengths-based" perspective that begins with thinking of your project as an opportunity to build on what is best instead of focusing on "solving a problem." This small distinction is why we refer to the capstone project as a **Positive Change Project** in which you are embarking on creating change from a position of strength and opportunity.

As seen throughout this book, it is also my belief that a capstone project provides a great deal more than the project itself. One of the fundamental drivers of this book is, in fact, the realization that most students who complete a capstone project successfully don't tend to focus on the "project" as much as they do the entire capstone experience. One of your challenges, in fact, will be learning to keep the momentum of your project moving forward while maintaining a steady gaze on the horizon of learning from the experience, most of which can occur long before any research or writing is underway!

Why a *Project* for a Capstone?

Business Curriculum Pedagogy

Let's reflect briefly on all those courses you have taken as part of your business program. If you haven't taken the time to complete the *Doing by Learning* activity asking you to list your courses according to the *Areas of Management Practice*, then it might be helpful to do so now. In each of your courses, based on the content and instructor, you used some fundamental methods for the learning and assessment of the course content. The most obvious method, used in many of your courses, is an examination. When done well, an examination provides not only a cognitive measurement of how much you know about a given topic but serves as a personal validation of your learning, builds self-confidence in your ability to apply the content in the future, allows deeper connections to other courses and content areas and provides an opportunity for reflection on how you have changed as a result of your "new" knowledge. That said, examinations do have their limitations and it is probably fair to say that most examinations are predominantly focused on cognitive skills of recall, blended with some application and integration of the course materials.

Business and Management Education Options

Henry Mintzberg, Professor of Management Studies at McGill University, is widely regarded as one of the world's leading experts in the field of management education. In his widely acclaimed book, *Managers Not MBA's, A Hard Look at the Soft Practice of Management Education* (2005), he looks critically at our practice of training students in management. This is, of course, directly aimed at business schools, of which he is a part! His criticism is grounded in the premise that management is, fundamentally, a practice that needs to be learned though experience and that management education, such as the typical MBA, has severe limitations. Given that our dependence on completely work-based and experiential learning for business and management studies has several structural and financial limitations, business schools depend on a variety of methodologies, including examinations, as learning activities.

Mintzberg maintains that it is the "authenticity" of a learning methodology that characterizes the level at which it contributes to true management education. By authentic, I believe that he means learning that includes all three of the basic types identified earlier (Cognitive, Affective and Professional Work Products). He identifies a range of five basic types of learning activities (other than tests and quizzes) used in business school that he ranks based on their "authenticity." They are seen in the following diagram and explained below.

Authenticity in Learning

Figure 1: Authenticity in Learning
Adapted from: Mintzberg, H. (2004) Managers, Not MBAs, p.266

- **Computer Simulations and Role Playing** – Often used in classes related to organizational behavior, ethics, management, strategy, policy or organizational development, these can provide an opportunity for students to see how various pieces of the organizational puzzle fit together and provide a "feeling" of real decision-making.

- **Projects by Students** – Projects allow a student to work independently or in teams on a project that is open-ended. Mintzberg is assuming that the student is doing an academic project that isn't necessarily grounded in the workplace, so it has the advantage of being a "real" problem to be understood but is still lacking in context.

- **Case Study Discussions** – Case studies are used frequently by many of the best business schools as an excellent means to bring more experiential and authentic learning into the classroom. Notice that Mintzberg includes the "Discussions" in this methodology and is sending a clear message that working to solve a case study collaboratively, with the valuable interaction and reflection that comes about through a discussion, is an extremely important ingredient in case studies when used for management development.

- **Action Learning by Managers** – Here, Mintzberg relies on Action Learning in its strictest definition: that of a team that is empowered to design, test, learn and repeat the process while learning at each iteration. It is learning that is collaborative and grounded in the consequences of making and learning from decisions and being trusted to continue the process based upon learning.

- **Experienced Reflection** – The key differentiator here is the level of reflection embedded into the decision-making process. Reflection, here, is taken to mean deep learning that addresses both the cognitive and affective domains of learning. Reflection is also taken to mean mindfully addressing opportunities and challenges with others in reflecting publicly in order to build on the collaborative Action Learning model.

This is directly relevant to the Experiential Business Capstone Model addressed by this book. By doing a project that is work-based and experiential, you are engaged in an activity that would fit on the higher end of the scale. By, first, building a network of mentors and colleagues to share your discovery and receive insights (discussions), and, second, taking an iterative and collaborative approach to your design of a solution to your opportunity or challenge (Action Learning), and then, third, including reflection as part of the overall set of competencies, your learning experience becomes the most authentic it can be. Because of this, you can be assured that, if approached as the opportunity that it truly is, you will be entering a "course" that is potentially more transformational than virtually any course taken to date.

This "work-based project" approach of your capstone is also supported by recent research on the most current direction of capstone types. Hauhart and Grahe (2015. p.119), for example, report that based on multiple studies, the research supports the idea that capstones are predominantly based on a **major project** or paper. They also refine their observations and identify the most typical types of capstones including "senior thesis," a research project, a portfolio (whether of illustrations, drawings or papers), or some form of **real-world problem-based learning**.

Integration is Job #1

The Competency of all Competencies

To "keep our eye on the ball," we need to refocus on what is one of the most important elements of any capstone, regardless of its structure, i.e., emphasis on type of learning or level of authenticity. In our own study of over sixty business and management capstones at both the undergraduate and graduate levels, the most frequently cited competency or course goal was the **integration of the entire business/management curriculum**, period. This is a big job! In their own research on capstones, Hauhart and Grahe (2015, p. 33) found the two most frequently cited purposes to be "Review and integrate learned material" and "It helps students extend and apply learned material." They also reported that other research supported the high-level importance of integration and synthesis within a student's academic major.

Many business courses make little effort to be cross-disciplinary with other business disciplines. The reason cited is generally that "there is already too much material to cover" or "that isn't the job of my course in (insert topic)." As a result, many business students come to their capstone course with little preparation in the kind of systems thinking required of managers. Instead, they bring to the table a collection of independent successes in each course in which they have responded to the course requirements but done little to synthesize and reconcile the learning with other courses that they have taken. This is a failure of many business programs since, really, the single most important competency of your business degree, whether stated in your program or not, **is the need for integration at all levels**. This means seeing the relationships between the technical areas (finance, marketing, operations management, etc.) but also those associated with management (organizational behavior, leadership, ethics/policy, etc.).

The Integration Process

The job of the capstone is often to provide a single integrative experience and to set the stage for your application of all you learned in an integrated way throughout your career. My own MBA, which I feel delivered a quality learning experience and is an AACSB accredited school of business program followed this model to the letter. Each course was very focused in the specific course content and was followed by a "Comprehensive Exam" in which we (team of graduating students) were given a broad strategic problem for a large, multi-national, publicly held corporation. After two weeks of preparation, we would sit for virtually a full day and respond to questions on all aspects of the business including Accounting, Marketing, Organization Design, Financial decisions, Operations Management, and more. This was truly integrative, for sure, but was also putting a big responsibility on one learning activity to ensure that we graduated with what is the most important competency of all, one that has been far more useful than many individual "lessons" in specific courses. I believe that a work-based project is similar in its role in your education.

Where to Begin

So how do you approach something so important, so broad and for which you may be feeling somewhat ill prepared? Take baby steps and use the tools provided here to guide your learning. By now you may have begun discussions at your internship site, workplace or "client" organization to scope out a potential project. While more detailed processes for project selection are expanded in later chapters, for now you might simply begin by looking at an opportunity that has made itself known. The short course is that whatever project you select, it undoubtedly falls into one of the Areas of Management Practice.

One of my favorite examples from a previous life, which you can probably relate to, was low sales volume. This obviously points to the area of Sales, Marketing and Customer Relationships and it certainly was, to start, so we began with looking at our customer communications and marketing/advertising. That's easy enough. It quickly brought about the need, however, for a more holistic approach. Looking at our marketing efforts quickly pointed to the call center, where we found opportunities to learn from some highly successful call center representatives on messaging. This knowledge and change caused reflection about our overall market position that, in turn, brought up some training changes needed even in the mindset of management and senior leadership. From there, we began to look at data captured by the call center to better understand customer perceptions and inquiries, then to information/reporting systems and eventually to the entire set of products and services, including pricing. I could go on, but I think you get the point. An opportunity for a positive change always has a home base that provides a starting point for subsequent thinking, testing and learning but quickly spreads to multiple *Areas of Management Practice*.

The challenge and reason for your Positive Change Project capstone is the systems or integrated thinking that every organizational member, regardless of "position" on the organizational chart, would benefit from. As a student of business and management, you will use your experiential capstone to jump-start your ability to do that by validating all that you have learned and building from that starting point.

Four Case Studies

Introducing Four Case Studies

Throughout this text, we will use four case studies repeatedly to demonstrate the application of the principles explained in each chapter. These case studies are compiled from multiple actual capstone projects that demonstrated excellence in their level of research, analysis, solutions, and reflections on learning. Each case study also demonstrates the application of the *Areas of Management Practice* model in multiple ways to display extraordinary integrated thinking. Below is a very brief introduction to each of the four cases which I have written from the perspective of the student/project owner. If you want to know more about these cases, don't worry, it's coming in the chapters that follow! This is just the outer skin of the onion…

CASE 1 – Inventory Management Improvement

We needed to improve our inventory management system so that it would ensure more accurate data, better error tracking, and usable real time reporting capability. The current system has opportunities for improvement in both reporting accuracy and timeliness of reports. We have been asking ourselves internally for years now how this could possibly be improved? This is what seems like a very basic problem but is constantly in need of improvement and more efficiencies, given the increasing scale and complexities of our products and the logistics behind our materials management.

CASE 2 – New Generation Target Market for Lending Institution
It was well known that our organization needed to increase its mortgage lending business. Even in the absence of new secondary research studies or any direct customer research by our marketing department, our instincts were that there was a lower than desired demand with the younger generation of first-time homebuyers. We know that the characteristics and priorities of the younger generation of potential homebuyers has been influenced by the home lending crises and other factors. A positive change would be to identify how to help younger potential home buyers fulfill their dream of home ownership.

CASE 3 – Employee Training and Development for less turnover and better customer service
My organization is a national and well-respected retail organization with approximately 40,000 employees. Our product depends heavily on knowledgeable employees who can engage with customers, provide technical assistance and encourage repeat sales. We find, however, that high employee turnover creates a vacuum needing to be perpetually refilled and that the gap in training and development is a never-ending game of catch-up. My capstone project could explore a positive change in employee training. Ultimately this might result in higher sales but-- just as importantly -- provide some assurance that well-trained employees will build trusted relationships with customers by providing excellent advice. In a nutshell, we might better understand how we can improve sales and customer management with more experienced and better trained employees. This might happen through lower turnover and improved training and development.

CASE 4 - Merging of multiple non-profits into one organization
My organization is a non-profit that delivers a vital service to a very special segment of the population in one of several regions in the United States. Like most non-profits, funding is always a challenge, and resources are generally subject to economic constraints. There are several other non-profits who deliver virtually the same service but in different geographical areas of the continental United States. Because we are all so similar in mission, service delivery, funding and organizational infrastructure, there may be benefits to merging at least two of the regional organizations. My positive change capstone would explore the advantages and challenges to a merger of all of these nearly identical but regional organizations into one entity serving the entire country.

Do any or all of the following as a means of beginning your Positive Change Project Capstone.

- *Prioritize your business program's competencies based on your interests by topic, course, models, or frameworks identified earlier.*

- *Appreciative perspective – now, at a more granular level, what learning area opportunities have been the most engaging to you?*
- *What competencies or Areas of Management Practice did you find yourself doing most enjoyably?*
- *Talk to a colleague or friend in your program (or not) and ask them to share their reflections on their most engaging competencies from their degree program and compare notes.*

CHAPTER 2
LEARNING THROUGH AND BUILDING ON EXPERIENCE

Overview

As you learned in the first chapter, your experiential capstone is very different from a typical course. The single greatest differentiator that sets your experientially-based capstones apart is the fact that it is built around a project that takes place at an existing or emerging organization. As you saw in the Four Case Studies, a project will typically begin by identifying some organizational need. From there, you will be researching and assessing the impact of that change whether it is a new or improved process, a customer acquisition strategy, a merger, or some other initiative to create positive change. As described earlier, where most courses are built around specific competencies and then provide learning experiences to support those competencies, the project-based capstone is deliberately not singly focused on any specific topic. Instead, you will be starting with some opportunity to make a change, explore that change itself within generally one *Area of Management Practice* and then approach the change more broadly into other *Areas of Management Practice*. In doing so, you will be drawing on your knowledge from many if not all of your business courses to address your proposed change.

This chapter seeks to expand your understanding of what exactly is meant when we toss around terms like Experiential Learning, Action Learning, Work-Based Learning and others. It is very important for you to understand these many perspectives on learning because they are what you will be living out in researching and developing your Positive Change Project. We begin by putting the learning into perspective with a model called Integrated Reflective Practice and then expand your understanding with several models of learning at the individual and organizational levels that will be the drivers behind your project.

Integrated Reflective Practice – The Experiential Capstone Model

The diagram below captures the three basic components of your capstone experience that, taken together, describe everything you will be doing in your capstone project. We describe this as Integrated Reflective Practice and the three components are:

- **Action Research/Positive Change Project** – This is the capstone project itself, along with your activities of researching your Positive Change Project, collaborating with others, proposing your ideas, obtaining feedback, engaging in dialogue and more. With respect to type of learning, this area is primarily about the creation of professional deliverables.

- **Areas of Management Practice** – As described earlier, this is a bundle of content areas that you have studied as part of your business curriculum. In the Areas of Management Practice model, we have simply bundled many of the courses into ten themes or "areas," so that you have a common framework regardless of your school, level (undergraduate or graduate) or program (business, leadership, etc.). With respect to types of learning, this area is primarily, although not exclusively, about cognitive learning and the knowledge and application of course competencies.
- **Reflective Practice** – This is the process of reflective learning that you will be going through as you engage in your project, build your own leadership skills in managing the project and become the expert on your change. It also includes everything to do with your learning experience, both independently and with others. With respect to types of learning, this area is primarily about affective, or social-emotional aspects, of the learning experience.

Integrated Reflective Practice

Figure 2: Integrated Reflective Practice

A successful capstone experience depends on all three of these components working together to support each other. As the arrows show, there is mutual strength between each of the three areas as it both supports and is supported by the other two. The section below explains these relationships in a bit more detail, showing how each of the three areas supports the other two.

1. *Action Research/Positive Change Project* (**Professional skills/deliverables) supports:**
   - **Areas of Management Practice** – The project provides a real problem and becomes the context and vehicle of the application of all course and curriculum content. This means that any of the models, frameworks, techniques and theories that have been studied sit idle until the project provides a home for their application.
   - **Reflective Practice** – The change project provides the experiences needed to create new learning and generate reflection. The project is an endless chain of new experiences, relationships and revised theory about what may work. More important, it stimulates reflection about personal learning, growth and professional development that results in transformational learning and self-efficacy.

2. *Areas of Management Practice* (**Cognitive and content areas) supports:**
   - **Action Research/Positive Change Project** – Course and curriculum content found

in the Areas of Management Practice provides content, theory, frameworks and models that can be applied to the project as needed. As the project develops more complexity, it inevitably migrates into multiple areas of practice, and as it does, additional content is used to facilitate the project's development.

- **Reflective Practice** – The content areas also come to be used at the more personal and affective level as you identify with careers and methods based on your own learning or personality styles. Content in Organizational and Leadership studies is especially important to the more affective learning and growth that comes from engaging in and reflecting on these materials.

3. *Reflective Practice* (**Affective**) **supports:**
- **Action Research/Positive Change Project Dialogue and Learning with others** – Personal reflection is an important part of the learning process and helps to steer the project's direction. This also includes all affective and social-emotional learning that are derived from the project.
- **Areas of Management Practice** – Reflection and deep affective learning drive choices about models and frameworks being accessed from the Areas of Management Practice. It also more directly supports the use of leadership models and ethical boundaries.

"Formal" Learning Frameworks

Our three-sided model above describes well both the rationale and learning process at a high level. It is important that you are aware of other models of learning in order to make sense of your capstone experience and to better manage your own learning. With this background you will be more capable of managing your own learning and more aware of how to ensure your own success. Each of these models will be given a brief introduction along with its direct relevance to your experiential capstone work. In reviewing these models, you should soon begin to see some crossover in the themes and recommended techniques to facilitate quality learning. Be sensitive to the ways in which you can make the best use of this information as you begin to map out your project or, more importantly, as you adapt to new information and the ambiguities and paradoxical situations that you will inevitably encounter.

How People Learn

This government funded research was the outcome of an initial two-year study that was done by the Committee on Developments in the Science of Learning. After an initial publication in 1999, the most recent version of *How People Learn* brings the research to the classroom to make it more relevant to education in all settings. There are two areas of this publication that have particular relevance to your capstone.

The first is the distinction between "experts'" and "novices'" understanding of a topic. For the purposes of this work I am treating students at the completion of a course as being "novices," for whom the organization of knowledge covers the important topics and problem-solving techniques but ends there.

Experts, on the other hand, have a more expansive understanding that goes beyond problem solving into the bigger ideas and uncertainties that surround problem solving, per se. The expert also retrieves information with a stronger filter for relevance while the novice is less selective and tends to use problem-solving techniques without the expert's broad perspective. The relevance here is that your struggle will be to move, real time and in a short time, from a novice's approach to that of an "expert".

A second outcome from the research is related to the transfer of knowledge, or the ability to use previous knowledge to learn a new topic or apply knowledge in the interest of developing new learning. The research maintains that transfer is directly related to the quality of the initial learning and the degree to which the learning was built only on memorization or, preferably, on a deeper understanding.

This is something to think about as you encounter the various parts of your project and try to reach back to courses. You will probably be the most successful in drawing on concepts in which your learning was more broadly applied and given more perspective than, for example, problem solving alone. This supports the initial broad questions provided for each of the *Areas of Management Practice* that rise above the more technical elements of particular courses and start with questions at a higher level. The relevance here is that taking the time to develop a deeper understanding of your topic area, in my experience, positions you to make better research decisions as you move forward.

Knowledge transfer is also impacted by your motivation and interest in the topic of study. This shouldn't be a surprise but can't be reiterated enough. It is one of the most frequently cited reasons why so many of the most successful capstone students finished their projects with the same level of enthusiasm as they had in the first week of class. According to the research, a subset to motivation is the opportunity to contribute to something bigger. This confirms our own research with capstone students and other research on perseverance (Duckworth, 2010): that we are all more motivated when our work is connected to purpose. Highly successful capstone students expressed this in many ways but certainly choosing a project that has a direct impact and will be used by the organization is a good place to start!

How Learning Works

One of my favorite models of "learning" that is also research-based is *How Learning Works* (2010) by Susan Ambrose et al. The research provides seven principles that, in my opinion, serve as a perfect "checklist" for any learning experience regardless of the learner's age or the context for learning. For our purposes, I recommend reflecting on each of these with respect to your best learning experiences, and I'm sure you will notice that the most memorable ones embodied many, most, or even all of these principles (Ambrose et al, 2010). The seven principles, with a short statement of its relevance to your capstone are:

1. **Students' prior knowledge can help or hinder learning.**
    As you choose a project, carefully consider those Areas of Practices in which it is most likely to predominantly reside, and then reflect on your learning experiences in the courses supporting those areas. Did you feel successful in learning those topics? Were the learning experiences rich, and were you left with a deep understanding of course content? As you select your project, be ready to spend some time refreshing yourself on courses that you may have taken years ago. Review the "big questions" provided in each appropriate Area of Management Practice in Chapter One and give yourself some time to make sense of the area of study. Doing this early in your process by reading or talking to experts is a great first step!

2. **How students organize knowledge influences how they learn and apply what they know.**
    As explained earlier in the How People Learn model, your organization of knowledge at this stage of your career is probably closer to "novice" than to "expert." Just knowing this, to me, is helpful because it forces you to ask yourself how you can acquire a more expert

perspective as quickly as possible. It also helps you to understand the emotional anxiety felt by most students heading into the capstone. With what is basically "novice" knowledge, you will soon become an "expert" in others' eyes on your topic. Gulp! This is also a point of differentiation between those who have taken their studies seriously or not. Did you take the time to study and really understand your coursework (getting beyond "good enough for the test")? Then you are starting on a well-built foundation. Congratulations! Regardless of the strength of your academic background, you should still do whatever you can to map out what you know, link some big questions to it, and reflect on how you will get to a future state.

3. **Students' motivation determines, directs, and sustains what they do to learn.**
Remember that a capstone project, even in teams but especially if your program is online, requires more self-motivation than you have experienced in any previous course. Period. You will be starting with nothing more than a blank slate and a few questions with a goal of researching and solving for a design solution to an opportunity or problem in only a few weeks.
Wow! To be clear, because my research had been, by design, strengths based, I can say with ease that those students who most easily persevered through the inevitable difficult times did so because of a level of motivation that was driven by their passion for the subject. Likewise, those students who waffled and struggled (even changing projects mid-semester) were those who put little time into finding a project, settled on a project in which they had little interest, and, as a result, found themselves extremely unmotivated when life became hard.

4. **To develop mastery, students must acquire component skills, practice integrating them, and know when to apply what they have learned.**
This principle echoes something we learned earlier from the "How People Learn" model, that expert knowledge is built upon a novice organization of knowledge. This principle expands on that theme by going beyond the organization of knowledge to, first, the mastery of basic skills and then the application of them in an integrated way. This suggests two avenues for you to consider. First, review and expand your knowledge of whatever domain you need to understand and do that as soon as possible, hopefully long before you actually begin working on the capstone, itself. Second, be prepared to stretch yourself and get out of your comfort zone as required in order to apply and integrate your "course" knowledge with the field. This is a major transition for most students!

5. **Goal-directed practice coupled with targeted feedback enhances the quality of students' learning.**
While it probably seems obvious that targeted feedback enhances learning, this has been built into your courses up until now in the form of quizzes, homework assignments, tests, papers and projects. In a capstone project, the feedback is less clear and will be coming from many sources other than the instructor. In fact, unless your instructor happens to be an expert in the subject matter of your project, most of your feedback will be coming from your primary and secondary research sources, mentor advice and reactions of those "in the field" who have knowledge about components of your project and with whom you may only

interact informally. My key advice here is to listen carefully for any message that informs your work and be ready to pivot, since this "learning" is an important part of field-based or work-based learning.

6. **Students' current level of development interacts with the social, emotional and intellectual climate of the course to impact learning.**

   In Chapter One we described a basic framework for learning that included the Affective domain. In your previous courses the responsibility for managing "climate" of the classroom or online course was owned by the instructor. Even if you worked in teams, the instructor was always there to manage the social, emotional and intellectual components of the course and your learning experiences. In an Experiential Capstone it is now your responsibility to build the climate of your project as if it were a small organization. As you work through the organization collecting data, doing interviews and proposing designs, you will be required, as the project owner, to manage the social-emotional context that begins by managing your own emotional well-being and builds to managing relationships, none of which can be taken for granted. In a later chapter, self-assessments will be suggested that can provide guidance on your own self-development in this area.

7. **To become self-directed learners, students must learn to monitor and adjust their approaches to learning.**

   Any capstone course done within an accredited institution of higher education will undoubtedly have a syllabus, course competencies or learning outcomes and a schedule of deliverables due throughout the semester. Beyond that, however, the "on-the-ground" learning will need to be managed by you. Given what we have already described about the nature of the learning that is less structured than traditional courses, it shouldn't come as a surprise that you need to manage and adjust your approach to learning. Showing learning agility and being an adaptive learner are two of the more recent popular terms used in the field of Organizational Development. Their importance is linked directly to the pace of change now seen in all industries and the need for all employees to be open to change, display leadership and pivot as new information continues to become available. In your previous courses there were probably limited opportunities for such interactive learning but the experiential capstone, which mimics the workplace in its learning approach, requires that you exhibit this skill.

Creating Significant Learning Experiences

My "go to" checklist for developing any course or new learning experience is found in Dee Fink's book, *Creating Significant Learning Experiences*. Fink's work reflects well my own philosophy of teaching that isn't about teaching at all but about building learning experiences for students. The difference, to me, is that "learning experiences" by definition need to include all dimensions of learning and address the tactics that help to ensure that any learning activity allows students to experience the course content in a holistic way that ensures, I believe, learning that is deeper and "sticky." Fink's model is a taxonomy that is well grounded in learning theory and reflects the wisdom of his research and experience in decades of helping faculty to ensure student success.

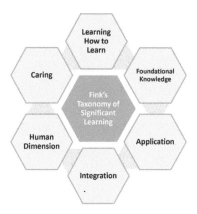

Figure 3: Taxonomy of Significant Learning
Adapted from: *A Taxonomy of Significant Learning*, Fink, Dee, (2003),
Creating Significant Learning Experiences, pp. 30, 33

Fink's taxonomy provides yet another important lens through which to reflect on both your previous learning experiences and the capstone sitting in front of you. Several parts of this model have been seen before (above) in slightly different form. While this model is directed at faculty developing learning experiences, I am using it here as a self-assessment tool for you as the owner of your own learning experience. Depending on your business curriculum and individual instructors, you probably have some variance in your competence in each of these components. Let's look at these with an eye towards you and your capstone…

Foundational Knowledge – As you decide on the topic of your capstone, you really need to ask yourself what your base of knowledge is and make any adjustments now either in your project selection or in building knowledge prior to launching your capstone work. Avoid, if possible, building foundational knowledge as you engage in your project.

Application – Because an experiential capstone project is "field based," you will be engaged in a more active learning process than you are accustomed to. This will be based on some level of inquiry and an iterative process of design, testing and learning. Are you comfortable with such an open-ended method of learning? How can you best prepare yourself for this experience?

Integration – As described in Chapter One, integration is one of the key objectives of virtually any business capstone. Our model of Areas of Management Practice provides a mechanism with which you can approach integration of your project components. Fink's model would suggest going even further and to be thinking about making connections at multiple levels (people, your home life and the project, and more).

Caring – We have described this earlier as having a passion. I like Fink's approach and, especially, his term "caring" because it seems to demystify the concept. Your capstone experience will be more productive if you care about your subject. I say that without the slightest hesitation. Ask yourself, please, if you really care about the topic of your capstone and, if not, go back and keep looking.

Human Dimension – Doing a capstone is more than dipping your toe into the waters of a work-based project and can be a truly transformational experience. If you immerse yourself in your project, open your eyes to new ways of learning, and listen carefully, you will be a different person at the end of the course. Guaranteed. Subsequent chapters will expand on the theme of leadership that supports the development of expert knowledge described earlier. In a nutshell, you will be put into one or more situations that may be uncomfortable and may provide more personal learning and growth than any other course in your program. Are you open to that and ready?

Learning How to Learn – Can you think back to some of your first courses in your business program? Remember how you struggled to adapt to the new expectations of your new level of school? Now fast forward to some of your most recent classes and how you so easily managed the learning. The difference is that you have *learned how to learn* and developed strategies to teach yourself, create feedback loops and manage your own learning. These same skills and others will be needed for the capstone as you engage in a new and very different learning experience. Are you ready for that?

Getting to Significant Learning – Fink's model is a wonderful tool for reflection on what your experiences have been in other learning situations. Significant learning sits at the intersection of all six areas as seen in the diagram above. If you haven't thought about your own learning process as you negotiated your way through your business degree, then now is the time. The capstone is different, and you are in the driver's seat to manage your own learning!

On a single page, make a left-hand column and there list the components of either the "How Learning Works" or the "Creating Significant Learning Experiences" model. Feel free to combine these models if desired.

At the top of the next three columns list the three business courses in which you had the most successful learning experiences. In deciding on which courses to list, ask yourself which had the greatest long-term impact on your life? Which course(s) encouraged you to think at a higher level and to begin to see the bigger picture of organizational success? Which courses encouraged you to learn how to learn in a more self-directed way?

Now, fill in the matrix in front of you asking yourself how each theme or learning principle in the left-hand column played out in each course. Give this some time and when you have finished, review your responses, reflecting on how you responded to various learning situations and models and what this means to you now that you are learning in a more "formal" learning situation such as an organized course.

Work-Based Learning Models

Informal and Incidental Learning

As you can see in the three "formal" models of learning, each pays attention in its own way to the social context of learning whether through application or through its more social-emotional aspects. We are using the umbrella of "informal learning" to enter the world of learning *in context* or, in your case, within the organizational setting of your capstone project. Learning in the workplace is the same but different. It is the same because many of the same elements of effective learning remain the same, and the learning practices of our three models introduced earlier provide a solid starting point.

Learning in the workplace is also different because so much learning is highly unstructured, extremely social in nature and really depends heavily on the context. Some of the most ground-breaking work in this area that, despite being several years old, is still the most relevant was done by Victoria Marsick and Karen Watkins in their research on informal and incidental learning. We should begin by reviewing a clear distinction between formal and informal learning as described by Marsick and Watkins:

> *Formal learning is typically institutionally sponsored, classroom-based, and highly structured. Informal learning, a category that includes incidental learning, may occur in institutions, but it is not typically classroom-based or highly structured, and control of learning rests primarily in the hands of the learner. Incidental learning is defined as a byproduct of some other activity, such as task accomplishment, interpersonal interaction, sensing the organizational culture, trial-and-error experimentation, or even formal learning. Informal learning can be deliberately encouraged by an organization or it can take place despite an environment not highly conducive to learning. Incidental learning, on the other hand, almost always takes place although people are not always conscious of it* (Marsick and Watkins, 1990, p.12).

This is an important point of departure for you and your capstone experience. While you are probably doing your capstone as a "formal" course, your learning will probably be heavily "informal" as you work to research a problem, understand the organization's culture, interview and test ideas with colleagues or employees or otherwise interact with the organization's members. A particularly important aspect of this type of learning is that it needs to be captured and many times is not at all explicit because it may be buried in emotional responses, what someone doesn't say, or even body language!

What Marsick and Watkins describe as incidental language may happen and you may not even realize it until well after your experience. This points to the importance of keeping a reflective journal or field notes in which to save these experiences, and by documenting your thinking about anything, no matter how seemingly insignificant it may be at the time.

Situated Learning and Communities of Practice

Closely related to informal and incidental learning is the social context of learning in a workplace situation. In my opinion, this may be one of the most important concepts underlying all internships, cooperative education positions and experiential capstones. In a nutshell, Jean Lave and Etienne Wagner's research speaks to the relationship between you and those in the workplace with whom you interact in developing your knowledge of the organization's practice. Lave and Wenger maintain that learning occurs as described by Marsick and Watkins, through the context of work activities and those engaged in work make up a "Community of Practice" (Lave and Wenger, 1991). What they add is that a newcomer, such as you, enters the community of practice, becomes part of the culture and moves from the periphery to the center of the practicing community. This social process of interaction that Lave and Wenger (1991) call "legitimate peripheral participation" is a very informal and subtle process that most often happens unintentionally as a new community member moves from the perimeter toward the center of the community. Why is this important? This will be your life over the next few months and being aware of where and when you need to pay attention to learning, how you manage your learning process, or where you stand with a community of practice, can provide a compass when you need one the most.

Experiential Learning*
Portions adapted from: *Workplace and Reflective Learning*, Haggerty, D. (2013a).

Getting Learning from Experience
Your capstone is deeply grounded in the philosophy of *experiential learning,* which is an area of study that can be, at the least, confusing and, at times, overwhelming. Like many areas of academic study, subsequent researchers often redefine the terms, and conceptual subtleties may be teased out by new research and then given new names. Regardless, the focus of the subject is always the same -- understanding how to enhance what you learn from your own experience (or how you can choose/design your experiences in order to enhance learning). In this section, we are simply taking the time to get you grounded in the philosophy and theory behind it, so you can better manage your career and personal development.

Kolb's Experiential Learning Cycle
While there are a variety of learning "models," it is the *experiential learning cycle* developed by David Kolb (1984) that is probably the best known and most widely adopted. Kolb's model is, simply put, huge in the world of learning! Without even knowing it, you have probably encountered classes or activities in which the cycles of action and reflection were used in a very deliberate way to enhance learning that comes from your experience.

Kolb's model outlines the fundamental process of learning from experience in which reflection is a key component to this and other similar models. His work is built on the work of earlier learning theorists including John Dewey, Jean Piaget, and Kurt Lewin. Kolb's model consists of a four-part experiential learning cycle that describes the stages by which one learns from experience. The four stages are *concrete experience, reflective observation, abstract conceptualization,* and *active experimentation.* These four phases of learning are also called *Learning Modes.* The cycle describes how experience is translated into concepts, which, themselves, become guides in the choice of new experiences.

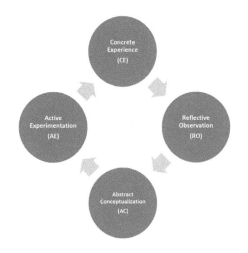

Figure 4: Experiential Learning Cycle
Adapted From: Kolb, D. (1984). *Experiential learning:*
Experience as the Ssource of Learning and Development, p. 42

Kolb's theory is based on the belief that learning from experience inevitably involves all four of these dimensions (or modes), although the starting point may be different depending on the experience and our own preferences. The directional arrows show the pathway that is typical for most learning experiences, although this can vary greatly. To be effective learners, however, we must be able to participate in all four phases that include:

- **Concrete Experience (CE)** – This is the immediate experience providing the opportunity for learning.
- **Reflective Observations (RO)** – The experience (above) serves as a source for observations and reflections.
- **Abstract Conceptualization (AC)** – Observations and reflections (above) are internalized and reframed into a theory or concept allowing inferences and tentative conclusions.
- **Active Experimentation (AE)** – The inferences and conclusions we draw (above) are now tested and become a basis for choosing new experiences.

Kolb's Learning Cycle, Part 1: Your Primary Learning Mode

The purpose of this section is to help you to better understand this theory by, first, understanding your own learning mode and learning style. As you might expect, Kolb has developed an assessment instrument called The Learning Style Inventory (LSI) that, when taken, will give you insights into your preferred learning mode and preferred learning style. In the absence of completing the complete self-assessment, we will walk through the concepts at a level that will allow you to make a "best guess" at both your learning mode and learning style.

I will highlight at the outset that there is no best way and no best style: examining and determining your learning style is carried out in the belief that we all currently use all four modes, but we all have preferences and, most importantly, *can develop* our style to learn more effectively from our experiences using all four modes.

Step One: Choose Your Learning Mode

The first step in identifying your Learning Style is to choose your Learning Mode or the single phase (of the four) that best describes your starting point for learning something new. Choosing one method over the other three only begins the process of understanding your learning style by saying, yes, of the four this is the one with which I would generally be most comfortable starting out my learning when faced with a new learning opportunity. The descriptions below provide a "high level" description of four modes.

Concrete Experience (CE)

This mode represents the more outwardly directed means of relating to an experience. In new situations, those who prefer this method would tend to "sense" or "feel" their way as opposed to "thinking" through a problem. Perception comes through the senses and through immersion in an experience, with a heavy reliance on intuition rather than a more analytical approach. Some of the characteristics that might fit a preference for Concrete Experience include:

- Being very oriented to the present
- Enjoying new experiences
- Being open to new ideas
- Preferring to be involved in things
- Being driven by feelings

Reflective Observation (RO)

Given a choice, those who prefer reflective observation would move more cautiously and prefer to reflect deeply first before taking any action. This differs from those who would prefer to "jump in" and take action. Some of the characteristics that might fit a preference for Reflective Observation include:

- Being tentative
- Watching or observing
- Acting in a reserved way
- Questioning
- Reflective

Abstract Conceptualization (AC)

While Concrete Experience suggests learning through tangible experience and Reflective Observation is characterized by contemplative observation, Abstract Conceptualization prefers thinking about, analyzing or systematically planning, rather than using intuition or reflection as a guide to a new learning opportunity.

Some of the characteristics that might fit a preference for Abstract Conceptualization include:

- Being analytical
- Being evaluative
- Being logical
- Being future-oriented
- Being rational

Active Experimentation (AE)

This is the learning mode of those who prefer trying things out as a starting point. Some of the characteristics that might fit a preference for Active Experimentation include:

- Risk-taking
- Going first
- Being active
- Valuing productivity
- Valuing relevance to the task

After reading these you might go back quickly and ask yourself which of these four best describes *how you might typically want to start a new learning opportunity.* Since we are using the Business Capstone as a context for learning, you might think about these four within the context of a likely capstone project. For example, would you prefer jumping right in, reflecting on the topic, finding an example to observe, or reading current theories? Again, there is no right or wrong and it is just a personal preference for how you like to begin your learning before moving to the other three modes.

Identifying your Learning Mode (see Doing by Learning activity below) is a first step in identifying your preferred Learning Style and only represents what you think of as your starting point in learning. It is helpful if you go back to a few of your most recent experiences in which you encountered a new learning situation. What was your first inclination, or general approach to engaging in learning? This does not mean that the other three modes are excluded but that one of the four is simply considered to be your most likely starting point.

"Doing by Learning" activity

Choosing your Learning Mode

*Experiential Learning is such an important concept that taking the time to step through **this activity is a "compulsory event!" After reading carefully through the four descriptions above, select the one that you feel best describes your entrance or starting point as a learner in a new learning situation.** Have you done that? Do you feel comfortable with your decision? **OK, it's time to move on...***

Kolb's Learning Cycle Part 2: Choosing Your Second Learning Mode
Two Fundamental Categories
The diagram below adds another level of understanding to Kolb's model. You will notice that the lines (two axes) have been added and labeled how based on two fundamental dimensions of learning from experience: how you perceive or "take in" and process or "deal with" a learning opportunity. Each of the four modes can now be viewed as belonging to these two fundamental categories. The vertical line represents how you prefer to *take in, or perceive, experience*, which can be either by direct involvement (Concrete Experience) or by a more passive and intellectually driven analysis (Abstract Conceptualization). The horizontal line represents how you prefer to *deal with, or process, the experience* through

either reflecting on the experience (Reflective Observation) or testing and experimenting (Active Experimentation).

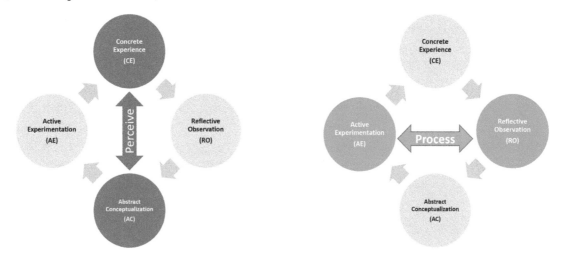

Figure 5: Perceive and Process Information
Vertical Axis = How we perceive, grasp or take-in information for learning
Adapted from LSI Report; Copyright: The Hayes Group.

Horizontal Axis = How we process, transform or deal with information for learning
Adapted from LSI Report; Copyright: The Hayes Group.

Your Second Learning Mode

When you chose your primary Learning Mode (above) you already selected a mode along one of the two dimensions of taking in or dealing with an experience. To get to your learning style, you will need to now choose your preferred method along whichever of the two dimensions you did not select for your primary learning mode. It would be helpful for you to briefly consider this by quickly reviewing the descriptions of all four modes (above) and selecting a second mode from the two modes along the axis that you have not yet selected. Here is an example: My learning mode, based on my initial assessment, is Reflective Observation, which is a method of transforming experience. For my second preference I need to choose from the two methods that are on "grasping experience" axis. Those two methods include Concrete Experience and Abstract Conceptualization. Based on my understanding of those two, I would select Concrete Experience. With that done, I can now say that my preference for Grasping Experience is Reflective Observation, and my preference for transforming experience is Concrete Experience.

Two Modes for a Learning Style

When we think about (or measure) our Learning Style, we actually measure our preferences along each of the two axes. In other words, we each fall somewhere along the vertical (CE/AC) "perceive" continuum, and *also* fall somewhere along the horizontal (AE/RO) "process" continuum. When you finally identify your learning style, you will really be identifying ***two preferences***: first, the way in which you take in (perceive) experience and then, the way you deal with (process) it, since both are required for learning to take place. The *combination of the two preferences* will indicate your overall preferred method of learning.

The theory is this. The four stages represent dialectically opposing forces: affect (concrete experiences) versus cognition (abstract conceptualization) and perception (reflective observation) versus behavior (active experimentation). Learning requires the resolution of conflicts between these dialectically opposed modes of adaptation to the world. In other words, to learn from an experience, an individual must progress through all four stages of the learning cycle. Kolb refers to this as integrative experience (Kolb, D., 1984).

Like choosing your initial mode, this second "compulsory event" requires choosing your second preference from the axis not used in your first choice (learning mode). You should now have two preferences with one from each of the two axes in the diagram above. With that done, you are now free to move on to identifying your learning style (below).

Kolb's Learning Cycle Part 3: Identifying Your Learning Style

With your two Learning Mode selections having been made (above), identifying your Learning Style is just a matter of putting them together into one "style." Remember that to find your learning style, *you need to select two preferences* (learning modes) for both how you take in (perceive or grasp) experience on the vertical axis (either Concrete Experience or Abstract Conceptualization) and how you deal with (process or transform) experience on the horizontal axis (reflective observation or active experimentation). It is *the combination that makes up your learning style* that, by definition, needs to include both grasping and transforming experience.

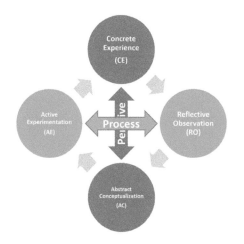

Figure 6: Learning Style Choices by Axis
Learning Style = Choosing one from each axis:
Vertical (perceive, grasp, take in)
and
Horizontal (process, transform, deal with)
Adapted from LSI Report; Copyright: The Hayes Group.

Choosing a Learning Style

To reiterate, the most important lesson of parts one and two above, choosing two preferred learning modes (one from each axis) is required to identify a Learning Style. Doing so allows you to then look at the *combination of those two modes which describes your Learning Style* that includes both how you "take in" (process) and "deal with" (perceive) information.

Understanding Your Learning Style

The descriptions below (Wentworth Institute, 2018) describe the four learning styles with enough detail that you can, hopefully, decide which fits you the best. Your starting point, of course, will be the two learning modes you have chosen from each of the two axes and chosen based on the descriptions found above. In your chosen description you should see some familiar characteristics since your Learning Style is just a blending of the two methods you chose earlier!

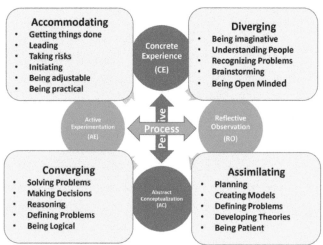

Learning Style
Figure 7: Learning Style
Adapted from LSI Report; Copyright: The Hayes Group

Accommodating Style (Concrete Experience and Active Experimentation)

Learners with this style like to work in teams and their approach to learning is more trial and error. When learning, they ask themselves "What if"-type questions.

- They like Concrete Experience (feeling) and Active Experimentation (doing) as dominant learning abilities.
- People with this learning style have the ability to learn primarily from hands-on experience.
- They enjoy carrying out plans and involving themselves in new and challenging experiences.
- They tend to act on gut feelings rather than logical analysis; they rely more heavily on people for information than on their own technical analysis.
- Learners with this style gravitate to action-oriented careers such as marketing or sales, business, social work, educational psychology, law, educational administration, architecture, psychology, education, medicine.
- As a formal learning style, these learners prefer to work with others to get assignments done, set goals, do field work, and test out different approaches to completing a project.

Diverging Style (Concrete Experience and Reflective Observation)

Learners with this style like to work in teams as well, but their approach to learning is about observing others and everything around them. When learning, they ask themselves "Why" type questions.

- They like Concrete Experience (feeling) and Reflective Observation (watching) as dominant learning abilities.
- People with this learning style are best at viewing concrete situations from many different points of view.
- Labeled "diverging" because a person with it performs better in situations that call for

generation of ideas, such as a brainstorming session.

- People with this style have broad cultural interests and like to gather information.
- People with this style are interested in people and tend to be imaginative and emotional.
- Learners with this style gravitate to dramatic arts, language, music, art, journalism, library science, philosophy, sociology, home economics, political science, anthropology, and physical education careers.
- As a formal learning style, these learners prefer to work in groups, listen with an open mind, and receive personalized feedback.

Assimilating Style (Reflective Observation and Abstract Conceptualization)

Learners with this style like to work independently (solo). They like to work on abstract concepts and prefer a logical approach.

- They like to plan and do research and like inductive reasoning. When learning, they ask themselves "What is there to know" type questions.
- They like Abstract Conceptualization (thinking) and Reflective Observation (watching) as dominant learning abilities.
- People with this learning style are best at understanding a wide range of information and putting it into a concise, logical form.
- People with this style are less focused on people and more interested in ideas and abstract concepts.
- They find it more important that a theory has logical soundness than that it has practical value.
- Learners with this style gravitate to science, geography, physiology, botany, agriculture/forestry, biochemistry, chemistry, mathematics, physics, and economics careers.
- As a formal learning style, these learners prefer reading, lectures, exploring analytical models, and having time to think things through.

Converging Style (Abstract Conceptualization and Active Experimentation)

Learners with this style like to work independently (solo). They like to work on problems, for example, technical tasks and theories and they like deductive reasoning. When learning, they ask themselves "how"-type questions.

- They like Abstract Conceptualization (thinking) and Active Experimentation (doing) as dominant learning abilities.
  - People with this learning style are best at finding practical uses for ideas and theories.
  - People with this style have the ability to solve problems and make decisions based on finding solutions to questions or problems.
  - They prefer to deal with technical tasks and problems rather than with social and interpersonal issues.
  - Learners with this style gravitate to technology, business, ecology, and engineering careers.
  - As a formal learning style, these learners prefer to experiment with new ideas, simulations, laboratory assignments, and practical applications.

"Doing by Learning" activity

Choosing your Learning Style

Read through the descriptions above and choose your best fit for Learning Style. Begin with the two learning methods (learning modes) chosen earlier. If necessary, cycle back to the two Doing by Learning activities on choosing your two best fit learning modes. When you have settled on those, then return to this activity to identify your Learning Style.

Why Learning Style?

Earlier in this chapter we reviewed several models of learning that all had one theme in common. To use Henry Mintzberg's term all these models in some way are working to make the learning *authentic*. Why? Because authenticity carries with it both the cognitive and affective sides of the learning equation and helps to explain why so many of our most vivid learning experiences have emotional memories associated with them. It is why we all work so hard to include real work experiences that are "hands on" and that help us to learn in the context of a real-life setting.

While formal education is still important for a variety of reasons, it is now widely recognized that experiential learning is invaluable, especially in any occupation that is practice oriented. Think for a minute about some of the most challenging occupations that expect excellence in performance under demanding conditions such as physicians or airplane pilots. These occupations, like many others, depend heavily on experiential education as a bridge between the classroom and the "real world." The world of business is similar and involves learning to juggle the many dimensions of any decision while carrying the weight of emotional learning as well.

Kolb's model of experiential learning is a bright line in the sand that clearly provides some intellectual grounding for how learning by doing or from experience works and why experiential learning is so valuable to your professional development. If you have taken the time to truly reflect on the three steps to the quick introduction to Learning Style, then you now have a great start for building on that understanding as you research and write your capstone.

Kolb's model should provide you, first, with an understanding of yourself as a learner when learning, especially when outside the classroom. Second, if you understand your own learning style and begin to extend your understanding to others (family, friends and colleagues), you can begin to paint a picture of how all of us work together on the job. This is especially important, for example, when you are heavily dependent on one or more people who have very different learning styles, from one another and from you, which can be both a real strength and detriment. It can also be used to examine larger groups or even an entire organization and to support the case for diversity of learning style to ensure that learning is balanced.

You can use this in your capstone as background to your experience. Understanding your learning style, for example, can help to free up a log jam in your workflow or thinking. If, for example, you tend to depend on the Divergent style and prefer to spend time observing and collecting data, then you may find that you really need to be more Convergent to bring things together with some decisions, after which you'll take some action. You will also find yourself depending on others for support, input and sharing their experiences. As you engage others, be aware of your differences in learning style, and it will help you to make every learning situation a great experience!

Organizational Knowledge Spiral Model*
*portions adapted from *The Champlain MBA*. Haggerty, D. and Stone, V. (2011)

While Kolb's model helps us to understand learning from experience at the individual or even the team level, it raises the question of how this scales up to an organization. At the organizational level, below is a learning model to do that called the ***Knowledge Spiral***. This comes to us from a great book titled *The Knowledge Creating Company* (Nonaka, I. and Takeuchi, H., 1995). While there are numerous "models" to explain organizational learning, I have chosen the Nonaka-Takeuchi model as the one that is most compatible with the pedagogy of experiential learning, action learning, reflective learning and reflective practice. This model is deeply grounded in the same theory of experiential learning but has been built to explain the important application of learning to the ***organizational*** context. This model explains the *knowledge creation* process from an experiential learning perspective and is, of course, applicable to any size group.

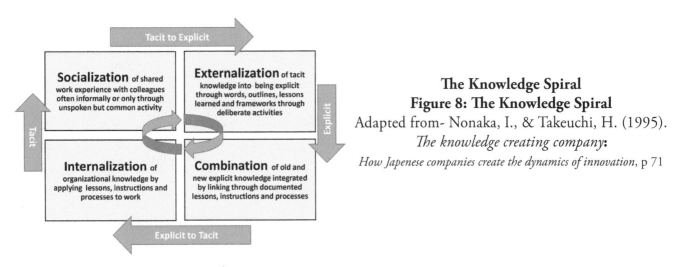

The Knowledge Spiral
Figure 8: The Knowledge Spiral
Adapted from- Nonaka, I., & Takeuchi, H. (1995).
The knowledge creating company:
How Japenese companies create the dynamics of innovation, p 71

The model begins with the premise that knowledge falls into one of two variables, *Sharing of Knowledge* and *Type of Knowledge*. *Sharing of Knowledge* is a function of (1) the degree to which knowledge is owned by one individual, and (2) the degree to which knowledge sharing among organizational members occurs. *Type of Knowledge* refers to the premise that knowledge is in two fundamental dimensions: tacit and explicit. *Tacit Knowledge* is known by the individual and as such is ***linked to an individual's mindset***, or mental model, which includes that person's deeply held values and beliefs. Explicit knowledge, on the other hand, is knowledge that is shared or known by multiple individuals and is exposed to ***multiple persons' values and beliefs***.

When placed on a grid of ***type*** of knowledge (horizontal axis) and degree of ***sharing*** (vertical axis), the result is four quadrants that explain knowledge conversion: Socialization, Externalization, Internalization, and Combination. Each is explained briefly below:

- *Socialization* is the process of quietly sharing knowledge without any direct use of language. It is a sharing of assumptions and beliefs when groups meet.
- *Externalization* is the process of articulating tacit knowledge to make it more explicit. This is done, typically, with the use of metaphors, analogies, concepts, hypotheses or models. It is often facilitated by dialogue or collective reflection.
- *Combination* is the process of systematizing concepts into knowledge systems. It is taking knowledge that is widely shared and institutionalizing it by categorizing, sorting or otherwise manipulating it.
- *Internalization* is the process of embodying explicit knowledge into tacit knowledge. It occurs when socialized, externalized, or combined types of knowledge become internalized, or owned, by an individual.

The model explains how knowledge is built as knowledge spirals within the four types of knowledge as it is made, combined, internalized, and socialized in an ongoing way (Nonaka and Takeuchi, 1995).

The quadrants with the four types of knowledge explained above are now used to explain the "process" of knowledge creation within an organization. We can think of it as how an organization or a group of people learns from their common experiences. While individuals may be undergoing their own "cycles of learning" from experience (Kolb model above), the people within the organization "build" knowledge together based on this model. Nonaka and Takeuchi propose that organizational knowledge creation takes place in spirals in which knowledge is externalized, combined, internalized, and socialized in an ongoing way.

This process is directly related to your capstone because of your role as the owner of a project that, presumably, is designed to create new knowledge about a given topic, whether it is characterized as an opportunity, a problem, or an academic exercise. Think of yourself as the "captain" of a "field team" of individuals who all understand pieces of the puzzle and in which you will be managing the learning process. You begin by, perhaps, interviewing and collecting data to build your own understanding of multiple dimensions of your topic. You then facilitate the socialization and externalization of individual pockets of knowledge by helping to make them explicit and combining them with what multiple parties contribute to the process.

When you have a proposed solution, even if temporary, then the results become internalized and the process begins again. What is important for you is to simply understand that your function as the project owner is NOT to collect some information, sequester yourself, write a plan and be done. Instead, *you will be the engine behind others' sharing and learning in an iterative process of learning.* This distinction and being clear about the "why" is one of the most important concepts behind successful capstone projects.

Action Learning Defined

What is Action Learning?

Welcome to the world of Action Learning! The purpose of this section is to build further on the models of Experiential Learning (Kolb) and Organizational Knowledge (Nonaka and Takeuchi) by giving you a tool in action learning as a methodology and mindset for learning and change in the workplace. At the highest level, action learning is simply a framework for working with others to understand an opportunity or solve problems collaboratively. As a problem-solving process, it may not seem significantly different from many other team processes. However, beneath the surface, it gets to the core of how best to approach any organizational problem or opportunity. What's special?

> *"Action Learning is a real-time learning experience that occurs on the job and with the dual and equally important purposes of addressing a business need and developing individuals by exposing them to important, challenging, and useful learning experiences."*
>
> *(Rothwell, W.J., The Action Learning Guidebook)*

When we peek below the surface, we find **four elements** that make Action Learning unique:

- First, the **deliberate reframing of problems** and the use of reflective inquiry is extremely important because it forces us to slow down the decision process and "get it right" by examining the problem thoroughly.
- Second, there is a strong **focus on learning** that, for most problem-solving processes, too often gets swept under the rug in the haste to get to a quick solution and then moving on to the next problem.
- Third, the process is built around **taking action and empowerment**. It allows those closest to the problem the freedom to solve the problem together and learn by implementing a solution.
- Fourth (which is the foundation for the first three), is the **high level of communication** required through conversations that are based on the principles of dialogue rather than debate.

In a nutshell, Action Learning is about people coming together as a team and solving problems collaboratively using communication that looks deeply at the underlying assumptions to reveal the root cause, develop potential solutions, take action, and learn from actions taken.

As Marquardt (1999) and others are often quick to point out, Action Learning is not just "teamwork," "Quality Circles," "job rotation," "project work," or "case studies." The focus, when applied in the workplace, is on real problems being solved with high levels of communication, learning, and reflection that all combine to make it more powerful than any of these initiatives alone. You might think of Action Learning as the implementation tool to enable the experiential learning processes addressed earlier in this chapter.

The Action Learning Cycle has several steps that dovetail nicely with other models described earlier in this chapter. In this model, the learner experiences a dissonant event, identifies a problem, reflects on the issue, experiments to find a solution, analyzes and generalizes for the experiment, plans a course of remedial action, tests the proposed solution, and then takes final action (Haggerty and Stone, 2011, p.5).

Action Learning Cycle
Figure 9: The Action Learning Cycle
Adapted from: Marquardt, Michael, 1999, *Action Learning in Action*, p. 36.

Action Learning is really the basis for much of the teamwork that goes on in today's workplaces. Because it is "work-based," it is highly unlikely that you would have experienced it in any academic setting where experiential learning has probably been "simulated" through problems and case studies. Because you are now bridging the gap between academic studies and the workplace through your capstone project, the principles of action learning especially related to selecting a problem, problem solving, reflection and learning are particularly relevant here. In this case, your "Action Learning Team" is really made up of your colleagues and the stakeholders in your project.

Action Learning in Management Education
Professionals working in the field of management education almost universally agree on the power of learning from experience. We have all heard, and probably said, that some of the best learning comes from applying knowledge to real situations. Understanding Action Learning, even if only at a high level, will provide you with some perspective, appreciation and knowledge of a model that has been the backbone of collaborative and experiential learning in the workplace for several decades. Your experiential capstone is an attempt to provide an Action Learning experience by giving you the opportunity to engage in a work-based project as a final "class" to your business program.

Despite agreement about the value of Action Learning, finding ways for its integration into business education courses is difficult. Your experiential capstone makes a deliberate attempt to connect the classroom and the workplace. How is your capstone using Action Learning? Here's how:

- First, for almost all capstone projects, it is highly unlikely that you will be working on it completely alone. This means that you will undoubtedly need to collaborate with others in your workplace or internship location. Even if no formally organized "team" exists, you will need to manage these relationships with inclusion and communication that follow the best practices of Action Learning.

- Second, if your experiential capstone is being done by a team of students, then you will need to collaborate on a single project(s) with classmates rather than working alone. Here, too, it is highly probable that you can benefit by taking an Action Learning perspective on learning and problem solving with your team.

- Third, in both the workplace and your capstone class, your classmates' projects will differ in their focus. This presents an opportunity for your class, itself, to become an action learning team in which you work together to the mutual benefit of all team members despite differences in your projects. In Action Learning this is referred to as an Open Group.

Appreciative Inquiry

Appreciative Inquiry (AI) Defined
One of the most useful concepts coming from the field of organizational development is that of Appreciative Inquiry (AI), which was originated in the 1980's by David Cooperrider at Case Western Reserve University. His fundamental concept, upon which he wrote his doctoral dissertation, was seemingly simple enough as "he was struck with the positivity generated when people were performing well together." (Stratton-Berkessel, R., 2010, p. 25). Following his initial work, Cooperrider continued to use Appreciative Inquiry as an organizational development tool that encouraged participants to build on their strengths. He found, along with other

AI proponents, that AI was "a powerfully effective way to enable organizations to learn about their systems in ways that result in transformative change, often literally, at the speed of imagination." (Watkins, J. et al, 2011, p. 23).

Jane Watkins, in *Appreciative Inquiry, Change at the Speed of Imagination,* proposes that AI can be thought of as three interconnected concepts (Watkins et al, 2011, p. 23):

1. AI is a philosophy of knowledge – a way of coming to understand the world.
2. AI is a principle-based intervention theory that emphasizes the role of language, dialogue, and story with a particular focus on the power of inquiry in the social construction of reality.
3. AI, embedded in its own philosophy and intervention theory, can be applied to any process and methodology for working in organizations.

AI Applied

In understanding AI, it is helpful to envision how it is used to facilitate groups or organizations moving forward together to change institutions from a more positive perspective versus a "problem" perspective. It is highly participatory and so has this and other characteristics in common with Action Learning. Its point of differentiation, however, is that its primary focus is to "discover the best in people and their organization" and to foster a deeply held belief that "every living system has something that works well already, where people have experienced some success, some satisfaction, something positive in their lives" (Stratton-Berkessel, 2010, p. 2). Imagine a session of stakeholders in which the entire focus of the conversation is about what is going well or what positive results need to be better understood and then leveraged across the organization.

AI's Strength

Using an Appreciative Inquiry perspective can mean a significant shift for many as it challenges one's most fundamental values, attitudes and beliefs. The overarching intention of the Appreciative Inquiry approach is to facilitate respectful inquiry into a selected topic to discover what strengths and capacities are already present in the group and the organization at large. The power of this approach, as opposed to more traditional "problem" and "root cause" methodologies is one of the most important defining characteristics because a conversation built on strengths, called the positive core, quickly becomes "easier" and more inspiring to embrace change and create organizational value.

Once participants have information and knowledge, it is a small step to imagine a future and then go about cooperatively designing ways to get there" (Stratton-Berkessel, 2010, p. 3).

AI Principles, Learning and Change

AI is based on five original principles to which a sixth has been added by several practitioners and about which there is general consensus:

1. **The Constructionist Principle** – Because organizational destiny is woven into the knowledge of an organization, we are always creating our organizational destiny through social interaction and dialogue, our agreed upon values and or acts of discovery.
2. **The Principle of Simultaneity** – Because change begins with the act of inquiry, it is imperative that our initial questions set the stage of discovery and positive intervention.
3. **The Anticipatory Principle** – Because change follows our collective imagination, it is

important then that our "habits of the mind, habits of the heart guide [our] images of the future." (Watkins et al, 2011, p. 73).

4. **The Poetic Principle** – Because stories hold both organizational facts and embedded emotional content and are constantly being co-authored and rewritten, we need to study our stories. "The organization's past, present and future are endless sources of learning, inspiration, interpretation and possibility" (Watkins et al, 2011, p. 74).

5. **The Positive Principle** – Taking a positive tact in any organizational change is just as contagious as a negative affect and cynical perspective. Because "human beings and organizations move in the direction of what they inquire about" (Watkins et al, 2011, p. 23), more long term and sustainable change is made possible by launching an inquiry process from a positive stance.

6. **The Overarching Principle of Wholeness** – Because AI is so deeply grounded in positivity and a strengths perspective, it leads to a very different way of thought from that seen in more negative stances.

AI is about building collaboratively and is therefore complimentary to Action Research, Action Learning and Design Thinking. AI supports innovation and change at the organizational level and helps to overcome negative conditions of the status quo or those obsessed with problems. At the end of the day, it is all about optimism. As Tim Brown, in *Change by Design* (2009) describes, "Without optimism – the unshakable belief that things could be better than they are – the will to experiment will be continually frustrated until it withers…To harvest the power of design thinking, individuals, teams and whole organizations have to cultivate optimism. People have to believe that it is within their power (or at least the power of their team) to create new ideas, that will serve unmet needs and that will have a positive impact" (Brown, 2009, p. 76). AI provides a much needed "philosophy" of change around which to build your capstone.

AI and Positive Change Project

A starting point in your learning is to adopt the frame of mind that your capstone will be a "Positive Change Project" that follows an experiential "learning" philosophy and is grounded in:

- **Experiential Learning** processes as defined by Kolb and others
- **Organizational Learning** processes as defined by Nonaka and Takeuchi
- **Action Learning** processes that empower employees to engage in a work-based system that puts problem-solving, experimentation and learning all on a level playing field
- **Appreciative Inquiry** that, itself, is a learning process of self-discovering organizational strengths through inquiry

All these models of "learning" have a common purpose in helping us to understand *how to learn from our workplace experiences in a productive and collaborative way*. It is important to absorb all these models as complements to each other and to use them as a foundation for your research and leadership on your project.

Four Case Studies

CASE 1 – Inventory Management

My three years of employment and experience working with existing inventory management systems are helpful in understanding the challenges of good inventory management. Others approaching this problem would need to substitute some more formal learning for a shorter term experience. My general approach is very much in the spirit of Action Research, with numerous management teams and employees being used as resources as I presented the fundamental challenges of obtaining accurate data. In order to make the conversations (and research) as generative as possible, I worked hard to reframe any questions from an Appreciative Inquiry perspective of looking for positive outliers and examples that could be used as positive benchmarks.

CASE 2 – New Generation Target Market for Lending Institution
Because I fit the profile of a relatively young first-time prospective homeowner, it was at least easy for me to empathize with this market segment. It certainly took some deep reflection on my part about what I might be capable of in researching and providing value added! Fortunately, I have an excellent relationship with numerous colleagues and senior leadership that provide a great starting point for action research and work-based learning that is built on a foundation of dialogue and communication. The need to design products and market to a younger generation is frequently discussed but only at a high level. Such reflective thought needs to be balanced by a more concrete experience in testing products and communications with a new market. It will take a more relational style to bring in other departments as this project will cut across organizational boundaries.

CASE 3 – Employee Training and Development for less turnover and better customer service
I wanted to take an "Appreciative Approach" and build from the strengths that we have in our current training programs. While not perfect, our training includes many excellent components that can set the bar for effective training. In terms of learning styles, my research may help us to reflect on what we have and where there are opportunities for change in the future, to understand from current employees what their needs are and begin to shift our training through small scale experiments in change. I work at the regional level, so I understand the magnitude of the opportunity that presents itself to develop a program that has an impact on the entire organization. That said, I also realize the level of effort it will take to design a program based on a wide enough set of data to address this opportunity at a corporate level. While I have felt the pain of managing underperforming employees, I have also reflected frequently on the magic between employee and customer when an outstanding employee engages with a customer and matches one of our products with his or her need.

CASE 4 – Merging of multiple non-profits into one organization
My career journey has been extremely experiential in nature. By that I mean that when working at a small non-profit there is virtually no "career path" per se and little in the way of formal training. My greatest learning has been through engaging in work projects, reflecting on my experiences, capturing the learning and repeating the process based on what I've learned. Informal learning, in the way of discussions with more senior employees at both my organization and in other regions has been instrumental. There have been times when motivation has been a challenge and when that has happened, it has always been my own self-management combined with carefully developed relationships that have kept things on track.

CHAPTER 3
A MINDSET TO LEAD LEARNING

Overview

One of the greatest lessons learned from the most highly successful capstone students has been the degree to which they felt that their leadership skills had been developed over such a short period of time. For undergraduate capstone students the capstone was one of their first "professional" experiences in which they were being asked to use their business training to make a positive contribution. For graduate students, many of whom have work experience and, in many cases, are employed where they are applying their capstone requirements, this can be just as true. This is because even fully employed students, if early in their careers, have few opportunities to take on a project that extends beyond the narrow scope of their job. Since a capstone project is, by definition, one that is comprehensive enough to extend to multiple *Areas of Management Practice*, it is often an unexpectedly huge growth opportunity.

The scale and scope of the capstone, then, for all students, undergraduate and graduate, will require a new mindset of leadership in facilitating a learning process. Keeping in mind the experiential learning models introduced earlier, and the need to serve as the owner of the project, you will have to develop a leadership mindset. In this chapter, we introduce several models of leadership that may help you in seeing yourself as a leader of learning! We are approaching leadership in two parts, here and in Chapter 9 which raises the bar to leading a change. In this chapter, our scope of leadership is limited but important as you assume a role and an identity of leadership almost immediately with every conversation!

Why Leadership?

Your Capstone and Leadership

Your capstone is probably the first opportunity for you to drill down and see clearly the iterative nature of workplace learning and problem solving. As you explore your topic, you will almost immediately be faced with the need for experimentation as a pathway to change. You will also see how your leadership is required just to explore a change and then build a roadmap to show how and why a change is necessary.

Students have repeatedly shared their surprise at how quickly this happened, even in very preliminary discussions about selecting a project. A typical reflection was that the capstone, as understood before taking the course, was about a big paper describing a project. After the course and the completion of the capstone project, however, students' big "aha moment" was that the capstone isn't at all about writing a big paper but about understanding *your role in the workplace as a knowledge creator, agent of change, and researcher-practitioner.*

This is only effective in view of the competencies of both your program and capstone course. If you recall, the competencies of the accrediting agencies that serve as our benchmark include reflective and integrated learning -- both of which tie in closely with "leadership" whether it is a project, process or people. Put a workplace learning filter on your new role, and it is obvious that you will need to lead learning through revisiting prior knowledge, testing assumptions, gathering evidence, identifying change, and engaging in a change process. This is very different from collecting research in the way of reports and journal articles to be summed into a large paper!

Leading in Learning

One of the tensions in any organization is the divide between what is "known" and the need to "learn." It creates a paradox in that we all spend so much time "learning" but -- that it could be argued -- little is ever truly "known," and everything is constantly challenged by new learning. This *Paradox of Learning* as described in Peter Jarvis's book, *The Practitioner Researcher* (1999), is that it is so temporary and needs to be constantly updated.

This is an important perspective for many students completing a research or work-based project to fulfill an academic requirement. There is a tendency to want to "solve the problem" and "identify a solution" and create a deliverable (capstone, thesis, dissertation, etc.) that is a permanent solution. What needs to be understood is a matter of perspective: that the project is always part of a bigger story of ongoing change at multiple levels within and external to the organization. It is quite typical for a business plan, for example, to be outdated by the time it is written. When defining a project, students, then, tend to think of the proposed change as "permanent" when in fact it is part of an ongoing story of change. Your role is to see both the immediate need for change along with specific recommendations, but also to see the big picture and the need for flexibility.

Leading learning, as you will be doing in your research project, is all about identifying ongoing change AND managing the day-to-day conversations about your proposed change. While your project focus is, admittedly, limited in scope, you are building leadership habits about understanding what shouldn't change, what can change, and also the likelihood of subsequent changes. The fast-moving and dynamic business environment of today requires a more adaptive style of "management" in which, regardless of what level we are working, we

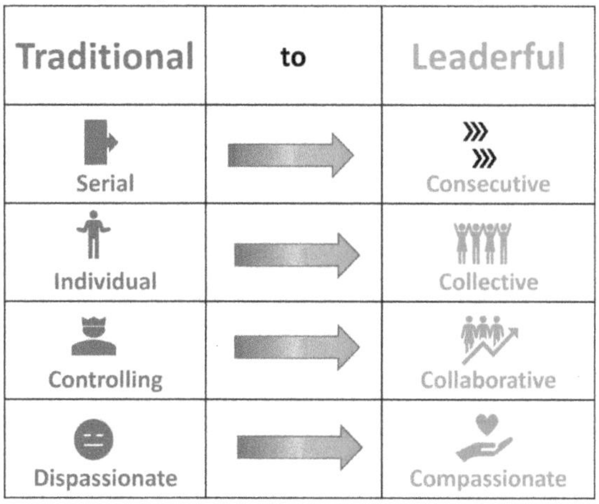

Traditional	to	Leaderful
Serial	→	»» »» Consecutive
Individual	→	Collective
Controlling	→	Collaborative
Dispassionate	→	Compassionate

his approach well in his "leaderful" model of leadership at all book, *Creating Leaderful Organizations* (2003).

Leaderful Model of Leadership
Figure 10: Leaderful Model of Leadership
Adapted from: *Creating Leaderful Organizations*, Joseph Raelin, (1999), p. 14.

Dr. Raelin's proposal represents the latest thinking in what it takes to be an innovative organization. His model characterizes four areas of leadership that contribute to a new era in management in which all employees need to assume more of a share in leadership. His model of collective leadership is important to understand because it describes the kind of leadership dynamics that may be going on in your organization either overtly or quietly. Here are his Four C's of Leaderful Practice (Raelin, 2003, p. 17):

- **Concurrent** leadership that replaces "Serial," meaning that the fast pace of decisions at all levels of the organization require multiple leaders to be working simultaneously rather than in sequence.
- **Collective** replaces "Individual," meaning that several people can work as leaders rather than the customary dependence on one leader.
- **Collaborative** replaces "Controlling," meaning that all members of an organization share in the responsibility for leadership.
- **Compassionate** replaces "Dispassionate," meaning that all stakeholders are respected and valued and that all voices are heard.

The fundamental point here is that as students you may not be aware that some very progressive styles of leadership that get beyond leadership behaviors and competencies are being used. This could impact your research as you define lines of accountability and ownership, as well as responsibility for leading change.

Ethical Leadership Perspective

One of the greatest challenges we all face every day in even the smallest of decisions is how to reconcile our personal values with that of the organization and what, exactly, the organizational values are. For any organization there is always a tension between the espoused values (what we say) and the actual values (what we do). As Razaki and Collier (2011, p. 3) point out in their article, "Ethics, The Soul of a Business Capstone Course," that ethical decision making "by its very nature is making a decision within the context of competing values." Your capstone is a great opportunity for you to exercise ethical decision making and awareness in practice!

Your business program has probably treated ethics in several ways, either as a stand-alone course, deliberately embedded into multiple courses or, in some cases, both. Wherever you encountered Ethics, hopefully it was taught in a way that has enhanced your perspective on how to go about your work in an ethical fashion and the need to be intentional about its application across the organization. Ethics can be very theoretical but it can also bring business to life when one chooses to put it front and center instead of backstage! For now, the most important thing to be aware of is its pervasiveness in every decision you make about your project including the organization you select, stakeholders you include, vendors or partners you recommend, research design and interpretation, economic valuation, strategic consequences (primary, secondary and tertiary) and any actions that you or your team recommended.

While hundreds of resources are at your disposal on the subject of Ethics, one stands out in its usability as a tool for building ethics into the DNA of your organization. David Gill's *It's About Excellence* (2010) takes a very positive, experiential and practical approach to the subject by using organizational excellence as a starting point. His fundamental premise is that "Ethics is first and foremost about *excellence…*and [that] most of the time, especially in the long term, sound ethics is a key factor in achieving and maintaining successful for-profit and non-profit organizations" (p. 12). As a capstone student, your perspective, of course, is also all *about excellence* in every way possible including how you interact with those providing you with information, how you handle confidentiality, and how you treat all your organization's stakeholders.

You also need to be thinking now, perhaps even before making a final decision about where and what your project will be and the ethical culture of organizations you are considering. I have seen too many students over the years who didn't perform any due diligence about the organization they signed on for and who found themselves in ethical dilemmas requiring that they terminate the relationship before finishing the project or the semester. If you are doing a capstone where you are employed, then the capstone may serve as a catalyst for your assessing the ethical strength of your organization. The important thing is to think about this now and to gather whatever information is available to you and to choose an organization that sees excellence in every way as a guiding principle.

In a general sense, it is important that you always understand the company values and mission. Beyond those, the next big questions are whether the company has a culture that encourages and motivates employees to "do the right thing." You might be asking what you should be looking for and what kinds of questions to ask. While Gill's book provides an excellent resource for understanding and measuring an organization's ethical quality, Gill (2010) also provides an Ethical Leadership Audit with a set of questions (shown here in two parts) that can easily be adapted to your situation.

Table 2: Ethical Health Audit	
Gill's Company Ethical Health Audit*	
Overall assessment of our organization's ethical health	**Rating 1-5** 1 = Strongly Disagree 5 = Strongly Agree
1. Overall, our company is ethically healthy – with clear values and principles, good leadership, and a commitment to do the right thing.	1 2 3 4 5
2. By comparison to its main business competitors, our company is stronger in terms of its ethics and values, commitments and practices	1 2 3 4 5
3. By comparison to other places I have worked, our company is stronger in terms of its ethics and values, commitments and practices.	1 2 3 4 5

* Source: It's About Excellence, David Gill (2010), p. 175

Table 3: Ethical Leadership Audit	
Gill's Company Ethical Leadership Audit*	
Does our company have gifted, effective ethical leadership in place and in training?	**Rating 1-5** 1 = Strongly Disagree 5 = Strongly Agree
1. Our current leaders and managers clearly know the values and ethics of our company and they "walk the talk" with integrity.	1 2 3 4 5
2. Our company leaders and managers frequently remind each other and employees of the core mission, values, and principles as planning takes place and important decisions are made.	1 2 3 4 5
3. Our company is committed to continuity of ethical leadership, and it actively identifies and mentors/trains future leaders within the company.	1 2 3 4 5
4. Compatibility with our mission, culture, values and ethics is an essential qualification for all prospective management and leadership candidates.	1 2 3 4 5
5. Our employees understand and carry out their responsibility to keep our company ethically healthy and set a good personal example to others.	1 2 3 4 5
6. Our company has in place systems, procedures, and policies that will help keep our ethics on track and healthy even during leadership transitions or failures.	1 2 3 4 5

* Source: It's About Excellence, David Gill (2010), p. 175

If you will be employed at your capstone project's location, then some of these may already be familiar to you since similar questions may be included in your annual employee engagement survey. I truly appreciate how difficult it is to ask these types of questions if you are external to an organization, such as an undergraduate student hoping to do a project linked to an internship. I have three suggestions.

First, do your best to research your prospective organization through its website and any other published material such as an annual report. Next, think reflectively about the questions above within the context of your relationship to the organization. If you know employees, selecting just two or three questions that address the organization overall and from a leadership perspective may be enough to get a conversation going. Third, you should consider including at least one question to address your interest in how the organization lives its values in order to assess your own compatibility with it.

Appreciative Leadership

In the previous chapter we introduced Appreciative Inquiry (AI). To summarize, Appreciative Inquiry is an approach to change that builds on an organization's strengths by asking questions about previous successes that may be appropriate to a potential change. From a leadership perspective, it is a very compelling approach because, unlike more negative "what's the problem?" approaches to change, it asks "what's possible?"

Appreciative Leadership is a very powerful approach for you to take as the "leader" of your research project because you have the power to set the tone when researching, whether it is through interviews, focus groups, surveys or any other research tool. In her book, *Appreciative Leadership* (2010), Diana Whitney et al. describe what their research shows in how positive power can be exercised at the highest levels of leadership. In her work with dozens of leadership teams working to introduce a more positive appreciative approach she has identified

Five Core Strategies of Appreciative Leadership (pp. 23-24) that may be helpful to your work:

- Inquiry – Asking positively powerful questions (lets people know that you value them and their contributions);
- Illumination – Bring out the best in people and situations (helps people understand how they can best contribute);
- Inclusion – Engage with people to co-author the future (gives people a sense of belonging);
- Inspiration – Awaken the creative spirit (provides people with a sense of direction);
- Integrity – Make choices for the good of the whole (lets people know they are expected to give their best for the greater good, and that they can trust others to do the same).

She goes on to describe how these five core strategies together allow you to mobilize "creative potential and turn it into positive power and set in motion positive ripples of confidence, energy, enthusiasm and performance to make a positive difference in the world" (p. 24). I must agree. Over the past three years I have had the pleasure of working directly with the David L. Cooperrider Center for Appreciative Inquiry, where I have seen first-hand how a powerful, positive approach has succeeded where more traditional organizational development efforts have failed.

Taking a deliberately positive approach at the outset is important because it sets a generative and emotionally positive tone for any inquiry. As we have all experienced, it is all too easy for any "change" project to easily head down a narrow and negative path that severely limits any creative or innovative thought. Appreciative Leadership's more **positive approach to your research** helps to neutralize unproductive negativity and what Angela Duckworth (2010) in her book, *Grit*, describes as "learned helplessness" and that overwhelming feeling of no possible solution because things are "just so bad!"

Framing issues from a positive perspective doesn't mean that problems are ignored but it does mean that setting a tone of growth, positive change and optimism is an important foundation for your project and your own emotional well-being when the project seems overwhelming. Instead, you want to set a tone of what Marty Seligman, in his book, *Learned Optimism* (2006), describes as a process, named after the book's title, in which we enact our ability to make *choices to be more deliberate about choosing a positive and more productive path to change.*

*While the book, Learned Optimism, by Marty Seligman is highly recommended, one quick way to understand the concept at a personal level is to take Stanford University's **Learned Optimism Test** that is based on Seligman's principles. It can be found at:*

https://web.stanford.edu/class/msande271/onlinetools/LearnedOpt.html

Take the self-assessment, reflect on your results and what it says about your sense of optimism. If possible, have a colleague, fellow student or close friend also take the test and then exchange your reflections on the results.

Deep Leadership

One of the most fascinating outcomes of our own research on successful capstones is the degree of transformational change that students undergo and their realization that they grew as "leaders" in managing their capstone project. Transformational, or Deep Change, is also a very powerful perspective on leadership. If you have taken a course or workshop on leadership, then you have probably done at least one leadership self-assessment. This is with good reason, because one of the fundamental prerequisites to leading others and managing change is to, first, develop the ability to change yourself, and it takes a conscientious effort. One of the timeless classics in this area of leadership development has been Robert Quinn's book, *Deep Change* (1996), in which he advocates strongly that leadership begins with personal change and that if we, as leaders, are unwilling to change, then it is fruitless to ask others to do so.

The concept of *Deep Change* is built around the dilemma that is found in most organizational settings: as the environment changes, we need to change proportionally or face what Quinn describes, very graphically, as the slow death. Most importantly, and the reason for including this resource at this point in your capstone, is that change isn't as easy as organizational restructuring (a favorite management tool) but must include the more difficult **personal changes on behalf of leadership at all levels**. The central point is that you need to begin thinking about the strong and unavoidable link between your capstone's organizational change and the personal change that may be required of all stakeholders. While, in some ways, the organization and its policies provide "excuses" for avoiding change, it is the individual who must take the initiative to push these boundaries from the inside out. As organization members, we have only a few choices: play it safe, leave, or push for change.

Your role as the project owner puts you in the unenviable position of discussing with people a change that may disrupt their lives. Just by asking questions and researching a change, you are seen as a potential disruption to the lives of everyone you encounter. While your change may be technical in nature, you will, like it or not, be in the organizational development business of helping others see the need for reflective personal change as a starting point for any organizational effort. Why? Even the greatest organizational transformation begins with its **people**.

Organization members need to adopt attitudes, knowledge, beliefs and values that make them open to doing things differently. This may mean a new set of behaviors and/or new ways of thinking. This has two direct applications. First, be prepared to change yourself as you encounter ideas, employees, vendors and more by being reflective and open to changes in your approach and project management style. Second, be aware that change doesn't come easily to people, so sensitivity and patience are attitudes to keep in mind as you launch your research! As the guru of organizational culture, Edgar Schein has repeatedly advocated in multiple publications that leadership *requires a willingness to take risks and change yourself*. Be ready!

Resonant Leadership

The capstone is an opportunity to accelerate your own leadership development in unexpected ways and build on Quinn's work. Being, worst case, just prepared for that change and, best case, being deliberate about your own leadership skills, is the career developing opportunity that sits in front of you. One widely acclaimed perspective on developing your own leadership competencies begins with a self-reflection on some fundamental skills in self-management and human relations.

Richard Boyatzis and Annie McKee, in their work, *Resonant Leadership* (2005), reiterate the need for authenticity and the use of Emotional Intelligence to build resonant relationships with others. Resonant leaders, they say, "are inspiring their organizations and communities to reach for dreams that even a few years ago were impossible" (p. 3). They propose a model of leadership consisting of ongoing personal renewal built on three key ingredients: mindfulness, hope and compassion. They define each as follows:

- *Mindfulness* as "living in a state of full and conscious awareness of one's whole self, other people and the context in which we live and work" (p. 71);
- *Hope* is to feel the excitement about the possible future that we feel is attainable;
- *Compassion* is being in tune with the people around us and understanding their wants and needs, while being motivated to act on our feelings.

Based on their work, Boyatzis and McKee conclude that these three are the cornerstones of leadership. Their work compliments other leadership concepts that we have examined in this chapter and others, such as Appreciative Inquiry, Action Research, Ethical Decisions and Emotional Intelligence. Boyatzis and McGee (2005, p. 82) have built a self-assessment on page eighty-two called "Your Moral Core" that requires you to select and rank your five top values from a list of ninety-five "Values, Beliefs or Desirable Personal Characteristics." It is instructive because it forces you to push yourself to the uncomfortable position of choosing values that may describe how you act or aspire to be in the future.

"Doing by Learning" activity

Values Self-Assessment

> *It is suggested that, as a first choice, you locate a copy of Resonant Leadership and use the self-assessment on "Your Moral Core." In the absence of this tool (which cannot be copied here due to copyright restrictions), search the Internet for a **Values Self-Assessment** Tool that works similarly. This is an especially useful tool to have when performing an Ethics Organizational Assessment described earlier in this chapter.*

A more recent resource with a similar perspective on leadership can be found in *Discovering Your True North* (2015) by Bill George. George advocates Authentic Leadership that is characterized by leaders "who are true to themselves and what they believe in", who "engender trust and develop genuine connections with others" and who "as servant leaders… are more concerned about serving people than about their own success or recognition" (p. 8). At this point you should begin to see a theme emerge from this chapter. YOU are no longer a passive recipient of knowledge in the classroom or even engaged in "active" learning (case studies, simulations, role playing) but are now stepping up to the "real deal" in which you are in the driver's seat. How you manage your project and your leadership of your project is not a mechanical process but rather is laden with the emotional white water that you must negotiate and manage.

Connective Leadership and Achievement*
*portions adapted from *Leadership Models for Change – American Leadership*. Haggerty, D. (2013k).

In understanding your personal "leadership style," you may find it helpful to think of it more broadly as "leading with others," rather than "leadership." Just for this reason, let me introduce you to Jean Lipman-Blumen's *Connective Leadership* model, from her book of the same name (1996), and what I have found to be one of the most intuitively helpful models of seeing how we "lead" from all levels of the organization. Her point of departure is that she refers to leadership as an *"**achievement**"* style. It might even be called a *"work* style." Whatever name you choose, the fundamental approach is the same: identifying the styles you have used throughout your life in all situations to succeed in "getting it done," whether in the workplace, helping a non-profit or managing a youth group.

The model's importance, and difference, is that it looks at the types of relationships used to achieve leadership. In today's fast-paced, innovative and collaborative work environment, applying this model could be the difference between capstone success and failure. While there is no designated assessment tool (questions and scoring), I have found that students comprehend the styles almost immediately and easily "see" examples drawn from their own work experiences. Studying the nine styles described below, identifying your preferred styles, and assessing the opportunities to expand your style repertoire is now your task. The first step in managing change is to understand what you are doing and why. This model helps you to do that!

The *Connective Leadership* model, seen below, has three fundamental styles, each of which has three additional subcategories of achievement styles. The diagrams below, adapted from the book, *Connective Leadership* by Lipman-Bluman (1996) are accompanied by a brief overview of each style.

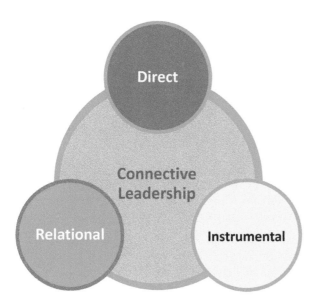

Connective Leadership
Figure 11: Connective Leadership
Adapted from: *Connective Leadership* by Jean Lipman-Blumen, (1996)

Direct – This style probably sounds familiar to most of us. It is highly individualistic and focused on the task at hand, using our personal skills and driven by personal objectives.

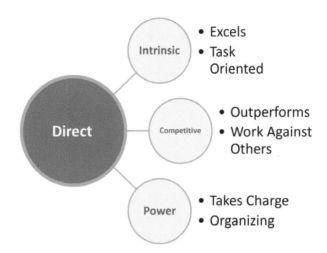

"Direct" Connective Leadership
Figure 12: Direct Connective Leadership
Adapted from: *Connective Leadership* by Jean Lipman-Blumen, (1996)

The three direct types are:

1. Intrinsic, in which the task itself is a source of excitement and challenge;
2. Competitive, in which the challenge of working against others is motivating; and
3. Power, in which taking charge, managing, coordinating and organizing is most important to us.

Relational – This style is less concerned with individual achievement and more focused on helping others to achieve their goals. It requires a high degree of interdependence.

"Relational" Connective Leadership
Figure 13: Relational Connective Leadership
Adapted from: *Connective Leadership* by Jean Lipman-Blumen, (1996)

The three relational types are:

1. Collaborative, in which teamwork and working jointly is found to be best;
2. Contributory, in which helping others to complete their tasks leads to satisfaction; and
3. Vicarious, in which mentoring, coaching or being a fan without any real direct participation is enough.

Instrumental – This style assumes that everyone is willing to help us to achieve our goals.

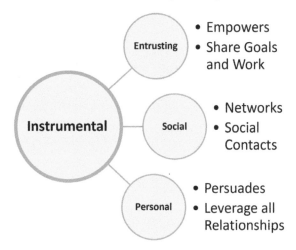

"Instrumental" Connective Leadership
Figure 14: Instrumental Connective Leadership
Adapted from: ***Connective Leadership*** by Jean Lipman-Blumen, (1996)

The three instrumental types are:

1. Personal, in which all stops are pulled in using any of our personal resources to help us achieve our goals;
2. Social, in which social contacts are approached to help the leader be effective in a situation; and
3. Entrusting, in which one consciously convinces others to share the goals.

There are two primary ways of using this model to enhance your understanding. One, and perhaps the most concrete, is to look at your own lifetime as a chain of personal growth incidents. For each moment of achievement, ask which style(s) contributed to your success. The second is to look around your workplace. Take a small sample of people who you know reasonably well and apply the model to them. Ask yourself how they accomplish their goals? How do they achieve?

Your own approach (or those of others) to achievement is probably not along a single path. For example, although your preference may be for one of the more individualistic **Direct** styles, you may find that a new project forces you to adapt to use some of the **Relational** or **Instrumental** styles. The important point is that you can improve your leadership by (1) understanding your own preferences, (2) being honest about your limitations and (3) developing the ability to consciously choose the style(s) that is (are) most appropriate for the organizational change that you are facing. That's the connective leadership!

The applicability to your capstone is this: it can be generally assumed that you as a student of business are either pre-career launch (undergraduate) or relatively early to mid-career (adult undergraduate or MBA). Even if early to mid-career, there is a good chance that at least some of your career has been in roles in which you were more of an individual contributor than a change agent. Working as an individual contributor, by its nature, tends to be more "Direct" than "Relational" or "Instrumental." Now here is the newsflash and hot tip you've been waiting for. *Your capstone project, by its nature, will be heavily dependent on others and probably require multiple styles to be successful.* If your capstone is a solo effort (not team based) you might think that it is going to be an individual effort. On the contrary, however, the most successful capstone students did the opposite and were noticeably relational and instrumental in their approach.

If you find yourself stuck after a few weeks into your capstone research, then look back at this model and reflect critically on your achievement style to unlock the log jam. How many relationships have you built around this project? Who have you talked to for advice? Even better, take this model and, once your project has been chosen, reflect on your current (preferred) styles and then *project yourself ahead to envision how other styles could be used* in your project. In either case, how you work, achieve, and "lead" your project will have a dramatic impact on its success and using the descriptions of the nine leadership styles as a basis for self-reflection is a perfect starting point.

Read through the descriptions of "Achievement Styles" above and identify your most likely styles that you would use in a workplace situation of being responsible for a project. If possible, rank all nine and reflect on what that says about your preferred styles. How is this a strength that can be leveraged? What opportunities might there be to increase your use of your less preferred styles?

Grit and Passion

Make no mistake about it – experiential capstone projects can be extremely challenging despite your previous track record of academic excellence in traditional courses. Why? Because you are being asked to learn in a way that you have not had to do in most of your previous academic work. Anxiety about being able to complete the capstone is always reflected in student surveys at both the beginning and end of the course. There is a tremendous uncertainty about how something so open ended will ever reach a finish line, and this, in turn, translates into somewhat justifiable anxiety. Because you are working independently, with self-imposed deadlines, subject to the contributions of others over whom you have little control, and on a short timeline, life can get very hard. The answer is simple to talk about but difficult to implement. Being motivated to push through the tough days and weeks will take strong determination and perseverance.

There are several ways to think about what competencies are needed for these times. Resilience, or the ability to rise up after setbacks, is important. Having perseverance or being able to apply continuous pressure to complete the task is also key. Both of these are embedded in a more recent term called "Grit" that is now associated with the work of Angela Duckworth in her book *Grit: The power of passion and perseverance* (2016), and is seen as *the ability to sustain interest and effort in reaching long term goals.* It is also associated with self-control and with deferring short-term gratification.

This is an area of study that is extremely important to a successful experiential capstone project. In a project that is so open-ended it is the degree to which you can persevere and overcome obstacles that will inevitably determine your success. In Duckworth's book, *Grit* (2016), she presents research supporting the importance of perseverance (Grit) in achievement. Her own research, and the survey instrument she used for the book, are based on the application of her *Grit Scale* of self-assessment, which consists of ten questions. When answered with honesty and candor, these questions can help you to measure your own Grit.

Take Angela Duckworth's Grit Survey and reflect on what this means to your capstone project. The survey is available online at the following website: https://angeladuckworth.com/grit-scale/

While resilience, perseverance, and Grit all have their obvious benefits to a capstone student engaged in a work-based project, I feel that Grit may be the most important of the three because it is based on passion. Based on my own research, those students who were the most successful in both completing and enjoying their capstone projects were those that reported having a *passion for their topic*. This fits perfectly with Duckworth's findings that passion is driven by both an *interest* and a *sense of purpose* about work. Like employees who are more engaged when they connect to an organization's purpose, students who are working from a foundation of deeply held beliefs about the work that they are doing are better able to be resilient and to persevere when learning and progress are going slowly or that stop altogether.

Duckworth's research also parallels several of our own findings about success factors:

- *Long term effort requires far more time than the minimum.* Grit research tells us that high levels of achievement take much more practice than one might feel necessary in order to become even competent or "successful." This aligns with the amount of pre-work, networking, and basic skill building done by high-achieving capstone students who put in significantly more hours than is ever required based on the credit hour requirements of the course.
- *Passion and Engagement get you through the tough times.* Grit research is very clear on the need to have a real self-driven interest and purpose behind it and serving as a basis for "passion." High-achieving capstone students routinely describe the higher purpose of their work not only to themselves but to their organization and the world. This higher purpose doesn't minimize the need to see relevant self-interest (such as career mobility) that is also seen in outstanding capstone students.
- *Stick to your plan.* Grit research refers to the ability to sustain an interest in your current project rather than moving on to the next big thing at the first opportunity. This is an extremely

important behavior to understand when you are involved in a project that is open and subject to change as you engage in action research. Knowing when to "stick to the knitting" or to change topics is one of the greatest attributes of the most successful capstone students. Switching topics with little justification is also the hallmark of capstone students who struggle the most with sustaining their interest.

- *Make Learning a Social Experience.* Duckworth refers to the need to serve others as a basis for the social experience of work. This links directly to our own capstone research in which we have seen that building your network of support and mentorship becomes a valuable resource for learning and reflection. This also aligns with the relational and instrumental achievement styles described earlier.

Obviously, it is the combination of sticking to your plan along with passion and a willingness to put in the long-term work effort that provides a magic formula, if there is one.

Leading Learning: Summary

Is the organization where your capstone resides following good "Leadership in Learning" practices? Are you? This chapter has opened seven doors for you to enter that all converge on the most recent thinking about leadership and organizational development. They could easily be bundled under the umbrella of an Innovative Mindset, because Innovation is all about learning. How you will apply each of these frameworks to your own capstone is your decision. To start you off, here is a checklist of where we have been in the past few pages:

- **Leaderful Organizations** are more collaborative and base decisions increasingly on the collective. What is true for organizational learning is true for your little capstone team!
- **All About Excellence** shows us that authentic ethical behavior is "baked in" at both your organization and your capstone levels. Are both the organization and you on board with such excellence?
- **Appreciative Leadership** is all about taking a more positive growth mindset that builds on strengths rather than obsessing on problems and weaknesses. How will you structure your own questions to be addressed in your capstone?
- **Deep Change** maintains that leaders need to change before asking others to do so. What will you be looking for in change at your organization? How will you approach change yourself as you engage in the capstone?
- **Resonant Leadership's** key concept is authenticity. Do you see such authenticity at your organization? Are you being authentic in your own search for answers to your proposed change?
- **Connective Edge** provides a map of the types of relationships used for achievement. How does this model fit your organization and how would it impact your project? How can this be used by you to structure your capstone relationships?
- **Grit** gets beyond determination and shows us that passion and purpose are the real drivers to getting it done when motivation becomes difficult. How much passion and purpose do you see at your organization? To what extent are you driven by passion and purpose?

All of the models presented in this chapter have the potential to provide a road map to success in your capstone by simply paying attention to your feelings, being honest about your effort, and, to the extent possible, using your experience to build and leverage strengths as you build new competencies.

Four Case Studies

CASE 1 – Inventory Management

Taking a positive and appreciative leadership position is instrumental. Based on my reflective learning style and a mostly direct achievement style, I would prefer to collect data forever and to work on my own, but it became evident early on that it was important to take action and drive the project with small iterations of collaborative design. This project required a deep investment in relationships from the outset and required also that I bring people up to speed regularly with my latest thinking. I have always had an interest in operations, and it has been something that I've cared about for the five years that I have worked in this area and built my career around the challenges of logistics and materials management. I appreciate that this project is so close to my interests and passion and that it offers me the opportunity to think deeply about how I would fit into this area of business in the long term. Perhaps most important is my belief in what we do. Our business is important to the world, and efficiency here in my shop has a ripple effect on other parts of the economy that affects many peoples' lives. In many ways, I find myself thinking differently about myself already as a leader as I engage with others on this project and learning and helping them to learn with me.

CASE 2 – New Generation Target Market for Lending Institution

It will take a more relational and collaborative style than I typically use to bring in other departments as this project will cut across organizational boundaries. Because of the changes to various data management systems, marketing budgets, operations and customer service centers, this project will take a higher level of persistence and "grit" by me and any of my leadership team. This is made easier, however, by my passion to get young families into homes that they own. In managing this project, I am finding that management is delightfully positive about the future and does not really dwell on the marketing failures of the past. I recognize also that my "Appreciative Leadership" perspective has begun to pay off, even in the preliminary conversations that I am leading in which I have successfully directed the conversation to building on our organizational strengths.

CASE 3 – Employee Training and Development for less turnover and better customer service

Because most of my work has been at either my immediate office or the local level, this project will give me an opportunity to exercise some leadership. At this point, my leadership role may be enhanced more later on by my final deliverable than during the course of my project inquiry. This is because so much of my research, while involving other employees, is asking about their perspective as followers rather than as leaders themselves as part of a system of collective and shared leadership. The need for leadership training has caught some people's attention as a bigger opportunity than just my project, and it is good to know that during the early stages of my project. What it does is it brings about a reflective perspective by even senior leadership's willingness to change. As someone who has always been interested in human relations and who works in Human Resources, I prefer a more relational achievement style, so this project is causing me to be more direct in my achievement style. The program design will begin with facilitated discussions with employees to have them share their biggest successes in leadership development on which to build a new program.

CASE 4 – Merging of multiple non-profits into one organization

While I would consider myself very early in my career (my first real job!), I do feel that my competencies match many that I have studied for self-leadership, always a first step in leading projects, processes or other people! In doing self-assessments and reflections, for example, I found that I had numerous strengths that characterized good leadership, not the least of which was a deep belief in a strengths-based approach to life that matched well with Appreciative Inquiry. This will drive my inquiry into this merger and will need to lead conversations that could all too easily head down a path of "we've tried it before" and "why this won't work." I do believe that, given the mission-driven nature of all the organizations, leadership does exhibit "Resonant Leadership" characteristics of authenticity and mindfulness, which constitute a great starting point for any dialogue. Also, given the nature of our work, all the stakeholders are committed to excellence and to doing the right thing, something that makes any ethical decision easier to make in the name of excellence.

"Doing by Learning" activity

Leader in Learning Self-Reflection

Review each of the seven Leading Learning models and, for each, write down the concepts that seem most important to you, preferably on one sheet of paper. Identify those concepts that have been the most important to you in your own working career. Can you think of specific examples when these concepts were exemplified by employees?

Now reflect on how your understanding of the concepts in this chapter will help you in approaching your project research as you engage with others and face obstacles and setbacks. Can you see yourself as a Leader of Learning?

CHAPTER 4
INQUIRY AND "DOING BY LEARNING"

Doing by Learning

Some of my favorite memories from my own career are of times when an opportunity presented itself about which little was known. At times like that you scramble to gather any information available, contact anyone you can unearth with even a nugget of insight and build from there. From those experiences you learn several things quickly. First, your business training provides some amazing guidance, but finding most of what you need to know lies ahead of you. Second, what you need to know probably isn't documented or very explicit, nor is it bundled nicely into even a few "reports" or white papers. Third, you need help in the form of collaborative relationships and networks that may provide important information in very subtle ways. There are other lessons, for sure, but the important point is that at every step of the way, you will need to inquire and question everything from the most basic assumptions to the tiniest detail.

In previous chapters I have provided you with a deeper understanding of what you know for business competencies, how you have achieved those competencies through various learning models, and finally how experiential or work-based learning differs from these. As a capstone owner and an emerging "leader of learning," you will need to develop competencies that allow you and others to learn about your topic.

These skills are more relational and include the ability to build a community around an emerging idea that is constructed through inquiry with others. While I am the first to appreciate the concept of *Learning by Doing*, or learning through "hands on" experience, I also have come to realize that much of the important learning in building new knowledge comes between those periods of action and in the form of inquiry and reflection. I call this *"Doing by Learning"* because it is the inquiry and the conceptualization of ideas that provide the foundation to any future action.

The World of Inquiry

Roots of Reflective Inquiry
Reflective Inquiry lies at the heart of everything we have presented in the previous chapters. It is the driver to taking action in our models of experiential learning (Kolb, D., 1984) and organizational knowledge creation (Nonaka, I., 1995). It is a cornerstone of both Action Learning and Action Research.

One way to think of Action Research, in fact, is that you are layering the experiential learning model onto the research process of making an inquiry into your organization. As learners, we all tend to underemphasize the reflection and observation part of the learning process. If you think about the models of workplace learning that have been introduced, they all are centered on some form of reflective inquiry.

So, what is reflection? One of the world's experts on Action Learning and management education, Joseph Raelin, in his classic book, *Work-Based Learning* (2008), calls reflection "the practice of pondering and expressing the meaning to self and to others in one's immediate environment of what has, will, or is happening (Raelin, 2008). This definition alone opens our eyes to the idea that reflection not being confined to being conducted after-the-fact. Reflective Inquiry can also occur in *advance* of an expected experience or happen *real-time* during an experience. But Reflective Inquiry doesn't just happen. It takes a deliberate effort to make space in our lives for real reflection that allows for learning that is meaningful because it opens the door to deeper, emotionally driven feelings. Individual reflection is the place where we allow ourselves to ask questions collaboratively that test even the most basic assumptions. The importance of group reflection, as well, cannot be overemphasized. Open reflection, such as the use of dialogue, is critical to "helping group members learn to appreciate contrary points of view, differing modes of interaction, and varying levels of commitment to the team" (Raelin, 2008). Reflective Inquiry, because it is deep learning, allows space for emotional learning, as well. Because of this, both individual and group reflection can support either cognitive or affective learning and, as such, suggest that reflective learning through inquiry can support quality learning associated with workplace experiences.

While reflection can be built into your research and learning process in numerous ways, the most important aspect of it is that you somehow capture your reflections and learning. One highly successful way to do this is journaling, which is a very reliable process for reflection during the Action Research process. Also called "field-notes," these notes to yourself are an invaluable resource as you move through the research process. Think of reflective journals as a method of collecting data that help discipline the research process, enabling you to integrate information and experiences as they occur throughout the project. It is important in virtually all Action Research to involve others in your process. Whether it is getting feedback on broadening or narrowing the scope of your research, brainstorming on preliminary findings, or examining data for themes and lessons learned – involving and collaborating with others is essential!

Inquiry
Your inquiry is driven by the assumption that you are trying to create value for multiple stakeholders in your organization. While we will discuss this further in subsequent chapters, let's acknowledge that you are now in the role of *agent of positive change* – a role that will evolve over time through your action research. As you engage in identifying a project, you will want to be as inclusive as possible, with a wide set of stakeholders with whom you will engage in a *process of mutual inquiry*. Experiential projects are a team sport!

Your role as a researcher-practitioner is based on inquiry which, itself, is a competence worth developing. As Warren Berger (2014), says in his book, *A More Beautiful Question*, "Because change is now a constant, the willingness to be comfortable with, and to even embrace, ambiguity is a critical skill for today's leaders" (p. 159). In your work doing research you are demonstrating both the organization's and your own willingness to *inquire into its current processes and business model*. This alone is a major step toward change. If you are not employed at the organization, then your "outside" perspective is valuable because it will allow you to see things with a fresh viewpoint.

As a student doing a capstone project, you may feel, at least initially, that you are creating little value. After all, you may be starting out with little knowledge about your topic, only a handful of resources and a very limited network of support. Underestimating your value would be a mistake. However, you may be far more valuable to the organization than you realize just because you are asking important questions! As Michael Marquardt explains in his book, *Leading with Questions* (2005), "Questions can be very powerful in focusing attention. When leaders ask questions, they send constituents on mental journey – quests -- in search of answers. These journeys can be positive and productive, inspiring creative problem solving, new insights, and fresh perspective" (p. 63). Marquardt goes on to describe what he calls empowering questions that "get people to think and allow them to discover their own answers, thus developing self-responsibility" and "build positive attitudes and self-esteem; they remove blocks and open people up to unexpected possibilities while inviting discovery, creativity and innovation" (p. 64). This has huge implications for you as a researcher. Even with little prior knowledge you are serving as a catalyst to inquiry and reflection by others in the workplace. Your inquiry is the launching pad for your organization's learning.

Questions, Questions, Questions!

Presumably, this role of being an Action Researcher is new to you. Consistent with our *Doing by Learning* mindset, you will need to be deliberate in your development of questions. As you engage with others through questions, you will be constantly pushing against the natural tendency for others to provide immediate solutions. While these may be well intended, you as a researcher will be working hard to open the inquiry to possibilities, looking for insights and making new connections rather than jumping on quickly assembled solutions. In short, good questions are the basis for good research data. How?

Marquardt (2005, p. 66) provides us with several benefits of great questions that include:

- Causing the person to focus and stretch
- Creating deep reflection
- Challenging taken-for-granted assumptions that prevent people from acting in new and forceful ways
- Generating courage and strength
- Leading to breakthrough thinking
- Containing the keys that open the door to great solutions
- Enabling people to better view the situation
- Opening doors in the mind and getting people to think more deeply
- Testing assumptions and causing individuals to explore why they act in the way that they do, as well as why they choose to take action
- Generating positive and powerful action

In most cases, people will want to help you by telling you how to fix the problem rather than helping you to understand the problem at a deeper level to reach a breakthrough. Your greatest challenge then is to develop compelling and powerful questions that encourage deep thinking and broaden the conversation.

Powerful Questions

So, what is a powerful question? To answer this, we will turn to several resources, so you have them at your disposal. In a white paper, *The Art of Powerful Questions* (2003) by Eric Vogt, some broad guidelines state that a powerful question:

- Generates curiosity in the listener
- Stimulates reflective conversation
- Is thought-provoking
- Surfaces underlying assumptions
- Invites creativity and new possibilities
- Generates energy and forward movement
- Channels attention and focuses inquiry
- Stays with participants
- Touches a deep meaning
- Evokes more questions

These guidelines are an excellent starting point to any interviews, however informal, that you are having about your project. Notice that each of these suggestions are divergent and look to expand the conversation and are NOT designed to look for solutions. While suggestions for solutions are welcome, they happen all too naturally and, once shared, tend to restrict the conversation from opening any more new and insightful possibilities.

Building Questions

How, you might be asking, do you begin building questions? Vogt (2003) also provides a model that structures the process into three "Dimensions" that may be helpful. They are presented below with brief elaboration.

1. **Construction** – The first step is to choose a basic opening to the question by selecting from the following list based on which one you feel would be the most powerful in opening up the response of your target audience (Who, When, Why, What, Where, How, Which). He suggests that Why/How/What are the most powerful; Who/When/Where the next most powerful and Which or Yes/No questions are the least powerful because they are the most limiting. In a nutshell, each of these (and other openings) set the stage for expanding or constraining the response, and the choice is yours to make before you engage in a conversation!

2. **Scope** – The second step is designed to stretch respondents by encouraging them to think beyond their immediate situation, something that is all too easy to slip into. The three choices here are simply representative of a typical range of scopes. They include work group, company, and supply chain. The important point is to expand the scope as much as possible in order to broaden the thinking, as well!

3. **Assumptions** – Frame possibilities based on assumptions. Here, your questions need to look at any of the underlying assumptions about the project. For example, if your project was about building a new formal leadership program, you might ask how leadership could be developed at your organization in the absence of a structured leadership program at all, in order to test the assumption that leadership needs a "program" to be successful.

How to Frame Better questions

The final piece from Vogt's paper (2003) is adapted then from Sally Ann Roth's *Public Conversations Project*

(1998). Below is a set of questions that can be used to ask yourself as you begin to frame a set of questions. These are used by the Public Conversations Project, a group that helps create constructive dialogue on divisive public issues.

- Is this question relevant to the real life and real work of the people who will be exploring it?
- Is this a genuine question — a question to which I/we really don't know the answer?
- What "work" do I want this question to do? That is, what kind of conversation, meanings, and feelings do I imagine this question will evoke in those who will be exploring it?
- Is this question likely to invite fresh thinking/feeling? Is it familiar enough to be recognizable and relevant — and different enough to call forward a new response?
- What assumptions or beliefs are embedded in the way this question is constructed?
- Is this question likely to generate hope, imagination, engagement, creative action, and new possibilities or is it likely to increase a focus on past problems and obstacles?
- Does this question leave room for new and different questions to be raised as the initial question is explored?

This list makes several points. First, it forces you, the researcher, to be on task and ensure that your question relates directly to your fundamental research question(s). Second, it checks on the expansiveness of your questions since the responses to constricting questions are difficult to expand after the fact! Third, it allows for emotional response to be explicit and be captured, something that is highly valuable for any insights into motivation and how people *truly feel*, despite what they may "say."

Sample Questions to Ponder
- "Why" questions – "Why do you think that?" or "Why did this work?"
- "Can that be done in any other way?"
- "What learning has come out of this so far?"
- "What other options can we think of?"
- "What resources have we never used?"
- "What other opportunities can you can see?"
- "What assumptions should we be rethinking?"
- "Are there any challenges around the corner that we should be prepared for?"
- "What do we expect to happen if we do that?"
- "What is stopping us?"
- "What are some possibilities that we haven't suggested so far?"
- "What happens if . . .?"
- "Have we ever thought of . . . ?"
- "What is this telling us about what is emerging?"

Deepening Questions
Because our objective is to be inquiry driven, make tacit knowledge explicit, and to expand our responses, it is helpful to have a repertoire of what I call qualifiers for your questions. This list below from Marquardt's book, *Action Learning in Action* (1999, p. 229), is highly useful in structuring your primary questions before engaging in an interview or focus group. Perhaps as importantly, they are highly useful to have top of mind to encourage elaboration, or when you need to redirect a respondent to provide a more expansive and deeper

response or to simply evoke a different perspective on a response.

- <u>Open</u> – Asked in such a way that it invites freedom in how to respond ("How do you make such decisions?")
- <u>Affective</u> – Invites the sharing of feelings ("How do you feel about…?")
- <u>Reflective</u> – Asks the other to say more about something he or she has said ("When you said there were difficulties, what kind were there?")
- <u>Probing</u> – Causes the person or group to consider greater depth or breadth on a topic ("Why is this happening?")
- <u>Fresh</u> – Challenges basic assumptions ("Why must it be that way?")
- <u>Connecting</u> – Creates a systems perspective that looks at interrelationships among features of the situation ("What are the consequences of these actions?")
- <u>Clarifying</u> – Results in further descriptions or explanations of something ("Are you saying that?")
- <u>Explorative</u> – Opens up new avenues and insights that the other may not have considered ("Have you explored…?")
- <u>Analytical</u> – Examines causes ("Why has this happened?")
- <u>Closed</u> – Asks for a yes or no answer, and should be used sparingly since they provide so little data. That said, it may be helpful to generate a conclusive and decisive response when needed.

Dialogue
*portions adapted from *Understanding Dialogue*. **Haggerty, D. (2013e)**

Welcome to the world of dialogue. One of my favorite quotes is from the forward of William Isaac's book, *Dialogue* (1999), in which he says that dialogue is described in Native American cultures as, "You talk and talk until the talk starts." This describes nicely both the challenge and opportunity in using real dialogue.

If your workplace has you pressured for results (and most do!), then it should be easy to see why real talk is so limited and has been replaced, instead, with fast-paced discussions and debates. In both discussions and debates, the objective is to get the "problem solved" and "action taken," often at the expense of understanding the real problem or opportunity. To get to the real issues, however, talk needs to be, if nothing else, more extended until, as the quote above says, the "talk" starts. We are beginning, then, by focusing on what continues to be the core workplace issue -- communication that is deep enough to facilitate learning that is reflective. At its best, this is called dialogue.

The diagram below provides some perspective on where Dialogue fits into our communication schema. Dialogue's most important distinction falls at the Fundamental Choice Point. Here is where normal discussion is generally driven by some major point to be made and defended in one of several ways (conversation, discussion, dialectic or debate). These defensive communication methods are directed at making a decision, solving a problem and coming to a conclusion. Dialogue, on the contrary, means that participants are open to listening without resistance and without a prior position to defend. From there, Dialogue is more open to learning, exploring any underlying assumptions and opening up to possibilities. In short, Dialogue is more in line with the nature of inquiry and research questions as we have described them earlier in this chapter.

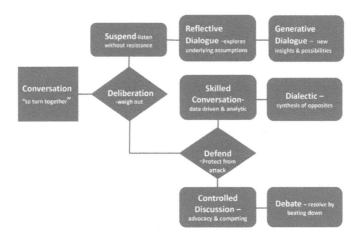

Figure 15: Dialogue vs. Debate

Adapted from: *Dialogue and the Art of Thinking Together,* William Isaacs, 1999, p.41

Dialogue works best in a small group and your use of it could prove limited, depending on your project and your immediate role at your organization. The chart below summarizes some of the characteristics of dialogue.

Table 4 – Discussion vs. Dialogue	
Discussion	**Dialogue**
Presenting a structure to propose or defend a proposition	Postpone immediate solutions – suspend judgment
Often characterized as a debate with all sides having defendable positions	Statements or additional questions designed to increase understanding about earlier questions
Positions proposed and defended	Working to speak to the center to the Center of the topic rather than assuming one position.
Seeking a solution	Inquiry-Based Understanding

With a basic understanding of Dialogue and where it sits as a communication tool, we will now explore two aspects of the topic. First, we will address the question of "Why dialogue?" Second, we will touch on some of the "Benefits of Dialogue." Hopefully, these will help you in your application of dialogue to your capstone and your life!

Why Dialogue?

Some of the "Why" of dialogue may have already been answered, in your mind, by the introduction above. As simple as it may seem, it is still very powerful. Why?

Because it is a Vehicle for Learning and Change – One of the most important things to remember about learning (whether individual, group or organizational) is that it is about change. Whether it is as simple as a new concept that replaces something learned earlier in life or a more complex and emotional experience that transforms your whole perspective, change is always in the learning picture. Dialogue, because it opens your mind and heart to the conversation, makes room for learning and change.

Because it is a Means of Interaction – While this is not a book or chapter on communication, per se, your success in the capstone will, to a large extent, depend on how you communicate with all of the stakeholders associated with your capstone project, including fellow classmates and instructors. Understanding *how and why dialogue works* is an important means of interaction because it provides a framework for getting to the real issues and assumptions that so often are hidden in our conversations.

Because it is a Foundation of Leadership – As the definition of "leadership" continues its ongoing evolution to a more collaborative and relational model, the need for highly effective communication increases. Dialogue provides a tool and a mindset about how to talk to each other, what language to use (or not), and how to behave in a management role. It goes beyond conversation to becoming a cornerstone for how to most effectively help people work together.

Because it is a Conduit for Public Reflection – As discussed earlier, *reflection* is probably not what you thought of as an important competency for completing a successful capstone. Especially in the workplace, *reflection* takes place, not only alone, but with others, or in "public." This *public reflection* is a critical component of learning in both the team and organizational environments because it takes the focus from just getting the job done (action) to really understanding why recommended actions are being taken (reflection). Dialogue is the conduit for that discussion because it deliberately and thoughtfully *slows the pace* from hasty (as happens all too frequently) to being focused and more thoughtful.

Because it is a Background for Organizational Learning – As current or prospective managers and leaders at all levels you will ultimately have a responsibility to an organization whether it be large or small. Even as entrepreneurs, our small businesses quickly take on a life of their own with their own need for *new knowledge* and ongoing learning. Dialogue disciplines the conversation to pay respect to all stakeholders and helps ensure organizational knowledge and decisions are based on the widest available input. In short, it ensures both diversity and that all voices are heard fairly.

Benefits of Dialogue

<u>*Problem identification*</u> is something that makes up much of our time in the workplace, and with good reason. When tasked with the job of correcting a situation, the most logical step is to look to the immediate cause of the specific problem and correct it. Too frequently this has the effect of band-aids and aspirin – it gets you through the moment but does not solve the underlying cause. Isaac, in his book, *Dialogue*, (1999), condemns our "dividing" a problem from this perspective; often the act of dividing a problem *incorrectly* has the result of focusing our attention on only the most obvious problem and failing to get to the *root cause*. Dialogue, or talking things through thoroughly and openly, allows the use of a mindset of *systems thinking* to be used that looks at all possible causes from a broader systems perspective. This supports, for example, your use of the *Areas of Management Practice* model, in which you need to probe for connections between your most immediate focus and other areas of the organization.

<u>Reflective dialogue</u> is just what it sounds like – dialogue that takes on a tone of *reflectivity and deep learning*. It is not until we get to the deep understanding of the core assumptions and beliefs behind a problem that we are able to truly generate innovations that have any long-term effects. The diagram above, from Isaac's (1999) book *Dialogue*, is extremely important in understanding what dialogue is all about. It clearly shows how dialogue is different from other conversations. For example, notice that most conversations (such as department meetings, project teams, etc.) are driven by each player "defending" a position, which even in a "controlled"

conversation ends up in "debate." Dialogue, on the other hand, is very different, because it is a conversation to unearth new information and reveal some fresh insights into the possibilities!

<u>Tacit knowledge</u> is described as the "unwritten and unexamined" knowledge that each of us has on various topics. Remember the module on experiential learning? In the spiral of knowledge creation, introduced in an earlier chapter, Nonaka (1995) points out the need for organizations to "pull" knowledge from individuals and get it socialized or shared. This is called making tacit knowledge *explicit* so that it is out in the open to be examined by everyone.

A decision made by one manager "thinking alone" without adequate dialogue, or a decision that gets "pushed" through a team meeting, does not get the benefit of *real* group input. Only through a more thorough process of mutual inquiry can the tacit or hidden reasons behind a decision be tested and understood. The concepts of *participation* and *action learning* are premised on the fact that, although many of our work-based problems are already understood (at a deep and tacit level), we fail to capture our own knowledge.

The theory posits that the best solutions are derived through being *reflective* about what we know. Dialogue is simply a means of being *reflective together* in order to build and make explicit our collective knowledge. Said another way, reflection opens our minds to multiple ways of thinking, and dialogue is simply a tool to get us there. It does this by asking us to do a few simple but difficult things. When the Nonaka describes it, however, as a *"quality of being"* (p. 75), he captures nicely the difficulty of learning something that is less a "method" with a rigid set of rules and practices, and more a "mindset" about how to approach a problem and treat each other!

Remember that dialogue is not an "all or nothing" practice that needs to be held in reserve for a serious problem or crisis. Your readings get you grounded in the philosophy and need for dialogue. I urge you to try it out (see "Practicing Dialogue" below) in teams at your workplace. I would suggest practicing in small groups of two to four members. With a few people, it is easier to learn how to maneuver the conversation away from a politically driven process to one that is more open…that's dialogue!

Practicing Dialogue
<u>Overview</u>
The best way to learn how to use dialogue is to try it! That said, developing this practice means, first, paying attention to the four practices of dialogue: *Listening, Respecting, Suspending, and Voicing*.

<u>Listening</u>
Isaacs (1999) describes the importance of developing a "fresh response" and truly listening to what is being said. I will not belabor you with the hundreds of examples of meetings I have been in where people were missing each other's thoughts by not REALLY listening! I am sure you can think of your own situations immediately! But why does that happen? Isaacs, I believe, is right on when he states that "much of our reaction to others *comes from memory*; it is *stored reaction, not fresh response* at all" (p. 92). Whether it is the pressure of the annual goals, project deadlines, or our busy personal lives in general, all too frequently we are not really *engaged* with what is being said, *miss the meaning* (or the details), and respond mechanistically. This same lack of thoughtfulness leads directly to the problem described in the concept of the *ladder of inferences*. This model explains how quickly we jump to what we think is true with little basis in fact. This is not a small issue!

The role of emotions also deserves some special attention. As will be highlighted in subsequent chapters, it is often difficult to separate the cognitive from the emotional issues when reacting to experiences (and team meetings are experiences!). I have witnessed, as I am sure you have, some extremely smart, capable, and well-educated managers who are completely hamstrung in their thinking by emotional attachment to an idea from which they simply cannot divorce themselves. *Asking questions* may seem like an oversimplification of the problem but it is a great first step in learning to create real dialogue. This works because it causes us to pause as we extract meaning from each response. Rather than looking for an opportunity to advocate (defending) a single position, questioning continually opens the conversation to more data and possibilities.

Respecting

Critical listening (above) is the highest form of respect. Conversely, opening and willingly sharing information is also a sign of respect. Both are important to dialogue.

Two concepts that seem to be at cross purposes but are deeply related are "listening to the flow" and "being participants, not observers of the conversation." In dialogue, we need to do both. By listening to the flow, we are being asked to detach ourselves from the conversation and to gain a perspective that is broad enough to allow for some free thinking. However, this does not mean that we are excused from participation! On the contrary, dialogue, by its nature, means active participation by everyone. If we were not online, we would meet in a circle – without any back row in which to hide out!

Suspending

The term "suspend" is easy to misinterpret. By suspending we may be sharing our perspectives but doing so in a non-judgmental way that allows for further questions. As Isaacs (1999) points out, we are, "for the sake of the conversation, suspending our certainty" (p. 147). It is fine to share a belief, but it is contrary to the principles of dialogue to overtly advocate it.

For obvious reasons, this is not easy to do, especially when the stakes are high. When careers, financial rewards, and our personal identities are on the line, it is difficult to not advocate and defend. It is for reasons like these that make something as "simple" as dialogue so difficult to implement in the workplace. It is also one of the key differences between a debate and a dialogue!

The term *"Reflection in Action"* comes up repeatedly in your readings in this book. The concept originated in the book, *The Reflective Practitioner* (Schön, 1983), which is a landmark in the field of organizational learning. It was mentioned in an earlier chapter. By *"Reflection in Action,"* Schön (and others) are describing the reflection that may not be part of a deliberate conversation but that is embedded in the way we work. It happens "on the fly" as we go about our work. In one research project I interviewed a manager to better understand how reflective learning could have possibly worked for him, since he spent his days in the middle of a busy production facility. Because he did not have the luxury of attending "meetings" in a comfortable room, he had no choice but to adapt and develop skills of "suspending" and holding reflective dialogue while huddled up with a handful of coworkers in the heat of battle. He was, incidentally, one of the most reflective workers that I ever encountered! Despite the hectic environment, he would routinely push the conversation well beyond seeking an immediate solution to problems and always looked for the real issues at a deeper level. He connected with people, listened, and held mini dialogues at a moment's notice! Wow!

In summary, suspending is all about asking questions such as:

- Why am I seeing things this way?
- Is there another question that could be asked of this question?
- Are there any underlying patterns or new connections to what is being asked or said?
- In what other ways could this topic be reframed?

<u>Voicing</u>

For many of us, it is difficult to find a voice, or the right thing to say, in the absence of traditional debate. We are so accustomed to advocating a "position" that to simply *"suspend" our certainty* leaves a vacuum in the matter of what exactly to talk about. Coming forward in such an environment requires a "leap of faith" to simply *talk about a problem to understand* it better. This is what Isaacs (1999) describes as "thinking in the moment" and speaking in a more improvisational way.

You can fill the void by addressing some fundamental questions:

- What needs to be expressed here?
- How can a pattern be described that would support the dialogue?
- Is there an emerging concept that hasn't yet been articulated?

The key principle here is that the conversation needs to be directed to a common purpose or meaning that unfolds slowly. It is, as Isaacs and others have described, a conversation directed to "the center."

Dialogue Summary

I particularly like Isaacs' (1999) approach to the topic of dialogue because he makes no pretense that dialogue is easy, and he gets to those four key practices above so clearly. They **are not** simple to implement and will require a lot of practice both in your respective workplaces and in your interviews, especially in groups. In the end, dialogue, like other "Leadership" topics, comes full circle back and brings us back to our own self-reflection and willingness to listen to our true selves. As Edgar Schein (2018) in his paper *The Process of Dialogue*, states about dialogue:

> *"This moment is critical. As we become more reflective, we begin to realize how much our initial perceptions can be colored by expectations based on our cultural learning and past experiences. We do not always accurately perceive what is "out there." [and] " what we perceive is often based on our needs, expectations, projections, and, most of all, our culturally learned assumptions and categories of thought. Thus, the first challenge of really listening to others is to identify the distortions and bias that filter our own cognitive processes. We have to learn to listen to ourselves before we can really understand others. Such internal listening is, of course, especially difficult if one is in the midst of an active, task-oriented discussion. Dialogue, however, opens up the space for such reflection to occur."*

Inquiry in Appreciative Inquiry (AI)

AI's Positive Core

Having already introduced Appreciative Inquiry in a previous chapter, we will now look in greater detail at how it can serve our process of inquiry. Appreciative Inquiry is used to build on the best of human experience, best practices, and strengths of the organization. As an approach to organizational development and strategic change, it is a highly useful tool for your Positive Change Project. Because it is based on the collective imagination of stakeholders, it begins any inquiry from a position of growth and hope. Approaching a situation from such a positive mindset isn't just hype. While problems are identified, they are addressed within the context of a more positive overall approach. It is grounded in the belief that an organization's direction is determined by what it chooses to focus on and study.

Appreciative Inquiry begins by selecting a positive topic. The topic selection, by itself, sets the stage for how you will approach all subsequent inquiry, so it is an important first step. An example might be a situation in which a "problem" of lack of leadership had been discussed as a potential topic. Instead of dwelling on leadership failures, a more positive research topic might be to explore "exemplary leadership characteristics in our organization that should be codified and shared." The "problem" topic, once translated into questions, is likely to become endless discussions about leadership failure but with no hope of resolution. *A more positive topic is far more likely to generate a discussion about what is working well that encourages thinking about other ways to do well.* One is stuck in the past and the other is about building a future! In the field of Appreciative Inquiry this is referred to as the "positive core" or the "Affirmative Topic."

Diana Whitney, in her excellent book, *Encyclopedia of Positive Questions* (2013), provides some guidance in selecting what she calls an Affirmative Topic. She begins by saying that you should select between three and five compelling "juicy" topics, all of them meeting the following criteria:

- They are affirmative or stated in the positive.
- They are desirable. You want to create more of them in your life at work or at home.
- You are genuinely curious about them and want to learn about them.
- They will take you where you want to go.

She goes on, asking us to remember the following principles:

- As human systems-people and organizations, we move in the direction of the images we hold of the future.
- Images of the future are informed by the conversations we have and the stories we tell.
- Conversations and stories are informed by the questions we ask, so:
- *The questions we ask are fateful*. They determine what we find, and they create the world as we know it.

AI's Positive Questions

With the positive topic, or positive core, having been established, the next step in AI is to develop positive questions that are built around your positive topic. First, everything discussed earlier about inquiry and questions is true for AI. For all the same purposes of expanding the conversation to possibilities, the same structure and processes apply. The difference is that AI questions need to be consistent with the positive direction set out by the positive topic. Some typical questions can be used to probe and more closely define positive topics such as:

- What's working well?
- What metaphors might describe current success?

- What might the future look like?
- How can we build on earlier success?
- What feelings were present when things went well?

The use of positive questions driven by a positive mindset may have originally been launched by the proponents of AI but it also fits into some of the latest thought leadership on new business development and organizational entrepreneurism. Eric Reis, in his recent book, *The Startup Way* (2017), describes successful entrepreneurial ventures that are housed within large and ongoing organizations. In reviewing success stories, he states that "In every case, senior leadership has a point of view – and conviction – that the leading indicators [that] the change agents are working toward point to good things ahead" (p. 175). What Reis is describing is a "growth" mindset that is best nurtured through generative questions.

Diana Whitney (2013) describes a positive question as "an affirmatively stated question – a question that seeks to uncover and bring out the best in a person, a situation or an organization. It is constructed around a topic that has been selected by a person or a group – a topic that is *fundamentally affirmative*" (p. 120). She goes on to describe the typical structure of a positive question as follows:

- The title of the affirmative topic
- A lead-in that introduces the topic and describes it as already existing
- A series of sub-questions (usually two to four) that explore different aspects of the topic

Some examples of typical positive questions are:

- Tell me about the work experience in which you learned the most. Tell me about the situation. Who was involved, and what did they do? What did you do to foster your own development? What made this a high point learning experience? (Whitney, 2013, p. 59)
- What are the three most important enhancements you would wish for in our current technology so that it could be of more service to you and our customers?

Flipping the Question

In beginning your capstone project, you will undoubtedly encounter stories of failure and negative topics being suggested for your research. These topics might be appropriate, for example, in both the Affirmative Topic, as well as your Positive Questions. In using Appreciative Inquiry as a framework for your Positive Change Project, you will frequently be given an initial set of "problems" and things that are "broken" and needing to be fixed. It will be your job to reframe those "problems" into positive topics by what, in AI language, is called "flipping the question". Here are some examples:

Table 5: Flipping the Question	
FROM (negative topics or questions)	**TO (positive topics or questions)**
Customer Complaints	Delighted customers and why?
Missed Deliveries	Deliveries that are exceptional in on-time, safe handling and customer satisfaction
Employee Turnover	Highly engaged and happy employees

The point becomes obvious very quickly. The topics on the left take us nowhere, are not energizing and suggest that resolving them will get us back to a state of acceptability. Those on the right are generative and invite excitement about researching the topic in an effort to build a better future.

AI 4-D Process

While a positive, or affirmative, topic and positive questions can be used in any number of processes, the practitioners of Appreciative Inquiry have given us a prescribed process to support your getting to a future state. Based on the use of a positive topic and positive questions, it includes:

- **Discovery** (valuing) – In this first stage you will be asking positive questions to build an understanding of what has happened in the past that is positive and upon which a future can be built.
- **Dream** (envisioning) – With an understanding of what has transpired that is positive, this stage uses the data from "Discovery" to imagine what could be.
- **Design** (dialogue) – With a clear vision of the future established in the Dream stage, you can now begin to design concrete solutions that might be exercised to build to the new vision.
- **Destiny** – (co-constructing the future) – This final stage is all about implementation and creating the future.

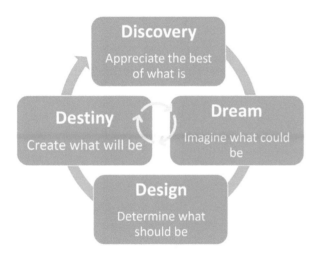

Appreciative Inquiry's 4-D Process
Figure 16: 4-D Process
Adapted from Whitney, D. (2008) Appreciative Leadership, p. 54

This 4-D Process is the primary structure when Appreciative Inquiry is used as a tool for organizational development and strategy. When applied in this way, it frequently includes the *whole system* of an organization in a large gathering of stakeholders that may extend into employees, suppliers, customers, community members, and more. These strategic gatherings are often referred to as *summits* by Appreciative Inquiry practitioners. Large meetings such as this typically extend over several days of inquiry done in small groups with the entire community's set of ideas being aggregated into one comprehensive set of priorities and initiatives that can then be used for strategic planning purposes. Often, potential projects may surface that are completely unexpected and result in new relationship building among the extended set of participants.

While a capstone project is unlikely to take on the scope of such a comprehensive planning process, the fundamental sequence can be used in doing your research. This is a very powerful way to direct your capstone work to a more positive and generative line of inquiry and to avoid the trap of negative and less productive conversations centered on problems alone. Instead, the 4-D Process sets a tone for more future-oriented conversations about the *possibilities* based on *successes* of the past. The value of this single attribute cannot be overemphasized and makes the 4-D Process a perfect filter to use as you define your overall topic and especially when building interview or survey questions for your primary research.

Action Research*
*portions adapted from *Action Research Cycle*. Haggerty, D. (2013g)

Action Research Overview
Action Research is presented here because it represents the basic research cycle of most capstone students engaged in an experiential or work-based project. Your project is, presumably, real and your process will be, out of necessity, cyclical as you collect data, make meaning of what you have, reflect on the project, move on to the next stage of research and repeat.

A more precise definition is provided by Coghlan and Brannick, in their book, *Doing Action Research in Your Organization* (2005, p. 7), in which they say, "Action Research focuses on knowledge in action." Accordingly, the knowledge created through Action Research is situational and out of praxis. In action research the data are contextually embedded and interpreted and the basis for validation is the conscious and deliberate enactment of the action research cycle. The action researcher is immersed in the research setting."

Action Research Cycle
Figure 17: Action Research Cycle
Adapted from: Coughlan and Brannick (2008),
Doing Research in Your Own Organization, p. 22

In your studies you may have used any of a number of iterations of the Action Research Cycle that are all very similar at their core. In *Action Research Essentials (2009)*, for example, Craig describes the process as having the following steps:

- Selecting a focus
- Reviewing helpful theories that apply to the problem
- Identifying research questions
- Narrowing the questions
- Identifying subjects and participants such as colleagues (and others)
- Selecting the method to best inform the inquiry
- Identifying the data sets
- Collecting the relevant data

- Analyzing the data
- Designing the action plan and taking informed action
- Reporting results to all parties involved to improve conditions and situations

While Craig's focus is primarily on educational Action Research, his steps are certainly compatible with any organizational setting in which research is being conducted within the organization. For now, it is important to see the relevance and compatibility of a disciplined method of inquiry joining forces with an equally disciplined set of questions. For your capstone, you might think of this as your primary cycle of events as you collect data, put ideas in front of people, ask them questions that generate new data and repeat.

Action Learning and Your Capstone*
*portions adapted from *An Overview of Action Learning*. **Haggerty, D. (2013d).**

Action Learning Revisited
We have introduced Action Learning in an earlier chapter. Its definition is nicely summarized by Rothwell (1999) in *The Action Learning Guidebook*, as "a real-time learning experience that occurs on the job and with the dual and equally important purposes of addressing a business need and developing individuals by exposing them to important, challenging, and useful learning experiences." Let's unpack this definition a bit to see the relationship of Action Learning to your capstone.

- *"Real-time learning experience"* – Unlike your previous case studies and simulations this is a project that has real consequences in an organization. That raises the bar for everything including the questions you ask, what data is used and how, who you talk to, how you conduct any surveys or formal structured research, how you manage any ethical decisions regarding your project, the recommendations you develop, and more.
- *"Occurs on the job"* – Unlike any course you have taken or even a project of studying an organization at arm's length, this project is part of actual decisions and operations. Any occasion when you take up people's time has a cost, and any recommendations you make may affect employees' lives. You will face unplanned constraints, suffer disappointing setbacks, encounter time delays that threaten your project's completion and perhaps run into paradoxical situations that seem to have no way out. All of this is part of learning "in context" and may affect what you are able to do and when.
- *"Dual and equally important purposes of addressing a business need and developing individuals"* – When used as a framework in the workplace, Action Learning provides space for employees to make decisions more freely, test out small-scale (or even large scale) changes, capture the learning and continue with professional development as a priority. What is different is that it deliberately makes **learning equal to problem solving** and puts employee learning ahead of the need to provide oversight. This empowerment in the name of learning is now considered to be "best practice" for many newer models of innovation. In your work your project may find itself being given freedom to explore or not depending on the learning culture of your organization.
- *"Exposing them to important, challenging, and useful learning experiences"* – If the priority of learning was not made clear enough in the description above, then this should resolve any questions you might have! The key concept is that better decisions are made by the people closest to the work, and the only way to develop employees' abilities is to be deliberate about

their learning experiences. This one concept has been the foundation of work-based executive education programs for the past fifty years.

Stages of Action Learning

By now the stages of an Action Learning Cycle should seem familiar and the model useful in guiding your process of inquiry at two levels.

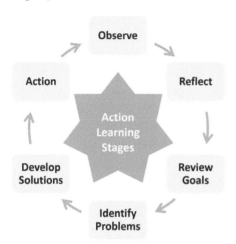

Typical Stages of Action Learning
Figure 18: Action Learning Stages

First, at the level of your work, it can be helpful to review an Action Learning Cycle by any of several authors and apply it to your own project work. For example, using the Action Learning Cycle above, you might ask yourself:

- What observation have I made about the nature of a capstone project, other successful students, or my organization's previous work with student projects?
- What reflections do I have regarding my own strengths and weaknesses to take on this project?
- Do I have specific goals about this project about which I am unwilling to compromise or that are important to reach for professional development purposes?
- Have I listened to others and identified problems needing to be resolved before I move on or that are likely to surface during the project?
- What recommendations, plans, and schemes do I have for getting this huge endeavor accomplished with my busy schedule?
- What actions can I take now to ensure my success?

Next, these types of questions can also be applied to the work-based Positive Change Project itself, whatever it is. Regarding your project, as you engage in research you often experience an overwhelming feeling of being buried in data.

- <u>Observation</u> might be equated with the first big round of research and after doing the first set of interviews or other data collection, you may have a feeling of accomplishment that also leaves you wondering what to do next. Just realizing that this is only the first of many stages gives you a sense of perspective and reassurance that you are not lost but just early in the journey.
- <u>Reflections</u> are an important part (perhaps the most important) of the learning process. Seeing

that it is a distinct stage that needs to be treated in a deliberate way helps to set aside that lost feeling that comes with a mountain of data! Assemble your interview notes, mark them up, make new notes about your data, look for insights, take a nap! All these feed on your reflections and doing this in a conscious way will liberate you to move on.

- Reviewing Goals at this point allows you to pull up from the depth of reflection and get some perspective on where your project data is beginning to answer some key questions related to your goals. With your goals assessed, you are now better able to continue looking at your research with fresh eyes.
- Identify "Problems" could just as easily be interpreted as identify "Strengths" (with which to take on a more Appreciative Inquiry approach). Think of this stage as one of making connections and finding insights from your data that suggest leverage points for solutions, improvements or a new product.
- Develop Solutions doesn't need to mean final solutions. Instead this could be an opportunity to "test" solutions in some low-cost way. What may be the most important lesson when you reach this stage is that identifying some possible solutions is where you wanted to be after completing some research but that it was impossible without deliberate work in each of the other stages. Understanding this, alone, BEFORE jumping into your capstone, better prepares you mentally for the challenge of doing this experiential capstone.

Action Learning Teams

So, you ask, "How does this fit with my capstone project?" This is a fair question, and the answer is somewhat dependent on the structure of your project and your relationship to the sponsoring organization.

If you are fortunate enough to have a team capstone format, then you might be thinking about how you will work together. Marquardt (1999) discusses several characteristics of effective action learning groups. These are quite useful, as they mirror those discussed in the general literature related to effective groups. They include:

- A shared commitment to solving the problem
- Clear, common purpose
- Willingness to work with others to develop strategies
- Courage to question others
- Clear and accepted norms
- Respect and support for others
- Willingness to learn and to help others learn

In general, however, you will find yourself going through some combination of the following stages:

1. *Formation of a group* -- The characteristics are: members appointed or volunteers, the group consists of members from the same organization with diverse components represented or representing many organizations, focused on a single common problem or the group members' individual problems, time frame, and frequency prescribed or determined by the group as it forms. This may be anything from a formal group with extensions to include others less formally as stakeholders in your project. The extension of a new "Inventory Management" project into other Areas of Practice such as Marketing or Information Systems is an excellent example of other stakeholders who are part of your "team."
2. *Presentation of problem(s) or task(s) to the group* -- Problem(s) need to be briefly presented to the group

and, in response, group members ask questions for deeper understanding. This stage is more powerful than it seems since inquiry is such an important part of your process in leading your formal and/or informal team. It is important that you open the conversations to encourage a dialogue about the true nature of the problem or opportunity.

3. ***Reframing the problem*** – Following the initial questions, all members reach a consensus about the most significant challenges or opportunities that emerge from the framing of the problem as it was originally presented. This, too, can't be overemphasized. What begins with sharing the problem to invite inquiry now continues with additional inquiry, dialogue and reframing of the original problem.

4. ***Determining the goals*** – After identifying the key challenges or opportunities, the group identifies the desired outcome or result that, if achieved, would solve the problem in the future in an optimal way. This is comparable to other models in which a "future state" or a "vision" is set for the project. Without a desired outcome to benchmark your progress, a project can too easily wander and find itself unable to reach any finish line because too many unfinished pathways have been used.

5. ***Developing the action strategies*** -- This aspect takes time and energy to identify and pilot-test possible action strategies using a process that integrates reflective inquiry and dialogue. You will be doing this throughout the project as you conceptualize possible solutions and share them for feedback.

6. ***Taking action*** -- Between sessions, the action learning group or its members collects information, identifies support, and implements strategies developed by the group. This may or may not occur as part of your capstone, only because of time constraints. That said, your work should certainly be of a quality that makes it possible to "test" solutions and learn iteratively. You may see a parallel here with the more recent thinking on entrepreneurism and corporate entrepreneurism.

7. ***Capturing learning*** -- Periodic reflective processes (after-action reviews) occur to support reflection on group process and performance on ways to improve the group's functioning. Because your capstone is being done within an educational institution, learning should, of course, be captured and documented for your final recommendations and reflections.

Design Thinking
A Model for Innovation

The final model I will include in your methods of inquiry is that of Design Thinking. Design Thinking has direct relevance to your capstone, especially if your focus is on developing a new product or innovative solution. The diagram below highlights the five steps considered to be the backbone of design thinking.

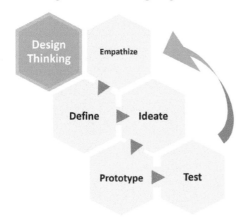

Design Thinking Process
Figure 19: Design Thinking
Adapted from: Brown, T. (2009) *Change by Design*

Empathize – The emphasis on Empathy is one of the key differences between Design Thinking and more traditional product development processes. Where other processes might depend on doing extensive marketing research and years of probing to understand a customer's needs, Design Thinking shortcuts that process by direct observation of customers' behavior now, in their current situation, in an effort to gain insights. The goal is to really understand your target audience.

Define – Based on the deep understanding of customer needs, the next step is to define what the customer needs are.

Ideate – Here the objective is to brainstorm as many solutions as possible without constraints of any kind. The key to this stage is to generate a volume of ideas under the theory that ideas, even those that may be impractical, may generate other ideas that have some usable components. At the conclusion of this stage the hope is that virtually all possible solutions have been entertained.

Prototype – After some process of selection, and without the benefit of exhaustive traditional research, a prototype needs to be built that can be "tested" by being put in front of users/customers. This prototype needn't be functional and could even be a sketch or mock-up model. The point is that feedback from customers and users about a real prototype will reveal reactions and insights that would otherwise be unavailable, especially in such a short timeline.

Test – The prototype is now shared with users/customers to receive feedback. Because it is a real prototype, the feedback can provide new insights into what would work or not. This last step is only the beginning since multiple loops will be required before any "final" design is produced on any scale.

Design Thinking Process

This process connects well with the use of inquiry, good questions and reflective learning described earlier. In each stage it is easy to see where inquiry supports the design process. From a project management perspective, Design Thinking represents the most recent thinking in Entrepreneurship, Business Modeling and Minimum Viable Product Development. The fundamental concepts of rapid turnaround and feedback combined with deep customer understanding are tools that can serve as the undercarriage of your capstone project. At the very least, some of the concepts at the highest level may be used to inform the process, questions and ideas you share as you engage in your Action Research. Below are some additional thoughts on Design Thinking that may be useful for you to reflect on.

In *Change by Design* (2009), Tim Brown nicely outlines several recommendations for the application of Design Thinking to the **organization** and your work. His work is summarized below:

Table 6: Design Thinking Characteristics	
Design Thinking Wisdom	**Quick Explanation**
Begin at the beginning	Begin with divergent thinking to generate a number of possibilities instead of narrowly focusing on just a few.
Take a human – centered approach	Look and listen carefully to human BEHAVIOR and how their environment conditions their reactions to a product or idea. Be open and actively listening for emotional content as well as what they say.
Fail early, fail often	Vibrant design thinking is characterized by prototyping as part of the creative process and not just a way of validating finished ideas.

Table 6: Design Thinking Characteristics	
Design Thinking Wisdom	**Quick Explanation**
Get Professional Help	Go outside your immediate group or organization and engage others –customers, stakeholders, partners or technical experts.
Share the inspiration	Use your networks to support inspiration and to stimulate the emergence of new ideas. Build using internal resources with people who you know and trust.
Blend big and small projects	Innovation depends on having a portfolio of possible innovations from short term incremental to longer term revolutionary ones.
Budget to the Pace of Innovation	Be prepared to build a budget for your innovation that is fast-paced and disruptive. The bureaucratic budget cycles probably won't fit with the pace of innovation.

Adapted from: Change by Design by Tim Brown, (2009, pp. 229-236)

Capstone Change Project Principles

At this point it may be helpful to reiterate and reflect upon the five principles shared earlier and that can be used to guide your work going forward:

1. *Question and listen carefully.*
2. *Look for strengths and know that your questions ARE the beginning of change.*
3. *Be prepared to pivot and modify your research approach and the need of additional data.*
4. *Engage others in a process of iterative change.*
5. *Be the leader of learning and positive change.*

"Doing by Learning" activity

Putting some Balls in the Air

While this book does its best to make the project a somewhat linear process, the reality is that you also must always be thinking about the project's many dimensions simultaneously. If you haven't begun to do so, it is now time to toss some "balls in the air" and think about them on, at least, a preliminary basis. So, you should probably be thinking about the need to develop:

- *A proposal or assessment of a positive organizational change for which you or your team (if this is a team-based capstone project) will become the "expert" demonstrating leadership skills.*

- *Focus on a change requires that the change be understood from multiple stakeholders' perspectives on others representing all areas of practice and the total set of competencies identified earlier.*
- *Figure out how your change will impact or be impacted by all areas of business, management and leadership – not just technical areas!*
- *For virtually all projects, some economic benefit will need to be identified to the extent feasible. Beyond the quantifiable economic benefit, the project will probably also need to demonstrate value in other ways, as well. These also will need to be measured and communicated.*
- *The use of less academic and more hands-on "experiential" and inquiry-based learning, which is supported by "literature" and "what is known," as well as internally generated information but heavily dependent on your own primary research which is context specific.*
- *What your role and relationship is to any change you are considering.*

"Doing by Learning" activity

Start Thinking about Change

Yes, it is time to start thinking about a change to your organization for your capstone project! As part of doing that, however, let's take an Appreciative perspective on successful change:

1.   Identify a change in your life in which you were engaged and inspired. What was going on and what were you and others doing that made it so successful?

2.   Think about opportunities for improvement by leveraging strengths in your current workplace and begin to talk to others about your thinking.

Four Case Studies

CASE 1 – Inventory Management
The project took on an Appreciative Inquiry perspective that blended nicely with Design Thinking as a tool and methodology. While I did not iteratively write code or sub-contract others to do so, I did find a more agile approach to managing the project.

CASE 2 – New Generation Target Market for Lending Institution
I took a design thinking perspective and interviewed prospective customers about hypothetical products to assess their interest. The project was also broken into several smaller components including the building and testing of chat, mobile and the web. Also, monitoring and assessment systems will be built ahead of the need for M&E.

CASE 3 – Employee Training and Development for less turnover and better customer service
My process did have iterations of possible changes and additions/deletions to the current training that I

shared with interviewees. That said, my approach took on less of a "design thinking" approach and more of a traditional process of conducting research that would build an understanding of employee needs as a basis for program design. I see this project itself as only the first iteration of understanding the change requirements that will feed into more experimentation with new training modules and learning for subsequent modules.

CASE 4 – Merging of multiple non-profits into one organization

I found this project to be an excellent conclusion to my business studies since I had dipped my toe into specific opportunities for change in my own organization as my class project in previous courses.

CHAPTER 5
PROJECT PLANNING

Project Planning in Action Research

Overview

For many students, the question "Where do I begin?" is the monster in the closet when they are faced with an open-ended, self-directed project that is also, paradoxically, constrained by the academic calendar. My experience has been that this tension between the workplace and academia puts a student squarely in the middle to reconcile the two. For one thing, calendars are not at all in alignment, and most organizations are not at all keyed into the semester or term as we know them. To the extent that your project sits outside of an organization's timeline, you are safe. But what happens when the VP of Marketing, who may be a key resource to interview, suddenly has a change of plans due to flight delays and has other priorities than your interview? In doing experiential capstones, these kinds of delays (and worse) happen routinely, so your planning must work around them.

If your project is following the lines of an experiential learning model such as Action Research, Action Learning, Appreciative Inquiry or Design Thinking, then planning based on traditional project management methods may be a struggle. While it is certainly recommended that you lay out major deliverables, milestones and work launch/completion dates, there will be adjustments given the iterative nature and flexibility inherent in these models.

Messiness of Action Research

One of the greatest lessons to be learned in applying all your training to a work-based project is what I simply refer to as its ever-present messiness. If you are designing anything that is truly new to your organization (or the world), you will be living a life of experimentation and learning. Remember those experiential learning cycles introduced several chapters ago? Let's look at just a sampling of the challenges inherent in experiential projects such as these:

- *Change* in the scale, scope or complexity is likely to come about as you learn more, test out ideas and collect more data.
- *Your role* may evolve over the course of the project from one of a neophyte to that of an expert. Yes, it happens and when it does, it affects how you think about the project, how others feel about you and how your project will move forward.

- *Politics* exists in any organization and, without knowing it, you may be crossing lines, offending stakeholders and stepping into ill-advised territories inadvertently as you make inquiries and propose changes.
- *Emotions* can easily drive stakeholders' participation and/or willingness to share data and their knowledge with you.

Long Lead Times

My proposed project plan shows what you may consider to be long lead times that precede the beginning of your actual course. Based on my research with the most successful capstone students, it is clear that a huge amount of preparatory work needs to be done in advance of the project itself. If you are currently employed and have received leadership training or have significant experience in managing work-based projects, then of course, this work could be reduced considerably. For most students, including part-time graduate students who are still early in their careers, this preparatory work is the difference between an outstanding project and one that is mediocre or unsuccessful.

The long lead time of preparatory work before your semester ever begins is there for three reasons: to develop a mindset of project leadership, to develop relationships, and to recognize the need for understanding the context and the iterative nature of your inquiry. The project leadership work included in this book is designed to prepare you for the greatest transformational change reported by the most successful students at which they were pleasantly surprised.

The need for relationships, explained in greater detail in another chapter, represents a major shift in learning methods compared to most traditional academic course work. You can't do a project like this alone, it doesn't happen in the school library, and relationships take time to develop. Finally, the iterative nature of any work-based research means that you will need to be capable of making decisions "on-the-fly" and of having a firm understanding of the organization, the industry, the scope and/or limitations of your proposed change, and the context. All this is extremely difficult to put in place within a semester. Launching your learning before your first class helps to ensure that you flourish in this learning experience!

Project Management 101

While the methods of Project Management as a discipline are outside the scope of this book, several major elements to the Work Breakdown are suggested here based on students' experiences. It should be emphasized that these elements are not sequential, and they represent, to the extent feasible, a somewhat linear approach, only to provide a sense of order and to make the work more approachable.

Choosing a Positive Change Project

Design and Implementation

In the same way that preliminary research may begin early as part of the project selection process (before you've really defined the project), so too implementation of an organizational change may begin as the research process unfolds. One example used by Coghlan & Brannick (2010) is that of an interview in which both the researcher (you) and the interviewee may come to reframe the definition of the needed change as the interview occurs (p. 73). Concurrent to this, you may have already set the wheels in motion for a change just by the act of creating awareness through the interview process! This is the beauty and challenge of Action Research. It is also especially challenging to use this methodology in research for a traditional graduate course, since time constraints work against the iterative process of spinning out revised research findings and a problem definition as data become available. Coghlan and Brannick, in *Doing Action Research in Your Own Organization* (2010, pp. 65-68) present a four-step Beckhard model for change that is useful. It includes:

1. Determining the need for change
2. Defining the future state
3. Assessing the present in terms of the future
4. Managing the transition

This model is almost a hand-off point for most projects done within the context of a graduate course, since implementation may take months or years to accomplish. The lesson here, however, is that the "research," while temporarily halted to meet the academic requirements of submitting a plan (paper), would continue iteratively as part of the change process. At some point, the research portion becomes redundant and the change is well enough understood that implementation becomes the focus.

Simultaneity

The Appreciative Inquiry principle of simultaneity is extremely relevant at this point in your planning process and reinforces the concept that change begins with the first question! Diane Watkins clarifies:

> *"These discussions about the focus of the work and the resulting topics to be explored are governed by the Principle of Simultaneity. As we seek to understand a situation by gathering data, the first question we ask is fateful. The organization will turn its energy in the direction of that first question, whether positive or negative. The seeds of change are embedded in the first question. Careful, thoughtful and informed choice of topics(s) is important as it defines the scope of the inquiry, providing the framework for subsequent interviews and data collection."*

> *(Watkins et al., Appreciative Inquiry, Change at the speed of Imagination, 2011, p. 121)*

The Capstone Project Plan

Twenty Steps to an Experientially Based Capstone

1. Develop a clear concept of Your Business Capstone requirements
Understanding the rationale for any project provides, if nothing else, a sense of security about where your work fits into the general schema of your new degree in Business, Management or Leadership. Comparing your specific course requirements and competencies to those in other capstones will help you to see the value of your work and make it easier to create a vision of where you are going. This step is all about seeing the forest through the trees and understanding the landscape before setting out on your journey.

This is best done by reviewing carefully the material in Chapter One, including the competencies and outcomes of the accrediting agencies. Look for anything in your own course requirements that should be found in your course syllabus. Is it clear to you what is expected and why? Does it fit with what you see as being relevant to your degree program? This is the time to seek clarification from your instructor before moving forward. To do this, begin with an assessment of your own Business or Management Program based on the Areas of Management Practice model as described in Chapter One.

2. **Launch your Network and Seek Project Suggestions**

   Finding a project, even for students who are currently employed, can be a challenge. As the chapters on Building a Network and Learning through Experience detail, it really does take a village to succeed in this kind of project. Due to the long lead time of both network building and final project selection, you really should begin this process months before the beginning of your semester. Beginning this process so far in advance with so little information or guidance may be one of the least comfortable steps in your project.

Like any major project, getting going can be the hardest part, so just start with some conversations with anyone who is the most knowledgeable about your educational experience, such as a colleague who has graduated from your program or who has done a similar project.

Cast a wide net and be prepared for insights into what might make a good project coming from unlikely sources. At this point, the goal is to engage in multiple conversations with as many people as possible to generate ideas. Think of this stage as the ideate portion of a Design Thinking process, in which every idea has merit because, at the very least, it may lead to or link to other ideas that get you closer to making your final project selection.

3. **Identify Positive Change Project possibilities (organizations and projects)**

   If you are a full-time student and not currently employed, then this process can be extremely time consuming, especially if you are "cold-calling" organizations looking for a site. Having a preexisting or current relationship is important, so look back at any places of employment (even part-time/summer) or internship locations. Very few students settle on a single project idea immediately but generally narrow the field down to a few and then carefully compare them in more detail.

This step is directly related to building your networks as described earlier. Starting this process early is key since there is really very little "slack" time built into a semester schedule. If you do nothing else before your first day of class, do this and begin the semester with your organization selected, set up meetings with your organization and have a clear project concept ready for presentation to your instructor. While you may need to make changes in the exact focus, scale and scope of your project, you will be able to do so quickly, having already begun the process with your sponsoring organization.

4. **Assess and articulate your Experiential Learning Style**

   This may feel like an extra step, but it does provide an important basis for self-reflection and assessment of the experience of doing a work-based project. Doing this is the first step in building your leadership competencies for managing this project and becoming the "expert" on your topic. Understanding experiential learning at the personal level is also the best way to understand thoroughly the more organizationally focused learning models described earlier in this book. Your prior knowledge of your own "learning style," combined with knowledge of organizational learning at a very "hands on" level, will allow you to better manage your relationships and the project itself.

Begin this step with doing one or more self-assessments, as described in the chapters on Learning through Experience and Leading Learning. Take this step seriously and reflect on your past experiences as a basis for understanding your learning style. Next, share your self-reflections with one or more people who know you well to get an external perspective. With this understanding, reflect forward to your project and consider now how you will use your preferred learning style to best launch and manage your project. How will you know that other less preferred learning styles might need to be used, as well? How can your self-awareness about learning style best support your work?

5. **Assess and articulate your Leader of Learning skills**

    Perhaps the most transformational aspect of an experiential capstone is the recognition that you are now seen, with good reason, as a leader on your topic. This doesn't happen magically at the conclusion of your project when you make your final presentation but grows organically with each conversation and iteration of your proposed solution(s). To the extent that any organization is on a continuous journey of learning, this puts you in a new role, one that I've called a Leader of Learning, described in a chapter of the same title. Your self-assessment of your Leader of Learning skills is a step that, first, builds your own awareness of this phenomenon and, second, allows you to take ownership of your role as you manage your project.

Like the self-assessment on your Experiential Learning Style described above, this begins with some simple self-assessment and reflection. Use the tools in that chapter as the basis for your consideration of your previous experiences in any experiential learning situation. If possible, share your insights with others who know you well. From there, reflect on how you see this self-awareness helping you in the future on your project.

6. **Select and frame the Positive Change Project**

    The process of framing a problem and selecting a research topic will vary widely, depending on your circumstances. In some cases, for example, where you are employed full time, there may be very little freedom to choose a topic, while in others you, your ideas, and your organization may be very welcome. For those projects in which you have a wide degree of freedom, it is important to recognize the *iterative* nature of "research" and "project selection."

Because you need to define a project within the context of an organization, it is highly likely that you will want to begin conversations and data collection to identify the problem. In doing this, the challenge is to remain open to the ideas and interpretations of the various stakeholders and participants as you begin conversing and collecting data. It is highly likely, for example, that you will get conflicting interpretations of issues and will need to balance various perspectives in further refining your research. Speaking of "issues," even the way that you think in terms of "issues," "problems," or "opportunities" can lead you down different paths. Being aware of your use of language and labels can mitigate their biasing influence.

Now let's look at framing through a different lens – one that conceptualizes the use of multiple frames. You can do this by consciously viewing your research topic through multiple frames that are included in the Areas of Management Practice model. While any issue is likely to have an agreed upon starting point (single frame), it is equally likely to have several secondary frames that may help to shape your exact definition of the research topic. What begins as a marketing related problem, for example, may quickly show itself to be a human resource or financial resources issue! Always be thinking of multiple frames!

7. **Research Industry/Organization/Product/Service for Context and Perspective**

It is difficult to measure the impact that years of experience in a given organization or industry has on employees. Suffice it to say that even in the most routine jobs you come to "know" how it all works, the competitive situation, what customers are expecting, how the economics drive profitability and so on. For newer employees such as students and recent graduates, this puts you at an extreme disadvantage in stepping on to the playing field and managing a project designed to recommend a positive change. Your ability to recommend a change begins with understanding the context both externally and internally.

Most courses in Business Strategy teach from exactly this perspective, conducting an external and internal analysis using assessment tools such as SWOT (strengths-weaknesses-opportunities-threats), PESTLE (political, economic, social, technological, legal and environmental), or SOAR (strengths, opportunities, aspirations and results), or others. While the level of detail here may vary considerably because of your own prior knowledge, experience suggests that virtually all students should do at least some research to understand the most current opportunities and challenges at both your organization and the "industry" in which it competes, however defined.

8. **Create a Vision of Success for you and your Positive Change Project**

Virtually all models of "success" at both the personal and organizational level have some form of "future state" or "vision" needing to be built early in the process. A clear vision of the future makes charting a pathway easier and provides continual guidance in a single direction that avoids "rabbit holes" and "dead ends." Highly successful students do this going into the capstone, determining where it will take them, how it fits into their professional development, and what a successful experience would be like.

Doing this doesn't need to be a complicated or laborious process. It does, however, require a deliberate reflection about what your own personal and professional aspirations are, even if they are slightly ambiguous. Success for your project depends on your starting point. For some new products, the capstone may serve as a starting point in accomplishing some exploratory research on the Customer Value Proposition. For other projects that are further along in their development, success may be more on the design and implementation end of the spectrum. At the personal level, this is an opportunity to take your previous self-assessments (experiential learning, leadership, etc.) and apply them to your situation, imagining a best case for yourself answering the question of what the most wildly amazing outcome of this project could be. Your personal and project visions of success should be written and used as guiding lights to your work.

9. **Select Positive Change Project's 3-5 key frame(s) in Areas of Management Practice**

One of the most important contributions that this book may have to your work is the careful disaggregation of a business problem into multiple Areas of Management Practice. This is grounded in the fundamental competency of "integration" described in earlier chapters. While it can easily be shown that virtually any project eventually touches upon all Areas of Management Practice, it is also true, of course, that a given project most easily fits into approximately three of them. A new Customer Relationship Management system, for example, will probably be most tightly connected to the areas of (1) Information Systems, (2) Customers, Sales and Marketing and (3) Operations and Performance Improvement. This step follows closely on the heels of or even simultaneous with your project selection.

This step begins with circling back to the Areas of Management Practice. Begin by reviewing the entire list and selecting approximately three of the Areas of Management Practice that you find to be the most appropriate. From there, for each selected Area of Management Practice questions, or other broad questions of your own design, begin to reflect on what the implications are for your project, particularly in terms of scale and scope. Make notes to yourself and share your thinking with others in your "network." The outcome of this step should be an emerging sense of clarity about what your project will be about and whether you have a manageable workload given your time constraints of one or more semesters.

10. Design Key Research Questions and Resources for key frames

A key part of any Positive Change Project is what questions need to be answered to fulfill your project's vision. While this begins with broad questions provided for each *Area of Management Practice*, more specific research questions also need to be formulated to guide your research. This is especially true for primary research such as interviews (individual and group) or surveys. In most cases, you will only get one opportunity to "ask the question," so clarity of the question ensures that your data will address the key issues.

Review your project, formulate some key questions in each of the three (or so) *Areas of Management Practice* you've identified, and rework them to build a hierarchy of questions with one being the "big question" and others falling under that as secondary questions. Refer to the section on Inquiry for question development and the development of positive questions. You should have one or more for each Area Management Practice. This provides a perfect starting and end point for your research! Once the questions have been developed, identify likely resources in the way of frameworks or big ideas that will help to inform those questions.

11. Reframe Positive Change Project based on all Areas of Management Practice

As described throughout this text, the integration of all areas of business is the single most important competency that needs to be demonstrated from this capstone. The step of moving from just a few *Areas of Management Practice* to the full set ensures that you will have successfully done that.

Using the full set of *Areas of Management Practice*, now go back to all of those remaining (not yet used in previous steps) and repeat the process used earlier. To summarize, review the broad questions in Chapter One and then develop a single research question for each Area of Management Practice. These serve as guideposts to your data collection as you move forward. While you may not be as focused on these secondary areas, they still have their importance when using that valuable "systems" or "integrated" perspective. For each new *Area of Management Practice*, identify at least one key question along with any appropriate resources needed to answer your questions.

It is at this point that you will need to be strong and avoid "Scope Creep" in your project. As you begin to explore your specific project and extend your analysis into other *Areas of Management Practice*, there will be a temptation to change the focus of your project. You need to balance your use of multiple areas of practice with the need to stay focused. Extending your project too deeply into another area of the business, for example, can quickly make your work overwhelming. Focus, focus, focus…

12. Create "Draft Report" Skeleton Outline

From the perspectives of good project management, minimizing stress and ensuring a quality learning experience, I've found that doing a "draft" report weeks before it is ever due can be a lifesaver! The outline generally follows the Areas of Management Practice and provides a place for you to collect your thoughts, begin to formulate what your data is telling you and to document how your project extends across all areas of the organization.

If your instructor doesn't require a draft report, then set yourself a goal of doing one for yourself so that is in line with the suggested timeline in the Experiential Business Capstone Planner found below. Remember that this first step in writing may feel uncomfortable at a level you haven't felt since your initial conversations in identifying an organization and project. But doing this now, weeks before any report is due, is invaluable in determining the ultimate quality of your final deliverable. While starting is a bit hand wrenching, once you've begun you will want to come back to it continually. This completely avoids the end-of-semester, "yikes, it's due soon" crisis.

13. Develop a Research Plan and Launch Preliminary Research

As described in more detail in the chapter on research, doing an experiential capstone generally takes you down the path of Action Research. Your goal at this point early in your project is to reach out to others, engage in general conversations about your topic, and get a sense of what information is likely to be needed or even available to inform your project. The easiest part of the research will be your literature review at your college library. I say "easy" not because it won't involve long hours or many circuitous routes of exploration like any academic research, but it will be structured, somewhat linear and even, I dare to say, predictable. For most work-related topics, from new products and revenue sources to customer service, and everything in between, you will unfortunately find a very limited number of relevant articles or reports. This absence of secondary research sources will demand that you use more primary research of your own.

Outside of any pre-existing internally generated reports and studies, your primary research will probably consist of interviews and surveys. As a rule, interviews are one of the primary tools used in various levels of formality and in both individual and group formats. Surveys are used routinely by students but do take some lead time, first, for approvals, and second, for response times. Your objective at this stage is to outline what you will do, including who you will talk to and why, what groups will be surveyed, what other parts of the organization (or partners) and stakeholders should have input, and more. The research plan is like a business plan – think of it as an opportunity to lay out a roadmap of your data collection efforts for the next few weeks of your life. Like any business plan, it is subject to change, but for now, do the best you can with what you know.

14. Assess and articulate your emergence as a Positive Change Leader

This book chose to split the topic of Leadership into two parts. The first, called Leader of Learning skills asks you to think about your approach to an experiential capstone and to build some awareness about how your role will be different in this course from any you've done before. In this second treatment of Leadership you are asked to be more tactical and given some models and frameworks from which to choose or combine into your own model of managing your leadership of your project. To reiterate the gestalt of that chapter: you will become the expert and your role is likely to be one of leadership in helping the organization to make your Positive Change Project happen. In this step of the project, you are asked to review and understand those models and frameworks, do some self-assessment and reflection, and put together an informal plan of your approach. Doing this while you are doing your project allows you to reflect-in-action and be better prepared for your new role, which may be happening sooner than you think.

15. Design preliminary Economic Value of Positive Change Project

One of the most necessary and elusive deliverables of a Positive Change Project is defining and quantifying the economic value of your positive change. As the chapter on the Economic Model points out, this is really driven by documenting the change and drivers of change in whatever metrics can be measured. From there, examining these drivers for changes in revenues or costs (increases or decreases) is the heart and soul of your economic model. Yes, some things are difficult or virtually impossible to quantify, and those can always be treated as strategic in nature. That said, doing this modeling, as painful as it is for most students, is both necessary and rewarding. Your goal at this point is to do the best you can to structure a model of the benefits and costs for your Positive Change Project. Generally, this is done in a worksheet (such as Excel) and doesn't need to be overly complex, but it does need to be a working model with some clarity about inputs, calculations and output. The acid test for this model is that it demonstrates clearly what the impact of your change is likely to be, based on stated assumptions. No more, no less.

16. Engage in an Action-oriented, iterative cycle of research, learning, testing, feedback, revision and reflection

While this is listed as a step in the project, it is, in reality, one that begins with your first conversation and extends over the duration of your project. The description of this step also really speaks also to the nature of your research process. Most experiential business and management capstones will not be controlled experiments based on statistical sampling and experimental design. Instead, they will be, as described in other parts of this book, "messy" and require that you keep a number of "balls in the air" before settling in with any sense of finality. This "step" of the project is, therefore, to engage, use the tools given to you in this book, keep your chin up during moments of discouragement (like cancelled interviews with the EVPs!), gather data, reflect and be persistent! Remember, it's all about grit!

17. Assess Economic Value of Positive Change Project

At this point later in the semester you have presumably begun to see how things are coming together. Surveys, interviews, reports and other data may give you more confidence in the workability of your proposed change. This is the time to put a stake in the ground and finalize (as much as anything is "final") your economic model. Yes, there is still some outstanding data and, yes, you don't have real numbers for two assumptions. My advice is simple and uncharacteristically direct – learn to live with it. There will ALWAYS be numbers based on assumptions needing revisions, and any model is only a plan that can be explained. Do the best you can, structure your model so that changes to assumptions are relatively easy to accommodate, take a deep sigh, and move forward.

18. Conclude Research and Analyze Data

All good things must come to an end, or at least to a temporary suspension. Your research has provided you with, hopefully, an abundance of both qualitative and quantitative data. This is the time to find a quiet corner and begin to make sense of it all. Look for themes, build hierarchies of concepts, use your Areas of Management Practice matrix as a framework for answering questions, resurrecting models and frameworks from other courses in your degree and, essentially, building your case for change. This is one of the most exciting and inspiring parts of the process when you realize that only a few weeks ago you had nothing but an idea and a few questions, and now you have data supporting a positive change. Make no mistake about this step – it may only cause you to do more work as some questions suddenly loom large as important but unanswered. Who can you talk to? What data would fill that hole? Push on, fill the gaps, make reasonable assumptions, document your work, and understand that this is how it works. Get comfortable moving forward with less than perfect information. Welcome to the world of leading change!

19. Create Draft report

When it comes to writing a draft report, I can't help but think about painting a house that has suffered from neglect. The work begins with replacing rotted trim and siding, scraping old paint, sanding major sections, applying caulk around windows and doors, priming with one or more coats over bare wood and then, finally, applying a fresh coat of paint. Writing the draft report is, as you have probably guessed, that fresh coat of paint. If you have followed the recommended processes in this book, you should have data, frameworks, and answers to key questions that are all anxiously waiting to be put into the report. You should now have sufficient clarity about the value of your project and enough confidence in your data so that there should be little "writer's cramp" or "waffling" about what to do next. Put on that paint, start filling out those chapters that you have been working towards since day one. You've got this!

20. Create Final Report and Economic Model

This is your last opportunity to reconcile your work. Outside of the mechanics of writing, there isn't much to say except give yourself plenty of time and look for integrity of the document and reconcile your economic model with your narrative report.

21. Create Your Presentation

The trick here is to remember that it is a presentation and needs to be kept to that level. Most audiences will not want or need all the details. That said, everyone will want to know the answers to a few key questions:
- What is the opportunity or problem?
- Why is this important and how do you know?
- What is your Positive Change Project (high level)?
- What did you do to make the case?
- How does this add value? (high level economic and any strategic)
- What confidence do you have and what uncertainties are there in your assumptions?
- How can this be moved forward? More research? Pilot? Testing? Implementation?

The "**Experiential Capstone Planner**" below uses the steps described above and puts them into a format with timelines for courses of various lengths. Negative signs indicate the number of weeks BEFORE the first day of the semester (or term) that the activity should be begun. A positive number indicates the week of the semester (or term) during which the activity should begin.

	Table 7 – Experiential Business Capstone Planner			
	Experiential Business Capstone Planner	Course Length (in weeks)		
		15	12	8
	Capstone Project Elements	Week # Relative to Course Week # 1		
1	Develop a clear concept of your Business Capstone requirements	-12	-12	-12
2	Launch your Network and seek Project Suggestions	-11	-11	-11
3	Identify Positive Change Project possibilities (organizations and projects)	-10	-10	-10
4	Assess and articulate your Experiential Learning Style	-10	-10	-10
5	Assess and articulate your Leader of Learning skills	-9	-9	-9
6	Select and Frame the Positive Change Project	-6	-6	-6
7	Research Industry and Organization for context and perspective	-5	-5	-5
8	Create a Vision of Success for you and your Positive Change Project	-4	-4	-4
9	Select Positive Change Project's 3-5 key frame(s) in Areas of Management Practice	-3	-3	-3
10	Design Key Research Questions needing to be answered for key frames	-2	-2	-2
11	Reframe Positive Change Project based on all Areas of Management Practice	1	1	1
12	Create "Draft Report" Skeleton Outline	1	1	1
13	Develop Research Plan and Launch Preliminary Research	2	3	2
14	Assess and articulate your emergence as a Positive Change Leader	4	2	3
15	Design preliminary Economic Value of Positive Change Project	5	5	4
16	Engage in Action-oriented iterative cycle of research, learning, testing, feedback, revision and reflection	6	4	4
17	Assess Updated Economic Value of Positive Change Project	9	6	6
18	Conclude Research and Analyze Data	10	9	7
19	Create draft report	12	10	7
20	Create Final Report and Economic Model	14	11	8
21	Create Presentation	15	12	8

Other Planning Tools

In response to the "messiness" of action research, you can find below a few tools for you to consider in managing your data.

Reflective Journal
Remembering that one of leadership competencies identified in both the accrediting agencies cited in Chapter One is reflection and learning reflectively, this may prove to be a highly useful tool. The cost and process can be very inexpensive and simple – a notebook (if paper) or a word/text file (if digital) in which you record

your thoughts and observations. This should be done daily or at least with some regularity and especially so immediately following any impactful event such as an interview or observation. These "field notes" will be a valuable resource when, after all is said and done, you are asked for a "Final Reflection" on your own learning process in managing this capstone.

Drawing

Drawing is always useful as a means to express ideas that need to be shared. There are several books on the market designed to encourage all of us to use simple drawings as a means of communication. Start with basic stick figure and geometric shapes supported by labels and work your way up from there! The important thing is to be brave and just do it! Remember that it isn't drawing for accuracy or to be judged but only as a means of sharing ideas. They may be useful, for example in interviews to convey a change in a process. As Tim Brown states in *Change by Design*, "Words and numbers are fine, but only drawing can simultaneously reveal both the functional characteristics of an idea and its emotional content" (Brown, 2009, p. 80).

Concept Mapping

Concept Mapping is also explained well in numerous sources both in print and online. For those unfamiliar with this tool, just think of it as "branching" in a diagram. A single concept might "branch" into several sub-categories of ideas, and each of those, in turn, may also branch into more detailed concepts. Although software is available for mapping concepts for many small uses (such as this project), it needn't be any more complicated than using, for example, MSWord by inserting little lines and text boxes that get dragged and built into a concept map.

Affinity Diagrams

If your project is feeling complex with concepts and ideas and needing some organization, here is an alternative to feeling overwhelmed. Put single concepts on "Post-it" notes of a reasonable size (3"x3" or larger) using a dark felt-tip pen that is visible from some distance. Find a large portion of unused wall space in your home, and stick ideas to it in no order initially. Once all ideas are on the wall, begin clustering ideas by theme and giving them some hierarchy. If themes emerge needing new notes, then add them. This process can be kept up for the duration of your project and used as a basis for your draft and final reports.

White Boards

It goes without saying that whiteboards are an invaluable tool for sharing ideas and collaborative thinking. If you have them at your disposal they can, of course, be used when doing research to share a concept or engage others in developing a concept. They also provide a good tool at the personal level to outline project components, your plan of research, or any other aspect of your project.

Legal Pads

While not exactly a novel approach, I feel compelled to mention good old-fashioned legal pads as a tool. In managing large projects, I frequently have a number of them going simultaneously. For concept mapping, list making, drawing, affinity diagraming and more they can be invaluable. Their advantage is that they can serve as mini-white boards that are portable. I find this helpful when I'm using both an office at work and a home office or for traveling.

Self-Management

I have decided to conclude this chapter by bringing your attention to what may be the most important project management tool of all – self-management and care. Given the potential importance and ambiguity of an experiential capstone, it is all too easy to "push through" and sacrifice both physical and mental health in the process. My only advice is to approach this work in as mindful a way as possible using all of the tools at your disposal including your network (remember them?). Other chapters in this book will bring attention to this in more detail.

*In your preferred electronic format, create your own **Experiential Project Planner** which has all the steps provided to you in this chapter. Based on your "best guess" at this point, insert the weeks (before or during your semester) in which you anticipate beginning each of the steps.*

Four Case Studies

CASE 1 – Inventory Management
The project has been in some ways ongoing, since we have been making smaller incremental changes over the past two years. That said, every step of the way took far more time than we expected to get things right. I am expecting to lay out a project plan with some milestones and deliverables over the next few months but couldn't possibly imagine this being fully implemented in that time. What I can hope for is to plan ahead for considerably more time in this project right now at the beginning than is needed just to get the job done.

CASE 2 – New Generation Target Market for Lending Institution
This project has taken longer than expected to get to this point. An agile approach to managing this project is being implemented to make allowance for changes along the way.

CASE 3 – Employee Training and Development for Less Turnover and Better Customer Service
This project seemed overwhelming at the outset since I had not really started on any of the research before the class began. Because this project has so much potential impact on my organization, I had great support and access to employees for interviews and follow-up. This greatly impacted my ability to maintain my project schedule and complete all stages of the analysis on time.

CASE 4 – Merging of Multiple Non-Profits into One Organization
While I found my project manageable during the designated capstone semester, I realize that, upon reflection, the amount of data collection, broad research on best practices, internal research on all operations and dialogue on overall performance goes back months and even years to my entire tenure here. This was due, at least in part, to my relative inexperience on the job. This project would have taken more time if I had done it as somebody outside the organization or as an intern.

There is just so much pre-work needed that goes beyond the scope of the project itself but is necessary to manage the project! I found, however, that my deep understanding of the organization (and the other regional organizations) allowed me to conceptualize possible "draft" ideas and solutions to "run up the flag pole" quickly for feedback and that this quick feedback loop really enhanced my ability to manage the project in a more agile way. I guess that the important lesson is that managing my project, while certainly driven by the timeline of the semester with key milestones and critical paths, was as much about engaging in the project with a deep understanding of the business we are in. That understanding brings clarity in making decisions about how to best allocate my time every day.

CHAPTER 6
CREATE A VISION OF SUCCESS

Vision of Personal Success

Overview

I'll admit it – I LOVE experiential capstones in Business and Management. Why? I've repeatedly seen that feeling of success for both undergraduate and graduate business students who have found a way to get the most out of the experience. I have seen students come to the table with a vague, broad concept of a topic and leave only a semester later with a new first job offer, career advancements or career mobility to a new organization or industry. Beyond the career advancement and professional development, there was always the big win, a new sense of self-efficacy about taking on an unknown challenge, starting from scratch and building something of value. This capstone is the opportunity of a lifetime to move your personal needle forward on so many levels!

Emotional Growth

Directly related to the sense of confidence -- and the best-hidden aspect of a successful capstone experience -- is the emotional growth that comes from success in accomplishing a project that is so large and has so much at stake. Whether completing a BA/BS or an MBA (including other related disciplines), the capstone can be a gateway to not only finally getting your degree for the years of hard work but also to the development of your emotional growth, as well. Why? The capstone, like virtually all experiential learning isn't only about cognitive learning but is also heavily affective. Because the capstone is such a deeply emotional experience, it is important to pay attention to and manage those emotions, in a positive way, early in the process. Understanding and tending to your emotional needs in this project is one of the most important steps in success later in the project when the work gets hard! While the topic of emotional competencies is discussed in more detail in a later chapter, for the time being you might keep in mind the four key areas of emotional intelligence that come out of the work of Daniel Goleman but which are the foundation of the book, *Emotional Intelligence 2.0,* by Travis Bradburry (2009).

- **Self-Awareness** – This area includes being aware of your emotions, understanding how your emotions affect others, your level of self-confidence, and your understanding of the ways others affect your emotional state.
- **Self-Management** – This area is the foundation of your relationship with others, by managing conflict and getting along with others, expressing your own feelings clearly and showing

empathy in your feeling towards others.
- **Social Awareness** – This builds on both self-awareness and self-management skills and lays the foundation for effective relationships. It includes the ability to sense the emotions of others, to care about others, and to really understand what others are saying.
- **Relationship Management** – This is the final and most "social" of these four areas as it builds on all the other three. It gets beyond getting along with others to include actually using empathy to build and manage relationships. It also includes successful relationship building and clearly sharing one's own feelings.

Why jump into the topic of Emotional Competencies so early in a discussion about creating a vision for your capstone? How does this fit in? It is really quite simple. There are two levels of "vision" needed for your capstone experience. The first, and the easier one really, is that you and your colleagues will pay attention to is the Positive Change Project, itself. Whether a process improvement or a new business plan, this work begins with a clear vision of the "future state." The second level of "vision," and the one most easily overlooked, is your personal vision of what you aspire to be at the end of this experience. The basis for building this vision is many of the emotional competencies found above. If you envision this capstone as something done in isolation, built on academic research alone, then this is the time to rethink that perspective. As you can see by the emphasis of this book, based on amazing success stories in business capstones, learning in the workplace is a social experience. If your vision is a work in progress, then consider this; it is incomplete if it doesn't recognize your development and use of these emotional skills. We will now build from there.

What's in it for YOU and your personal "Why?"
One of the reasons why an experiential capstone is so emotionally charged is that it carries so much of your emotional commitment to your degree itself. Reflect on what your graduation means to you, and you will probably find that it quickly extends to others who have supported you along the way. Your success is their success. For example, are you, like many, myself included, the first- generation college graduate or the first in your family with a master's degree? Did your parents or others make any sacrifices to ensure that you had the opportunity for higher education? If you are a part-time student with a full-time job and responsible to a spouse, partner or dependents, then clearly it isn't all about you! What was your personal motivation and personal dream for obtaining your degree? Whatever that vision is, this capstone presents itself, unfortunately, as the single remaining hurdle to reaching your goal and fulfilling your dream. Reflect on your "Why" and write it down, revise it, and share it with those close to you until you really feel that you've got it right!

Career Growth and Enthusiasm for Learning
While it takes on many faces, the ability to manage your career and find meaningful work is one of our deepest needs. The most anxiety-producing event in achieving this goal is the job interview in which you are given a limited amount of time to share your experiences, help others to understand who you are, and understand the organization with which you are interviewing. Imagine yourself in an interview for a dream position that you would really like to be offered. Now, as part of that interview let's say that you are asked to "describe a project over which you had ownership or in which you took on a leadership role." This isn't an unusual question and there is no right or wrong answer, since it relies on your simply sharing your experience. The point of such a question is less frequently about the technical material in your project and more focused on how you managed the learning and social and emotional relationships with others in building new knowledge in a motivated

and self-directed way.

Like life, what is really important is less about the outcome and more about how you managed the experience. You see, career counselors and corporate hiring experts all tend to agree that they are looking for employees who are engaged as learners, so the best response is one that is candid in describing learning behavior that is flexible, persistent and detailed about how you managed the learning process working with others – in short, your enthusiasm and ability to carry out a self-directed learning project and inspire others to work with you. Yes, technical skills are important, but today's business environment requires adaptive learners and leaders. Behavioral questions now used in interviews are designed to provide you with the opportunity to share your experience in taking control of the learning and assuming leadership as we have defined it throughout this book. Your vision of yourself post-capstone will be enhanced to the extent that you see your capstone as an opportunity to become, as described in an earlier chapter, an enthusiastic leader of learning!

Following a Passion
Work-based capstones can be a risky adventure. Over the years I've had dozens of students for whom things really (I mean really) unraveled. Typically, the cause is some major shift in management roles, organizational structure or leadership, and the result is a major shift in management support requiring a redesign of the research, or even the scope of the project. In some cases, a new organization and project must be identified midway into the semester. When I follow -up with students who have succeeded despite these setbacks, I tend to receive one answer in common – passion for the experience or general topic and that feeds into a personal vision of success.

Identifying your passion may seem like an overwhelming task and may feel all too much like the eternal question to all students from those annual gatherings of relatives asking, "What do you want to do when you graduate?" But feeling a passion is a little like being in touch with your emotions – it may seem difficult but just takes a deliberate effort. Beginning by identifying your key interests may be a more approachable goal. Look at your outside activities, hobbies, and those of others. Think back to part-time jobs that you've held and look for things that have sparked your interest. Look at others who you admire and examine why.

Selecting a *topic in which you have a strong interest* is repeatedly cited by the most successful capstone students as what kept them motivated when the research and work seemed overwhelming. Those same students frequently began their search for a capstone organization and topic early and engaged others in talking through possibilities for their project focus. It is the PROCESS of talking it through with others that will generate your own reflections and self-awareness about what topic(s) are meaningful to you. Begin there and find your passion as another component of your personal vision!

Professional Relationships
One of the greatest outcomes of capstone projects is the development of relationships that increase your awareness of other professionals in your organization and beyond. These happen in numerous ways. For one, just the process of finding an organization and a capstone project may put you in front of people who you would never have met otherwise. These exploratory meetings provide "data" about each organization's vision, culture, what it does, and how it accomplishes its mission.

At a more personal level, your connection may create a future opportunity even if it isn't your choice for this project. It's a small world, and in my own career it has happened, more often than I would ever have imagined, that some previous contact became a part of my life years down the road. There is a case to be made even for relationships that never develop much further, because you learn about the world and yourself with every meeting. You are still learning about professional interaction, applying those emotional intelligence skills (above), sharing your story and developing an understanding about another professional's world. This, too, is another important part of building your vision.

Professional Persona

Creating your own sense of professionalism and expertise on a subject is something that can't be taught in the classroom. The capstone provides you with the opportunity to come up to speed and "own" a subject. While the topic may still seem new to you as you launch your research and build a deeper understanding of the topic, remember that, generally, no one else knows more about your specific topic in this context than you! This feeling about yourself and awareness of having developed a professional persona is one of the most rewarding outcomes of a capstone.

Whether you are an undergraduate student ready to launch a career or an MBA student relatively early in your career, you are just beginning to build this persona. It isn't in books or in the library database but only comes from the experience of applying some of the skills described earlier such as emotional competencies, relationship building, identifying a passion, learning to lead learning projects, and more. It is who you are to others in a professional setting. Consider what your Professional Persona is and what it will be in the future.

Self-Confidence

There is no getting around the intimidating nature of a self-directed capstone project and the fear of failure from not being able to get to the finish line. This fear will slowly disappear throughout the semester as you move from one project stage to another. It is also one of the best reasons to follow a "plan" for your project and to see little "failures" along the way as opportunities for new and greater learning.

Imagine the level of self-confidence that comes from overcoming the capstone challenge and assuming responsibility for success. It doesn't tend to come from one specific accomplishment but from the intersection of having achieved the completion of the project, grown in your understanding, developed relationships and more. This is perhaps the most inclusive and long-lasting impact of your capstone because it demonstrates your character and strength as a potential leader in the future. This should definitely be on your short list of qualifications for a personal vision of success.

Creative Confidence

Today's business environment of shortened product life cycles, technological improvements and digitization requires a more adaptive and creative mindset. This requirement pops up in many ways – organizational design, industry disruption, emerging leadership skills, and more. Creativity is a key competency that is increasingly finding its way to all types of organizational settings. To build in creativity, we all need to leave behind definitions of creativity that limit its use to those "creative types." With the advent of the work of the Stanford School of Design, IDEO, and other creative-oriented centers, creativity is now front and center for any organization's future in innovation. In their book, *Creative Confidence* (2014), Kelley and Kelley provide insights into the breadth of creativity's impact on organizations:

In the business world, creativity manifests itself as innovation. Tech starts such as Google, Facebook, and Twitter have unleashed their employees' creativity to change the lives of billions of people. Today, in every department – from customer service to finance – people have opportunities to experiment with new solutions. Companies desperately need employees' insights from across the organization. No individual or executive holds a monopoly on new ideas. (Kelley, T. and Kelley, D., 2014, p. 3).

This, of course, has implications for how you think about your own future in which creativity and innovation will undoubtedly be a part. There is no hiding behind jobs that are routine, technologies that are stable, or cultures that are stagnant. Kelly and Kelly go on:

But innovation – whether driven by an individual or a team – can happen anywhere. It's fueled by restless intellectual curiosity, deep optimism, the ability to accept repeated failure as the price of ultimate success, a relentless work ethic, and a mindset that encourages not just ideas, but action (Kelley, T. and Kelley, D., 2014, p. 74).

But how can this be applied to your capstone and personal vision of success? Kelley and Kelley have outlined several effective strategies to help you get from the blank page to insight:

1. **Choose Creativity** – To be more creative, the first step is to decide you want to make it happen.
2. **Think like a traveler** – As if you were a visitor to a foreign land, try turning fresh eyes on your surroundings, no matter how mundane or familiar. Don't wait around for a spark to magically appear. Expose yourself to new ideas and experiences.
3. **Engage Relaxed Attention** – Flashes of insight often come when your mind is relaxed and not focused on completing a specific task, allowing the mind to make new connections between seemingly unrelated ideas.
4. **Empathize with your end User** – You come up with more innovative ideas when you better understand the needs and the background of the people you are creating solutions for.
5. **Do Observations in the Field** – When you observe others with the skills of an anthropologist, you might discover new opportunities hidden in plain sight.
6. **Ask Questions, Starting with "Why?"** – A series of "why?" questions can brush by surface details and get to the heart of the matter. For example, if you ask someone why they are still using a fading technology (think landline phones), the answers might have more to do with psychology than practicality.
7. **Reframe Challenges** – Sometimes the first step toward a great solution is to reframe the question. Starting from a different point of view can help you get to the essence of a problem.
8. **Build a Creative Support Network** – Creativity can flow more easily and be more fun when you have others with whom to collaborate with and bounce ideas off. (Kelley, T. and Kelley, D., 2014, p. 74).

What is most interesting is the degree of overlap with many of the key skills identified through our own research on successful capstone students! It can certainly be said that Creative Confidence summarizes many of the most important personal characteristics you want to capture and develop as you engage in your capstone.

These, too, provide some additional material for reflection on your vision of the future and how to get the most out of your capstone.

Designing Your Life

We introduced Design Thinking as a framework for approaching work in an earlier chapter. A framework similar to Creative Confidence has been developed by Burnett and Evans (2016) who, in their book, *Designing Your Life,* adopt a Design Thinking philosophy to help you manage your life (Burnett and Evans, 2016, p.xxvi). They have distilled their own research into five mind-sets that can be used to design tools to build your life and may be helpful in looking towards the future as part of your personal vision. They include:

- **Be Curious** – Being constantly exploratory "makes everything play."
- **Try Stuff** – Have a bias to action and try things as part of the design process.
- **Reframe Problems** – Step back, examine your assumptions and biases and reframe as a way of thinking!
- **Know It's a Process** – Know that mistakes will be made, prototypes are what they sound like, and your first idea is never the final iteration on your way to a great idea.
- **Ask for help** – You are not alone, and any good design requires what Burnett and Evans call radical collaboration; design is a collaborative process.

The five mind-sets above dovetail nicely with some of the concepts introduced earlier in the chapter on Leading Learning. They all approach work from a broad learning mindset of curiosity and socially based learning. Again, while directed generally at an individual's mindset at work, they translate well into a short list of behaviors that can easily be adapted to your capstone work with the goal of seeing improvement in these areas as viable end points for your own visioning process. To that end, Burnett and Evans (2016) provide some supportive concepts that may be useful in developing your own creative mindset:

- **Approaching with a beginner's mind** (Burnett and Evans, 2016, p. 7)
- **Being clear about why you work** (work view reflection) what, to you, work is for and what it means (Burnett and Evans, 2016, p. 35)
- **Flow and total engagement** by totally immersing yourself into the work (Burnett and Evans, 2016, p. 45)
    - Experiencing complete involvement in the activity
    - Feeling a sense of ecstasy or euphoria
    - Having great inner clarity – knowing just what to do and how to do it
    - Being totally calm and at peace
    - Feeling as if time were standing still – or disappearing in an instant

I find their work useful because it moves us into the psychological domain of being mindful about your work that is inextricably linked to the emotional competencies discussed at the beginning of this chapter. Coming full circle is a good stopping point but this also becomes your starting point in developing your personal vision. The materials and concepts presented are designed to give you a robust set of ideas about how you might want to be as a result of this capstone. The energy coming out of this experience is directly related to that going into it. Take the time to reflect forward and set a personal vision of success that you can be proud to achieve.

"Doing by Learning" activity

Build a Vision of Personal Success

1. *Think back to a successful personal success in any venue. What did it feel like? What level of ownership did you have over the situation? How did ou negotiate challenges and seek out opportunities?*
2. *Review the first portion of this chapter on a Vision of **Personal** Success and make notes on those concepts that resonate with your most positive experiences in your own learning and growth or concepts that you see as particularly relevant to your current learning and growth.*
3. *Building on #1 & #2 above, can you describe a Vision of **Personal** Success that you would hope to achieve as a result of successfully completing this capstone project?*
4. *Share your vision with a close friend or colleague and discuss it before refining it as a vision to take forward with this project.*

Vision of Project Success

In this section we want to provide some tools and concepts to help you build a successful Positive Change Project in the same way you will build your Personal Vision of Success. The fundamental concept here is to think big and imagine your project as something more than a capstone project. Imagine that it could have a dramatic effect on the organization, the industry or the world.

More than a Big Paper

How you see your capstone makes a difference and seeing it as a huge opportunity in any number of ways is another hidden secret shared by some of our most successful students. While the end product of a capstone is undeniably a written document that may be more voluminous than any single project you've done in your previous classes, defining the work in front of you as a "big paper" does a disservice to a project that deserves to be so much more. Approaching your work as a "big paper," for example, defines your project very narrowly and does nothing to motivate you beyond just "getting it done." Such a definition also takes on a somewhat transactional spirit that does nothing to convey the excitement of making a real change that contributes to your organization's success. In short, this provides no fuel to build a flame of passion and a vision.

Provide Value to the Organization and the World

The starting point of any project is that it clearly provides value to the organization. Whether performing a project as an outsider to an organization, as an intern or as an employee, nothing is more rewarding than making a positive contribution to an organization you care about. Careful attention to project definition, boundaries, and your ability to interact with the right people will all contribute to this end point. One key word here is *purpose*. Identifying a project that has a clear purpose and provides value by making an organization more productive helps the world, as well as helping you. Finding this purpose is an important first step in defining your project's vision.

Meeting Professional Standards

One of most difficult measures of success is to establish what the standards are for professional successes in the workplace. This is something that is learned "on the job" and varies by organization, depending on communication styles, information flow and culture. Meeting professional standards may also be different than meeting "academic" standards for your capstone. This may even mean writing a final deliverable in two forms to address the needs of different audiences. Capstone students are frequently torn between creating a work product that is appropriate for communicating efficiently to advance an organizational change and fully documenting it to academic standards. This is an issue that should be addressed early in the process with your professor, your mentor, and your organization. Clarity about your professional standards and using those standards will give you a deliverable that you are proud of and a learning project that you can safely share with prospective employers. This feeds directly into a quality project vision!

Leading Organizational Change

In the same way that you, as an emerging professional, demonstrate leadership and your personal vision so, too, your project itself is a catalyst for positive change. Toward that end, your project will need to understand and provide analyses for workplace-specific variables that go beyond any academic treatment of the subject. In many ways, this *real time data* collection is a fundamental difference between an *experiential capstone,* such as yours and a less experiential capstone such as a seminar class based on case studies. Your project is, in some ways, its own change agent as you demonstrate through your own leadership skills a way forward in a positive change. Including the potential to effect major change, then, is an absolute necessity to include in your project's vision.

Just the Beginning

We've already introduced some models of change such as Action Learning, Action Research, Appreciative Inquiry, and Design Thinking. All of those models have many things in common but most importantly they are, at the highest level, all cyclical. None of those models even implies that you would somehow arrive at "the" answer. When taking on a project, there is a strong desire to "figure it out" and "solve the problem." While this is a laudable goal, it needs to be balanced against the fact that for many workplace change opportunities your project is only one iteration in an endless chain of ongoing change.

This isn't to diminish the importance of your project, but only to help you recognize that it is always part of a bigger story and is really, itself, an iteration. Knowing this is important because it provides a sense of perspective about expectations and encourages innovation based on prototyping rather than driving to a single solution. As Burnett and Evans state, "Once you've done this prototype-iteration cycle a number of times, you will really enjoy the process of learning via the prototype encounters that other people call failure." (2016, p.183).

This has implications for your vision of your project -- that it be dynamic in both its approach and end game. Approach your project's vision as part of a larger story that has a past, your current addition to the field, and a future that, by definition, will move beyond even your best work. Even slow-moving academic research takes this perspective by building on previous research and demonstrating a new theory but always looking ahead to what the next phase of research can add to this discovery.

It's an Adventure

The vision you build for your project is not an academic or wasted exercise. Seeing your project as something that is dynamic and yet provides a positive change and that fulfills a greater purpose will motivate you to build with excellence in every step. As Burnett and Evans (2016, p. 79) point out "designers don't agonize or dream about what could have been. And they don't waste their futures by hoping for a better past. Life designers see the adventure in whatever life they are currently building and living into."

"Doing by Learning" activity

Build a Vision of Project Success

1. *Think back to a successful project or deliverable. What were the uncertainties, and how did it feel to have resolved them? How did it feel to have a leadership role and have your project provide such positive impact on an organization?*
2. *Review the first portion of this chapter on a Vision of **Project** Success and make notes on those concepts that resonate with your most positive experiences in your own learning and growth or concepts that you see as particularly relevant to your current learning and growth.*
3. *Building on #1 & #2 above, can you describe a Vision of **Project** Success that you would hope to achieve as a result of successfully completing this capstone project?*
4. *Share your vision with a close friend or colleague and discuss it before refining it as a vision to take forward with this project.*

Four Case Studies

CASE 1 – Inventory Management
This project provides a platform to take my technical and leadership skills to the next level. The project is truly the final integration of work that began at the beginning of my business studies. The vision is that this project would continue the transformational process of my studies in a work-based project.

CASE 2 – New Generation Target Market for Lending Institution
This project fits my vison of my career in marketing because it represents the types of challenges that I will always have in front of me. Finding a "package" that meets changing customer needs will always be a challenge that I see myself enjoying. Bringing about the opportunity for young adults to own their own home I see as a benefit to my community and the world, as these customers of our lending services grow in their commitment to their respective communities.

CASE 3 – Employee Training and Development for less turnover and better customer service
I greatly enjoy my organization since I so easily embrace its principles, values and the level to which I feel supported in my career growth. Because of that, this project serves a greater need in helping to build an organization that embodies values of sustainability and building a better world!

CASE 4 – Merging of multiple non-profits into one organization
This organization has a mission and values to which I have been deeply aligned. I took a position here in a relatively small organization because I saw myself developing my career in organizations that directly contribute

to making a better world. It was very important to me that I put my efforts into an organization where I would be forced to take on numerous roles and projects without fear of failure and with the flexibility to pivot and regroup based on experimentation, reflection and learning. Still, the most important thing to me is that I am engaged in building a career in which I am having a direct positive impact on the world and this will be my driving force, regardless of where I am employed.

CHAPTER 7
BUILDING YOUR COLLABORATIVE NETWORK

Why You Network

Learning is a social experience!

If you have read the earlier chapters on Learning through Experience, Leading Learning, and Work-Based Learning, then this chapter's title can't be too much of a surprise. How important is it? I would refer you to the project planning chapter in which building your network is one of the first and earliest project steps. In this chapter, we will look at that process in a bit more detail.

Owning the Topic

To begin this section, let's reiterate some important points about the nature of your learning in doing an experiential business capstone. Even if your capstone project is not done with a team of students and you are working individually, it will still be very much a team effort. As with any team effort, it requires both a qualified team and good communication among team members, and as we know from our earlier readings, the days of the "lone ranger" in the innovation-driven workplaces of today are long gone. As Tim Brown, in *Change by Design*, says:

> "*The complexity of most of today's projects is fast relegating [individual/lone inventor design] this type of practice to the margins...As design begins to tackle a wider range of problem -- -and to move upstream in the innovation process -- the lone designer, sitting alone in a studio and meditating upon the relation between form and function, has yielded to the interdisciplinary team*". (Brown, 2009, p. 26)

As the leader of your virtual "design" team, your first obligation is, of course, to take ownership of your topic by learning the fundamental terms, concepts, frameworks and variables that will impact any proposed change. From that starting point, your task becomes that of what we have described as a Learning Leader, whose work includes building an understanding, sharing your work, receiving feedback and new information, and revising your "solution" iteratively in an endless cycle. Your role is to be the center point, becoming the "expert," but in a collaborative sense as you manage a process of learning together.

Building your Language

One of the most important parts of "becoming" a professional in any setting is learning the language of your area of expertise, organization and industry. Like many topics addressed in this book, it is very iterative, and requires you to "bootstrap" with fundamental concepts and language, then build from there. In the Capstone Project Planner chapter this begins by looking broadly at your industry, organization and area(s) of possible exploration. Your resources are limited only by your imagination and may include reading online, observing videos, finding some inexpensive used books and engaging with others. This is especially true if your project involves areas of study or practice in which you, or others with whom you are engaging, don't yet have expertise in the topic. In such cases you will be immediately responsible for educating them on what is known, what you have learned, and what you see as needing to be better understood.

One challenge is that you may find that much of the academic literature is too detailed or focused on topics that seem obscure or irrelevant to your work. Many of these publications may be better used later in the process, once a specific topic and prospective change are better defined. Early in the process, what is most helpful is an overview to get a sense of the landscape. In my personal experience, this is where I have found online sellers such as Amazon/Barnes & Noble to be invaluable resources.

While libraries (even university libraries) are wonderful repositories, the constraints of limited collections and resources checked out by others makes doing research under your time constraints problematic. Yes, there are costs to purchasing one or two books online but the time saved and the appropriateness of the material makes it more than worthwhile. You can also be assured that all possible resources are listed and that the listing will include everything from out-of-publication (used) to those recently or about to be published. If nothing else, the search itself will provide an overview of availability (or not) on your topic including reviews, key authors and related topics.

Building your Network
The road to exploratory research on either choosing a topic or, if chosen, getting up to speed on key issues begins with your network. One of the major reasons for the importance of network building so far in advance of your actual course is to engage in conversations about your areas of interest and to ensure that you know the landscape of possible topics needing a better understanding. While e-mail and social media may be used for supplemental knowledge sharing, it will probably still be important that you make connections and schedule face-to-face meetings or, at the very least, telephone conversations for interviews and ongoing dialogue with your network.

Building a social network of others to support your effort is frequently a new role for students, especially at the undergraduate level. One perspective reviewed earlier in the chapter on Leading Learning that may be helpful is to think about your current "Achievement Style" in how you approach work and what other styles may need to be developed. To reiterate, this comes from the Connective Edge model of leadership seen in the diagram below showing the nine achievement styles. For most students or early career professionals, the three direct styles tend to be the most used. For the network building suggested here many of the relational and instrumental styles may be more appropriate.

What this means to you is that the capstone project that appears to be a herculean solo effort is not that at all. Instead, it is most successful when done through a network of support and through dialogue and inquiry that become both the research, your pathway to learning, and designing your proposed change as it unfolds.

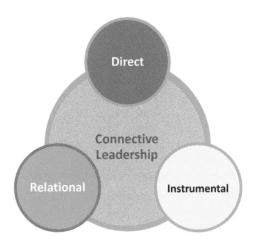

Figure 11 (repeat) Connective Leadership
Adapted from: ***Connective Leadership***, Lipman-Blumen, J. (1996)

Collaboration

It isn't news that teams provide the backbone for work to be accomplished in even the most conservative and hierarchical organizations. That said, most early career job opportunities will still be primarily task focused, with most of the work centered on a limited scope of activities and with little external "cross-functional" interaction outside of the immediate job requirements.

A business capstone project, given its integrative nature, will create opportunities to extend yourself beyond your immediate department or teams to solicit input, share data, and serve as screening for feedback for any of your interim proposals. This means that collaboration becomes the basis for at least part of your network. This is important both for your project and your professional growth, because, as Burnett & Evans share, "We design our lives in collaboration and connection with others because we is always stronger than I – it's as simple as that." They go on to say that when you design your life, you are engaging in an act of co-creation. When you use design thinking, the mindset is completely different from "career development" or "strategic planning" or even "life coaching." One key difference is the role of the community. If you're the sole architect of your brilliant future, then you heroically bring it into being – it's all about you. Life design is about your life but it's not all about you – it's all about us. (Burnett and Evans, *Designing Your Life*, 2016, p. 199).

If collaboration hasn't been your priority up until now, or if you haven't had the opportunity to "break out" of your immediate job, then this is your golden opportunity to develop an amazingly powerful professional skill and ensure a quality capstone project at the same time.

Network Resources

As I hope has been made clear, an experiential capstone doesn't happen by sequestering yourself in the library and reviewing the literature, except as a foundation to your work. On the contrary, if done well, you will need to "be out there" by building a team of support, and to embrace a wide diversity of participants, range of expertise, and competencies. Depending on your immediate situation, your network may vary considerably. In online programs, for example, you may have a more limited relationship to faculty or other experts at your school but may have contacts in your local community.

If you are in a traditional undergraduate program with only part-time or summer employment in your background, then you well may not have the immediate support of someone working full time but may have more connections with on-campus faculty or centers of excellence associated with your school. Even for those fully employed, a major factor is the length of time you have been with an organization or in your position. Many students switch organizations, for example, while completing their MBA part-time and may find themselves facing a capstone after only a few months, weeks or days with their new employer. This can be a disadvantage that is also an opportunity to reach out and build relationships rather quickly across the organization that may not have happened for years, if ever.

Remember that in assembling your network you are building a wide range of support that includes a variety of expertise and emotional support, as well. A mentor, for example, may not be someone with direct knowledge about your topic but still has enough broad business or management experience to provide a highly valuable perspective. The expectations of a mentor, in terms of specific time commitment and input, will also vary depending on your program and capstone course.

You might be asking yourself, "So, who can I turn to?" The range of stakeholders is far more wide-ranging than you might expect and can include everyone from experts in your field to a friend with little to no business experience. Some examples of network members who students have typically included are:

- **Your Instructor** – Meetings are really important so take the time to initiate some meetings or ask for advice outside the scope of your course. I routinely respond to questions or meet with students who take the time to reach out for up to a year before their actual capstone course.
- **Faculty** – This is an obvious choice and their availability varies by school, course, goals of program and specific instructor. It is most helpful, of course, if your faculty has real-world experience in your general area of focus. As an online MBA instructor, I also welcome e-mails from former students seeking advice and support, and I know that most of my colleagues feel the same.
- **Guest speakers** – Speakers who have come to your campus or class or who have provided workshops and lectures in your local community are often doing so because they are motivated to reach out into their community. Take them up on their generosity and obvious community spirit and view the relationship as a two-way street. From their perspective, they are making a connection with an aspiring professional (you) and are also given insight into a project that they wouldn't see in their normal work. Helping you becomes a learning experience for them!
- **Experienced Professionals** – Professionals in the field are, of course, one of the most highly desirable contributors and are often more willing than you might expect. They are frequently honored to be asked and, like all people, love to share their story when invited to do so. They are often willing to even serve as a "mentor" if the expectations are both clear and reasonable.
- **Friends** – While they may or may not have direct experience in your area of research, they can be a valuable sounding board for your approach to the project, help you through difficult times, and lend support by finding a community member who can assist you for a specific need.
- **Relatives** – One of the easiest groups to overlook and yet most highly used connection is that of parents, aunts and uncles. Because you know them as "uncle" or "cousin" you frequently don't see their "professional" side. Since you know them well, you can expect honest feedback that, itself, may be a precious commodity. You may also be pleasantly surprised to see how

much insight can be provided by "Aunt Emma" who has owned a bakery business for twenty years!

- **Spouse/Partner** – I've listed spouse/partner separately from "relatives" to emphasize, first, that they can SO easily be overlooked and, second, because of their importance. While you have undoubtedly had many shared "moments" of writing papers and preparing for examinations, the capstone presents a whole new dynamic in terms of stress and the need for emotional support. Including those closest to you as early and frequently as possible is good business!

- **Business Owners or Managers** – Small business owners are similar to experienced professionals but may be less experienced in your specific topic only because, as an owner, the job demands that you quickly become a "generalist" and manage all aspects of a business. That said, their experience in business has probably caused them to encounter at least some of the opportunities and challenges you are exploring, and their perspective on the "integration" of seeing business from all Areas of Management Practice is what they do every day. Like some other categories of network support above, very frequently they see your project as an opportunity to help you and to also learn themselves, making them highly engaged partners in your project.

- **Other Departments** – Reaching out to multiple departments in your organization that are beyond the immediate scope of your project is a given. Your connections with other parts of the organization are a resource that cannot be overemphasized in their potential contribution. Going back to the Areas of Management Practice in previous chapters, your connections with other departments may also provide you with some of the most valuable experiences of your entire capstone project. When reflecting on the capstone experience, it is not uncommon for students to point out that their visibility and connections to the rest of the organization were among the most surprising benefits of their project. My advice is to reach out early and often to this most valuable resource!

- **Immediate Supervisors** – The person to whom you report directly is, for obvious reasons, the most frequently used "Mentor" for those who are employed, or doing an internship, in an organization. Here, the success depends heavily on your relationship and how your project is viewed by your supervisor and how the project is being treated by the organization. One of the biggest constraints on using your supervisor is simply finding dedicated time to focus on your project since there is always work to be done that, despite your best efforts to contain it, takes precedent over scheduled "capstone" time to discuss your project. That said, getting your supervisor on board at some level is almost a prerequisite to a successful capstone if it is being done at your place of employment.

- **Colleagues or Fellow Students** – Your fellow students can be a highly valuable resource, despite being "in the same boat!" You and your classmates have an opportunity to support each other because of the differences in your experiences and the deep sense of empathy you all carry for each other because of being in the same situation. Engaging with fellow students in your capstone course, for example, also provides feedback on how you are doing; it can also help to bolster your own self-confidence about your progress while you are sharing how to overcome obstacles and develop strategies for moving forward when your progress seems to be slow.

- **Retired Executives** – This is a resource that can be extremely valuable. They are most easily accessed in state-sponsored business development organizations such as SCORE or similar connections through the Small Business Administration. Retired business professionals are an excellent choice, particularly if your project is focused on a new business opportunity and they have no competing agenda except to help you in the best way possible!

The Courage to Ask

Asking for assistance from total strangers may seem audacious to you, and that is understandable. It is clear, however, that overcoming this hurdle may be easier than you think once you make some initial contacts. With every successful new connection, it gets easier to ask the next one as you feel your confidence level and motivation to make connections increase with every new conversation. Here are some suggestions on your approach.

Start Small – Approaching an organization or even a colleague with the need for volumes of information, or to ask this person to serve as your mentor, is unreasonable unless you have a strong pre-existing relationship. What does work, when starting with a new relationship, is to engage in small conversations about your topic focused on one or two simple questions as you flesh out your idea. You can build from there as you learn more and share your progress in subsequent meetings. Again, this happens well before the beginning of your semester and supports the need to develop your network over time as your project idea matures.

School Career Resources – Presumably you are completing this capstone as part of your degree requirements at a college or university with career-oriented resources such as a Career Center and/or Career Counseling. Remember that these career "services" that help you map out a career plan are only the most visible part of their business. Offices such as these are really in the business of maintaining relationships with all types of organizations in both the for-profit and non-profit world, as well as government agencies and NGOs! Especially if you are in an undergraduate program with limited connections, one of your first stops should be the administrators, counselors and staff at your career center. These professionals can offer immediate support in building a list of possible organizations for your selection. Along those lines, consider, for example, that any organization's posting for an intern or even a job opening is really a call for help. Your offer to provide your services, while researching a capstone project that meets your interests and also helps an organization meet its needs, may be well received and, of course, may even lead to other opportunities in the future.

Cold Calling – This is, for many students, the most difficult option of network building and identifying a project. You have to be prepared for being told "no," leaving messages that never get returned or having conversations that are dead ends. That said, I have been repeatedly amazed at how students' persistence in seeking out organizations in which they have an interest has paid off with an opportunity to complete a great capstone project and even a job offer based on the capstone! When cold calling you need to be very clear and strategic about explaining concisely what you offer in the kind of work that can be done in a capstone (maybe even have a suggested topic or two), how you can add value, and that you are not interested in just doing busywork.

Social Media – If you actively manage your social media accounts and can identify some solid connections, then this may be useful, as well. Most student success in using Social Media has been in more of a supportive role as a resource to identify connections that can then be leveraged into more solid relationships.

Build an Inner Circle – Even for those who are in part-time or online programs and working full time where you intend to do your capstone, challenges can arise. At your workplace, start with an inner circle, branch out to other departments, your boss, colleagues. If you take nothing else away from this chapter, it is to "be inclusive" and to "reach out" as you begin this experience. This is supported not only by my own work-based learning experience but by my own capstone students, as well as decades of research on how learning works experientially. Enjoy the experience and don't do it alone!

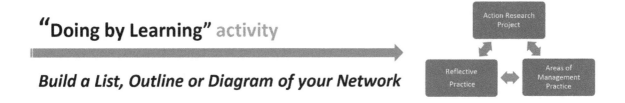

Your **Collaborative Network** *is the secret to your success in this project.*

1. *Think back to your biggest successes in any venue (not just work) and the extensive network of collaboration and support that existed. List two of your most memorable successes and for each, write down who was involved and how that collaboration and support felt.*
2. *As an activity, you should build a "plan" of who might be in your support network for this project. While it will change over time, this serves as a starting point. It also commits you to connecting with whoever you write down, assuming that it makes sense.*

Four Case Studies

CASE 1 – Inventory Management
The relationships of a data-driven project to other areas of the organization guided my selection of research partners within the organization. Secondary resources included a study of all appropriate management systems along with a number of internal reports on possible improvements still needing to be addressed but which might fit under the umbrella of this project. Internal research partners included personnel in several areas that would be affected including Customer Service, Accounting (Accounts Receivable, Accounts Payable, Budgets and Planning), Operations, Procurement and a number of leadership positions.

CASE 2 – New Generation Target Market for Lending Institution
I realized early in this project how little I knew about the technical requirements of other areas of the organization that I needed to support my efforts. My initial conversations began months before the capstone course and allowed me to reflect on the relationships not only between my project and those areas but others between those areas (such as billing systems and customer service). Given the nature of this project, I also extended my reach to community members and younger community members to get a clear sense of how they feel about home ownership and the mortgage process as part of the ownership experience.

CASE 3 – Employee Training and Development for less turnover and better customer service
My network is very extensive, since it includes both management (which is very supportive) and both past and current employees. My relationship with my employees reflects the respectful nature of my organization.

CASE 4 – Merging of multiple non-profits into one organization
Since my organization is made up of only a few employees, it may seem that I would be isolated in doing my capstone project. Actually, this turned out to be far from true for several reasons. First, I purposefully shared

every step of my project with close friends and relatives many of whom have significant experience whether in business, education or non-profits. This network alone allowed me to "test out" my thinking and clarify my direction with no risk and completely open and honest feedback. Second, I had easy access to employees given our organization's size which meant that feedback wasn't evaluative but merely advice and could be frequent enough to test ideas with colleagues who had a deeper appreciation for the opportunities and challenges. Third, the other regional organizations faced similar constraints to managing costs and growth, so they were extremely helpful in providing feedback, both informally and in more structured interviews. The sum total of these three layers really provided a diverse set of eyes and ears (and brains) that gave me multiple perspectives and a community of learning. It really does take a village!

CHAPTER 8
THE POSITIVE CHANGE PROJECT

Looking for a Change

The Stage is Set

Wow, after seven chapters, isn't it about time that we began discussing the structure of the project itself? Well, yes and no. The concepts, assessments, and processes provided in the first chapters of this book are based on research showing what makes a great experiential capstone project. Most of those chapters answer the question of "What is there about how the most successful capstone students managed their experience to be so extraordinary?" Consistent with our house painting example used earlier, the longevity of a house painting has at least as much to do with the weeks of prep work as it does the final coat of paint. On the foundation of those earlier chapters, and in a way that builds off of them, we will now begin building the capstone project itself!

The Beginning

With your personal and project visions of success completed and the network building under way, we now begin thinking more concretely about the topic for your capstone. Because your capstone is experientially based, I will be bold enough to suggest that it will always mean an organizational change at some level. As you have engaged with others in defining a positive change, two considerations should have surfaced immediately: the *magnitude* of your change project and your *role* in this change. If, for example, you are doing your project as a pro-bono service to a non-profit organization, then your role is very different from that of managing a change that is critical to your success in your own workplace. At this point it is important to reiterate our five principles of experiential capstone projects that you:

- Question and listen carefully;
- Look for strengths and know that your questions ARE the beginning of change;
- Be prepared to pivot and modify your research approach and determine whether you need for additional data;
- Engage others in a process of iterative change; and
- Be the leader of learning and positive change.

As a business student doing research in an organization in which you already have a relationship, you are in fact in two different roles as both a practitioner and a researcher. This is not an immediate conflict of interest and is actually a strength of action research, but it does challenge you to manage the convergence of these two roles. As Coughlan and Brannick (*Doing Action Research in Your Own Organization*, 2005, p. 64) note:

> *"Your organizational relationships are typically lodged and enmeshed in a network of membership affiliation, as you have been and continue to be a participant in the organization. These friendships and research ties can vary in character from openness to restrictiveness"* and these relations can affect *"the character of the data…"*

Change Drivers

In the Capstone Project Planner, it was recommended that long before starting your semester and even before your final project selection you do some preliminary research on the industry, your organization and, to the extent feasible, your possible change. The rationale is simple enough; the more you know about the context, the more capable you will be in designing and managing your proposed change. It should be mentioned that this does not provide any "internal" assessment of the organization itself which should also be done as part of any change project.

While you have presumably encountered the model below, called PESTLE, in your Business or Management studies, I include it here to ensure that you have at least one structured "model" for looking externally to your organization. PESTLE is an acronym for six areas needing to be understood when performing what is called an "external" analysis of the situation outside an organization. It stands for: Political, Economic, Social, Technological, Legal and Ecological, each of which is described briefly below.

Political

The political dynamics have the potential to affect any industry or organization and need to be understood at the global, national, and even regional level. An understanding of how current power distribution is affecting your industry and in what direction power will be heading is important. The fundamental questions include:
- Who is in power?
- What changes as a result?
- What changes are likely in the political landscape? Who wins/who loses as a result of any changes seen in the future?

Economic

The macroeconomic environment has an obvious effect on all business activity and even on non-profit funding. There is an abundance of freely available information from government sources to measure anything from very broad measurements of performance to the smallest leading indicators. Some fundamental questions include:
- Is the economy growing? Shrinking? Stable?
- What is the effect of such basic indicators as inflation, energy costs, or economic cycles?

Social

The topic of social and cultural phenomena addresses a very broad array of data on the collective human behaviors of groups. It might include everything from quantitative measurements such as birthrates and demographics to more sociocultural phenomena such as attitudes toward religion or human rights. Some fundamental questions might include:

- Are values and attitudes changing? How?
- Are demographic shifts occurring? Who is affected?
- Where is society heading with regard to its approach to health, education and human fulfilment?

Technological

Given the amount of change that has occurred in the digitization of products, services, and processes, it is hard to avoid the impact of technology on any organization. Shortened product life cycles and an extremely competitive global environment, for example, are both at least partially driven by technological change. Some fundamental questions might include:

- Is our technology current or obsolete/aging?
- Do we have any proprietary tech? Do our competitors?
- Are new, disruptive technologies on the horizon?

Legal

Laws and regulations are changing constantly; being aware of those changes could make a difference in whether a product or service will be viable in the future. Legal decisions are constantly being made that affect your organization.

- What legislation is in process?
- Will it affect us? Our customers? Our competitors? In what ways?

Ecological

Because of the increasing emphasis on the environmental impact of producing goods and services, the ecological impact should be measured.

- Is the physical environment changing?
- Does this present opportunities or threats to us? To our competitors?

The PESTLE model may not be included in your capstone project itself but does provide a nice starting point for subsequent work. If your capstone is at your place of employment, then you probably have a strong understanding of most of the PESTLE model. If, on the other hand, the organization and industry of your capstone is new to you, then it is hard to imagine proposing any change without at least a basic understanding of these six areas.

Choosing a Project

Your selection of a topic for your Positive Change project hopefully began long before you actually started your course. If you have followed the methodology outlined in the first few chapters of this book, then you are already having discussions with your organization's stakeholders some of whom have suggested changes that promise to create "value" in the form of higher revenues or lowered costs. That said, if you are just beginning your search now, concurrent to your actual course or ramping up after a slow broad search, it is time to add some structure to the process.

Typically, no organization or workplace is likely to have a shortage of ideas about where improvement is needed. The constraint, and the reason for not pursuing those ideas, is generally as simple as availability of resources to at least investigate an idea's feasibility. In your discussions with colleagues or stakeholders in your chosen organization you will probably find yourself needing to select from among a number of competing ideas. These ideas will need to be screened for their viability and whether they are within the scale and scope of your own resources and time limitations.

Refining the Change
Triangulate an Idea

Grabbing smoke is how I describe beginning an undefined project from scratch. Just reflect for a moment on how different your capstone is from a "normal" course in which your instructor lays out the resources, case studies, discussion topics, class or online activities, and methods of assessment. In your capstone, virtually all of this is up to you! Facing this challenge and the prospect of having to choose an organization and topic is one of the most stressful parts of this experience. Done well, this one decision (or sequence of decisions) also has the greatest impact on the enjoyment and success you will experience in this venture.

As with any creative process, it is unrealistic to expect that it will come immediately in a "flash" of insight immediately but will take some "cycles" of learning and reflection just to choose a topic. In this case the more actionable input happens through your preliminary "research" and your interaction with others. Use your network, reflect deeply on every new piece of information, and surround any single idea with possibilities. Said more succinctly, you need to triangulate your idea iteratively. As you become more comfortable with an idea, define a potential project as a proposed opportunity for change in a short explanation, and share your thinking!

An almost inevitable part of refining your topic will be to scale it back to a more reasonable level you can cope with. Remember that you are not alone and that most students begin with a project idea that is simply too large for a single course.

A Change Project's Value

Any discussions about a potential project will immediately center on the positive value coming out of any change. Your first job is to understand the nature of any value that might be seen from the change. Your perspective should cast a wide net for defining value, using criteria such as the *Balanced Scorecard* (Kaplan and Norton, 1996) or some other organizationally specific set of metrics. These will set a course for subsequent analysis. Keep in mind that "value" may be easily measurable and have economic value but may also be very difficult. It isn't unusual for a project to provide value that is more strategic in nature and may have obvious contributions but is not easily quantified, especially over a short time period. Other projects such as process improvements may generate changes and may be easily measured but difficult to link to changes in revenues or costs.

Understanding how value is created by your change will quickly become your responsibility. As the researcher, your job will be to understand and test any and all assumptions that are inherent in the proposed change. At the outset, it is fine to simply "accept" assumptions that may come from secondary and primary data or even conversations taken at face value. When you are beginning the process, these assumptions can even be used to bootstrap a simple economic model. As you learn more and obtain updated or more accurate information about these fundamental assumptions, however, you will then need to assess the legitimacy of earlier values, rework line items in your economic model and continue to build from there. The paradox, of course, is that you need some sense of the potential value to be created as you select your project in the first place. When you are in this position, it is likely that you will have to sketch out a rough idea of potential value just to begin the selection process.

Identifying a Need

Identifying a change for which there is a real and definable need is easier said than done. If you think about your project, for example, as a new product, then the question might be which market research suggests that customers care about what you offer. Admittedly, in many cases your change project has a documented need but one that simply hasn't been given the attention it needs to move forward.

In other cases, however, where the need is less well understood, it may be part of your job to establish a need or at least clarify it before moving into the design stage. An example might be a leadership program in which some employees have requested, and which members of senior management believe it should happen but no one has really asked employees what leadership skills they see as needed.

One "model" that may be useful early in your process is the "Jobs to be Done" perspective that has been developed by several authors recently. One of the most widely used is that created by the Strategyzer group as part of their Business Model Canvas business modeling process. Their model, called the Customer Value Proposition and found in the book, *Value Proposition Design* (Osterwalder, 2014), describes a very clear and visually-oriented process for identifying customer needs. This may be a helpful resource if you are at the "customer requirements" stage of a project.

The beauty of this model is that it circumvents many of the normal traps of endless research on "market" needs and gets directly to some key questions about the "customer." After identifying what exactly the identified customer segment wants to do (the "job to be done"), you identify the "pains" a customer is trying to avoid and "gains" a customer is working to increase. These very straightforward questions lead quickly to identifying ways to relive customer pains and create customer gains. With these understood clearly it is possible to map out the products and services that would provide a "customer value proposition."

If your project requires that you do primary research to establish a customer need, then I highly recommend obtaining a copy of this book and visiting the Strategyzer.com website for additional information including free videos and resources. Short introductions to the Value Proposition Canvas can be easily found on You Tube, as well. The process is designed for collaborative work and is consistent with all the latest thinking presented in this book, such as the Business Model Canvas, Lean Startup and Design Thinking.

Scale of Change

Scale of Change will need to be defined as closely as possible to ensure that you take on a meaningful project and that you will be able to reach a satisfactory conclusion by the end of your semester or term. A good method of screening is to use a framework developed by Anderson and Anderson in their book, *A Change Leader's Roadmap* (2001). Here they have categorized changes as developmental, transitional and transformational, along with several "drivers" of change that can be used to better understand the nature of the change you are potentially taking on.

Developmental Change – Change that has very low uncertainty and is just a matter of execution. Many projects in the workplace have a history despite never having been executed or needing little to be done outside of the change itself. A small change in the customer billing process, for example, if done within the boundaries of existing software, billing calculations, and revenue calculation but moving from print to online billing might be such a change.

Transitional Change – Change in which the movement from an old state to a new state is understood and the pathway is clear, organized and controlled. Sticking with our current billing system, a change in the bill calculations from, perhaps, monthly to quarterly customer bills along with changes in customer interface and moving to a new software system to accomplish all of this might be transitional.

Transformational Change – Change that is much less certain, and that may have periods of stepping back, reassessing the change and then moving forward again with revised assumptions. Again, staying on the revenue and billing side of the business let's imagine that the billing system is unchanged but that the business model is under pressure to change. Changing a business model can be very iterative through numerous fits and starts with stress to the core business systems and processes. The endpoint isn't clear so there will be numerous stages to an uncertain future!

Scope of Change

Like the scale of your change, the project scope also needs to be understood early in the project's life. It isn't unusual at all for a student to begin a project and discover that "scope creep" has occurred and that the project has grown far beyond its original intent. Again, we turn to Anderson and Anderson's work for their model of change imperatives. This is shown in the accompanying diagram, adapted from *The Change Leader's Roadmap: How to Navigate Your Organization's Transformation,* Linda S. Ackerman Anderson and Dean Anderson (2018):

Figure 20: Levels of Change

I like this model because I believe that it captures seven levels of change that can be applied to any change project. A brief description of each level is offered:

Environment – This is the most broad dimension of change and includes what, in many strategic frameworks, is the external environment such as the familiar and widely used PESTLE model of political, economic, social, technological, legal and environmental (as in climate and sustainability).

Marketplace Requirements – Within the greater Environment sits the customer defined market. Using the requirements of a well-defined customer segment is, again, linked to the best thinking from classical strategy to the most recent models of business modeling and entrepreneurship.

Business Imperatives – In response to the Marketplace a business needs to create a strategy that is dynamic and responds to ongoing change in customer needs.

Organizational Imperatives – In response to changes in strategy, the organization itself is under a continuous evolution and faces an ongoing need to know how it does business in everything from human resources to business processes and the newest technologies.

Cultural Imperatives – The forces of the Environment, Marketplace, Strategy and Organizational imperatives all drive the organizational culture. The important idea is that the organizational culture changes in direct response to the larger forces of change and includes everything about how people work with and treat each other.

Leader and Employee Behavior – Within all the imperatives above sits the behaviors of all organizational members but especially leadership that also serve to define the culture in an ongoing cycle.

Leader and Employee Mindset – Perhaps the deepest and most difficult change is moving beyond behavior and into the realm of mindset. This mindset includes organization members' deepest values, attitudes, and beliefs and drives behavior.

Applying this model is useful EARLY in your project because it provides a framework for where your prospective change sits on the scale and what forces are at work within or out of your control. Understanding this ahead of time allows you to assess where your boundaries are and what influences need to be managed to effect change.

"Gotta Do It" Projects

In any organization, there are projects that may not necessarily meet any pre-existing financial benchmark but just need to be done for strategic, competitive, technological, regulatory or other compelling reasons. Such a change may fit under the model of Anderson and Anderson above, for example, as driven by new industry technology standards, where you really have no choice but to stay with the pack. Regulatory or certification requirements (such as ISO, etc.) may also play a role in driving a change. The research to support such a change is no different from a more traditional project but it is made within the context of a prior decision. The only difference is that if there is little or no clear economic impact, then you may need to define the strategic benefits in the most explicit way possible. This topic is addressed in more detail in the chapter on Economic Value.

Projects with Purpose

Few people would disagree that having a strong interest in your project's topic is helpful in keeping you motivated and making the learning fun. In choosing a project, then, it makes sense to select an area which you have a strong personal desire to learn about and a topic in which you have some vested interest. But how do you do that? If one thing is clear, it is that finding a topic can take more time than you ever expect, and you may easily need several months of exploring and meeting with organizations or, if at your place of employment, other departments, many of which may be in another arm of your organization in another state or country. As you explore options, you certainly want to begin with the highest of expectations and identify a project with purpose. When students are asked about the key factors in their being able to push through the tough times, one of the top reasons was consistently "passion" driven by seeing a bigger picture and a greater good beyond your project's immediate scope of work. More succinctly, it is working with purpose that pulls them through.

Value Chain

Another useful model, with which you should be familiar, is Michael Porter's Value Chain (Porter, M., 1998). It is customarily used in business strategy to assess the internal relationships between areas of an organization to aid in understanding how each is adding value. As a quick refresher, remember that the "Primary Activities" in the lower portion of the diagram represent those activities that contribute direct value to whatever product or service your organization delivers. In the upper section are the "Support Activities" that are necessary to the overall functioning of the organization but not directly contributing to the product's or service's value. All of these together make up the "Value Chain" that moves from left to right.

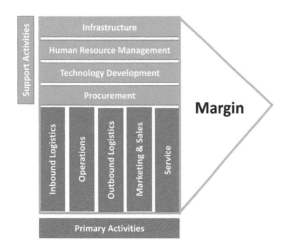

Porter's Value Chain
Figure 21: Value Chain
Adapted from: Porter, M. (1998),
Competitive Advantage, Creating and Sustaining Superior
Performance

This serves as a handy screening tool for your project because it provides a visual that can be used to identify the primary location of your change project. For example, a new Research and Development process under Technology Management would be very different from a new Market Testing Process harbored in the Marketing and Sales function. You might also begin to think about how all these areas might contribute to the value created by a change that is primarily located in one part of the chain. This links directly to the *Areas of Management Practice* Model.

Top Three *Areas of Management Practice*

The *Areas of Management Practice* (repeated below) have provided guidance on the structure to your capstone throughout this book. Once your project has been selected, it is generally easy to identify the primary area of study. For example, the development of a new Customer Relationship Management system might be considered to be primarily an *Information Systems* project. Beyond that, its secondary and tertiary areas might be *Products, Services, Marketing and Sales* and *Processes Improved or Added*, respectively. Once those have been identified, you can begin to pinpoint the nature of the change and relate it to your studies. As a resource to jump-start this process, go back to the questions for each of the Areas of Management Practice as introduced in chapter one and the competencies, models, and frameworks that came out of your courses. These, combined with some preliminary research and a few conversations, is enough to get you going on defining some of the big opportunities and challenges. The upward cycle of learning and change has begun!

1. *Alignment of Mission, Values and Strategy*
2. *Products, Services, Marketing and Sales*
3. *Processes Improved or Added*
4. *Information Systems*

5. *Organizational Impact and Change Management*
6. *Leadership Capabilities and Requirements*
7. *Economic Business Case*
8. *Project Implementation*
9. *Economic Modeling*
10. *Reflections on Learning*

Time to Write Something

At this point you are probably further ahead than you think. If you have built a network, done some preliminary research, and spent some time identifying a topic that you care about, the battle is already halfway won. To begin with, you have a topic, the major opportunities and constraints, and the people with whom you will connect throughout the project as they become increasingly clear. It is important to develop a short synopsis of what your project is all about. As Tim Brown in *Change by Design* (2009) describes it, you will want a "brief" that is "a set of mental constraints that gives the project team a framework from which to begin, benchmarks by which they can measure progress, and a set of objectives to be realized (p. xx) ." Remember that this isn't the final word in defining your project scope, the research required, or the ultimate end point in recommended actions.

"Doing by Learning" activity

Write a Project Overview

Write a Project Overview to share with colleagues and your collaborative network for feedback. It should contain just the basics such as:

- *Project name*
- *Opportunity or Problem*
- *Customer Pains and Gains supporting the need*
- *How this adds value to the organization*
- *What needs to be understood (key questions driving your research)*
- *Drivers of Change*
- *Scale and Scope*
- *Other, depending on context*

In writing this overview of your project you want to be clear about the possible benefits based on what you know to date. While it is clearly too early in the process to express any financial measurements, such as breakeven, ROI, etc., it is time to put a first stake in the ground on what the value might be in the form of at least the greatest and most obvious benefit. Doing this early in your process helps to shape your thinking and give direction to the questions you ask and the quality of the data you collect. Your change will ultimately provide some level of economic gain through revenue enhancement, cost reductions, or both. Cost reductions will generally be tied to the complete or partial reduction of one or more activities, reduced labor, or digitization at some level. Any higher expenses and/or additional required investment are likely to be caused by new or expanded activities and/or infrastructure needed to support the change.

As described earlier in the sections on Action Research, Design Thinking, and Lean Entrepreneurism, making use of your easiest and least expensive data to create an inexpensive way to test your ideas, or a "Minimum Viable Product," can't be overemphasized. The game isn't necessarily to research, research, research, complete an exhaustive analysis and then make a decision. Instead, think of this as a game of researching, analyzing, testing, learning and then repeating the process to constantly be refining your ideas. Feasibility analysis and concept testing make up both the starting and ending point.

Remember the discussion on Emotional Intelligence? The time is now…Pay attention to the *feelings* of both you and members of your network as you make your inquiries. Don't forget that how you and others feel about the project is relevant data that shouldn't be dismissed out of hand. Be asking yourself what sources of data are subtle and have more to do with what people aren't saying rather than what they are telling you.

Focus

I hope this chapter gave you some lenses to help you frame your positive change project and to get airborne with a basic project description and a well-defined scale and scope.

Four Case Studies

CASE 1 – Inventory Management

The project had a pretty clear focus from the start and looked to improve a few key metrics in managing our inventory. The change would provide benefits to employees, the organization itself, its operations and its customers. To the extent that it might lower expenses and, hence, customer costs, it also links directly to our organizational strategy.

CASE 2 – New Generation Target Market for Lending Institution

This project took somewhat definite form quickly given the obvious nature of our business requirements for growth. What wasn't as obvious was how to approach a younger market with different needs and communication styles from our current customer mix. Being able to help these young adults to enjoy the benefits of home ownership in a way that fits their needs became the positive change that I wanted our organization to be able to provide.

CASE 3 – Employee Training and Development for Less Turnover and Better Customer Service

This project did not change from its original emphasis on the positive impact that an improved training plan would have on employees, retail locations sales and the organization overall.

CASE 4 - Merging of Multiple Non-profits into One Organization

Because I was doing my project for a non-profit with a clear values-based mission, there was little doubt that my project was all about making a positive change in the world. If I could develop a plan that allowed several regional organizations to flourish as a result of efficiencies gained through merging, then I would have certainly met that goal! While such a merger is a long-term project, my deep grounding in the separate areas of the organization allowed me to create a "plan" that was extremely comprehensive and tied to actual data and employee input. If implemented correctly and with a spirit of a true growth mindset, this project can absolutely have a positive impact.

CHAPTER 9
LEADING POSITIVE CHANGE

From Leading Learning to Leading Change

Beyond a Leader of Learning

In an earlier chapter, we discussed some skills required for your new role as a Leader of Learning, especially early in your research process. In this chapter we build on those skills by providing some tools that will help you to build additional leadership skills more closely related to proposing your change and, in some cases, actually leading the change! Like the previous "leadership" chapter, this material is not designed to be read like a novel but to be used to do some deep personal reflection and then to be applied to your capstone project in its later stages of development.

Look Inward Reflectively

As you sit here, with your project topic only recently having been defined, it is time to jump ahead and make you aware of what is about to happen. In only a few short weeks, following your research, interviews and other work, you will become the expert on leading the change being studied. While you are now only at the threshold of understanding this change, you will suddenly find yourself as the "point person" who is educating others as you do your research. This began when you started to build your language based on some preliminary research and will accelerate with every new piece of data that you review, digest and make part of your study. Gulp, congratulations as you are about to assume the role of a change leader!

Your position of expertise will vary, depending on both your background in the organization and on the opportunity that you are researching. In describing a worker's position relative to the organizational community Lave and Wagner (1991), in their book, *Situated Learning*, refer to the process of developing expertise as "Legitimate peripheral participation provides a way to speak about the relations between newcomers and old timers, about activities, identities and communities of knowledge and practice" (p. 29).

It is important to understand this now because of its importance to your overall success and because it builds on the "Visions of Success" (both personal and project) that were described in the previous chapter. Seeing yourself now in a leadership role reinforces the professional value of an experiential capstone. This isn't an academic exercise but an opportunity to engage in the building of leadership capability for a positive change, something that you may not have imagined before beginning the course!

First, Self-Reflection

Values Alignment

Finding an organization that aligns with your personal values is extremely important to many students. Even when they are in the same industry or serve the same customers, organizations can vary tremendously in their organizational culture and relationship to their stakeholders, and especially to their employees. In your role of providing your study it is important that you feel comfortable and aligned with any potential organization. This begins with doing some basic research as you build your network. Look first to the organization's website, press releases and external communications. Begin immediately to ask others, including your school's career center, about the organization, and listen carefully to what is said. If, for example, you are visiting an organization for an initial face-to-face interview, then your visit is an opportunity to do some ethnographic research through observation of how people interact, the level of formality, openness, and candor or transparency. Edgar Schein, the world's guru on assessing organizational culture advocates, in numerous publications, how observing "artifacts" really make up the atmosphere. These might include wall hangings, office layout, etc.

Identifying organizations that align with your values and interests also presumes that you have personally made explicit what values are most important to you. If not, then one tool that may be helpful (yes, another self-assessment) is called the VIA Survey (http://www.viacharacter.org/www/Character-Strengths-Survey), which "provides a wealth of information to help you understand your core characteristics" because it "focuses on your best qualities." (From VIA Website). The VIA survey is a valuable tool in clarifying your own priorities by helping you understand how the "24 VIA character strengths are the pathways to each of the 5 areas of well-being (PERMA)". They underpin each element – deploying your highest strengths leads to:

- P – More positive emotion
- E – More engagement
- R – Better relationships
- M –More meaning
- A – More accomplishments

"Doing by Learning" activity

Complete the VIA Character Strengths Survey

1. *Go to the VIA Survey website and complete the survey. (*http://www.viacharacter.org/www/Character-Strengths-Survey *)*
2. *Review your results and reflect on how your strengths have been used successfully in the past.*
3. *Reflect on how your strengths will support your work in this capstone.*

Leadership Self-Assessment -- Resources

Your leadership role is, of course, supported by a number of your personal and professional strengths and leadership competencies. While this is a big topic (Amazon book search on leadership results in over 100,000 results!), a few of today's most widely used resources may be useful to you. Many of you have had one or more courses in leadership and have probably done one or more self-assessments. If not, then you might consider one additional resource that is also very turnkey because, as found in the book *Emotional Intelligence 2.0*, it is packaged with an explanatory book, so it doesn't require any certified facilitator or coach.

- *Strengths 2.0* – This book is based on the widely used Clifton Strength Finder and is a wonderful supplement to or replacement for the VIA Strengths Survey discussed above.

Leading Change

Leadership Challenge Model*
*portions adapted from *Leadership Models for Change*. Haggerty, D. (2013k).

One approach to leadership is found in Kouzes and Posner's classic book (now in its sixth edition), *The Leadership Challenge* (2017) in which they have identified some key competencies for effective leadership. This model is based on extensive research that is both broad (cross-sectional) and deep (longitudinal). The research is based on a fundamental question: *In cases where leaders accomplished extraordinary things (a major change) what behaviors did they exhibit? How did it happen?* The study, or sequence of studies, identified five "practices" of leadership, which are each broken into two "commitments" of leadership (see model below). This is also one of the few leadership studies in which both constituents and leaders were interviewed to understand each party's expectations, as well as leadership competencies.

The Leadership Challenge model (Five Practices and Ten Commitments):

Challenging the Process
1. Search out challenging opportunities to challenge, grow, innovate, and improve.
2. Experiment, take risks, and learn from the accompanying mistakes.

Inspiring a Shared Vision
3. Envision an uplifting and ennobling future.
4. Enlist others in a common vision by appealing to their values, interests, hopes, and dreams.

Enabling Others to Act
5. Foster collaborations by promoting cooperative goals and building trust.
6. Strengthen people by giving power away, providing choice, developing competence, assigning critical tasks, and offering visible support.

Modeling the Way
7. Set the example by behaving in ways that are consistent with shared values.
8. Achieve small wins that promote consistent progress and build commitment.

Encouraging the Heart
9. Recognize individual contributions to the success of every project.
10. Celebrate team accomplishments regularly.
   Source: *The Leadership Challenge* (Kouzes and Posner, 6th edition, 2017)

This is an important study and should become one of your key "takeaways" from the material in this book as your leadership role emerges out of this project. While a Leadership Practices Inventory self-assessment is available, it is outside the scope of our application. For you, as a student launching a new capstone project, it is suggested that you simply stop and carefully review each of the Five Practices and Ten Commitments. I strongly encourage you to think about how each practice and commitment might be useful in your emerging role as a leader of your own project. This is particularly true once the project is completed, at which point your organization's expectations may catapult you into an unexpected leadership role. Reflect critically on your strengths and areas where improvement might be helpful. You might also make linkages to other models, such as the Connective Edge introduced in the "Leading Learning" chapter. Also ask yourself how they are different and how your abilities and preferences might work together for you to make up your own unique "style" of achievement and leadership.

The Leadership Practices model above can be used immediately in your project work. While it can be interpreted as a model of leadership characteristics, it is also useful as a template for some considerations in developing a change, whether it is for an entire organization or a specific project, such as yours. Try applying it to your immediate situation and see both how you measure up and how it can support your capstone project.

The Heart of Change*
*portions adapted from *Heart of Change Summary*. Haggerty, D. (2013j).

Another of my favorite (and classic) models of leadership is based on John Kotter's work which is, unlike much of the management press, research based. His newer work, *The Heart of Change*, builds some new learning upon the earlier research. What's fun is that he does it through carefully selected stories and case studies making it easy to read and enjoyable to apply.

It is important to remind ourselves about Kotter's fundamental research question: If an organization has successfully undergone a large-scale or transformational change, then how did it happen? What was the process and what leadership skills supported that process? His response tells us how people succeeded at all levels in the organization (not just senior management) in successfully designing and implementing change.

His "model" consists of eight "steps," although he is quick to point out that they are not necessarily sequential and will probably overlap. They can also be thought of from two perspectives: as a process or as skills. As a process, the inclusion of all eight probably makes sense for most change plans and provides an excellent framework with which to start. As a set of skills, each can be thought of as a distinct competency requiring its own little bundle of competencies in assessment, research, communication, motivation or negotiation.

The most significant piece of new information, since the original research about six years earlier than this book, is the author's increased emphasis on the *emotional side of change*, even in an organizational setting. Kotter is pushing hard against the traditional analytical and financial model in favor of one that goes beyond that to reach people's feelings. He is proposing that when people change, it is because they have been *moved emotionally* and, generally, not because of traditional analysis. While the analysis still needs to be done, it is simply not the driver of change. This is an important message for you as a student of change management and as an emerging change leader!

I have summarized and commented on the eight-step process below the diagram that follows. But first, let me make a couple of small suggestions. Before you launch into reading about the eight steps, choose an activity or change effort in which you are involved at work or you know from a case study. As you read, continue to use this example and apply each step to it. At times, the connection may seem weak but don't give up; hang in there and be mentally tough, even if it makes your head hurt! Also, each chapter of the book has a nice summary in bullet form that you should look at and reflect on before moving on to the next chapter.

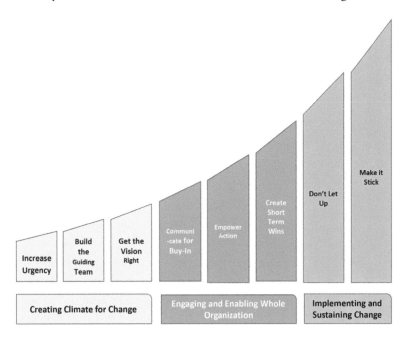

Eight Steps for Successful Large-Scale Change
Figure 22: Eight Steps to Change
Adapted from: Kotter, (2002), *Heart of Change, p.6.*

Kotter's Eight Steps for Change
1. **Increase Urgency** – This is among the most difficult of tasks because it draws on skills that many of us have little time to cultivate. However, thinking back, for example, to the various leadership styles that you have explored, it should be easy to see how this skill fits with many of the more relational or interdependent styles. The exercise on pages 34-35 is a good start in applying the material to your own situation!
2. **Build the Guiding Team** – Don't get hung up on the "organizational" scale of the book and many of the "transformational changes" presented. The "team" can be small and unique to your area of an organization BUT it needs to meet some fundamental criteria like recognition! Also, this is a great example of overlap. Building the team may begin before or after the urgency building and, in fact, both may evolve as the vision is created, as well!
3. **Get the Vision Right** – As we go through various models of leadership and change management, the need for a forward-looking and clear vision will keep resurfacing in your life. This is with good reason, since a vision provides clarity and focus in the information-overloaded lives of both you and your co-workers. It also provides a screen for decisions about what to do (or not to do) and will become the backbone of any communications plan. Again, the key word is clarity. Can I emphasize this

enough? That's C-L-A-R-I-T-Y, and without it, you will be wasting your hard-earned change effort dollars!

4. **Communicate for Buy-In** – If you paid attention to the paragraph immediately above, then the communication plan is half finished! If we believe Kotter, then the communication plan needs to be consistent with his findings in two ways. First, communications need to be succinct and focused on the fundamental message. Second, it needs to be emotionally driven. Emotionally-based communication isn't just for Nike and McDonalds, it is for your organization, as well!

5. **Empower Action** – While the "empower" word may be as overused now as "paradigm" was a decade ago, that shouldn't diminish its importance. Virtually every significant research piece on team building or organizational change suggests, usually somewhat forcefully, that delegating and sharing authority is a good thing. This is especially true in any change effort in which people are taking risks (remember Deep Change???). Doing so with little or no support for taking action dooms a change effort to failure!

6. **Create Short Term Wins** – Creating change in baby steps consisting of short-term wins is consistent with the most advanced thinking on strategic planning. While some "high-level" strategic planning is, of course, necessary, so too are revised plans based on new learning. Short-term wins, coming from experimentation and testing, provide that learning. Whether called a test, a pilot, a phase, a stage or a project, the result is concrete evidence that can be used for focus, participation, shared success, proof of concept, or celebration!

7. **Don't Let Up** – This is an interesting "step" since it is probably the least identifiable but among the most important of the eight. This is a second example of overlap since this issue will come up early and repeatedly throughout the change process. I think of this as the "innovation- applied" step, since no matter how well or poorly it is going, it is necessary to keep reflecting on what can be done better to reinforce your earlier efforts!

8. **Make Change Stick** – The key word here is "fragile," since any change effort can slip backwards in a flash! The key to preventing this is cultural change. While you will explore cultural change in more detail later in the course, the material and examples provided by Kotter should give you a sense of its importance.

I encourage you to breathe deeply and look over the Kotter eight-step model again. Think about the barriers at each step, the interrelationships of all steps and how it all applies to your immediate situation. You did apply each one to your situation, right? If not, go back and do that now. Your goal is to feel comfortable enough with this model that it can provide a framework for your capstone project.

See, Feel, Change

Underlying the eight steps is Kotter's fundamental proposition that it is the emotional buy-in that drives people to willfully engage in change. One key thing to remember as you engage others in a change is that people don't get emotionally engaged by being shown a spreadsheet. Instead, they need to be shown a vision that they can see and that allows them to feel the need for the possibilities coming from a change. This represents one of the most important contributions of Kotter's work – it provides a model of leadership and change that demonstrates the conceptual movement from a rational-only model to one that embraces the value of an emotional connection to an idea or prospective change.

While the broad and important topic of leadership may be outside the scope of this book, it is important enough that you should either revisit any leadership development program that you have completed or take it upon yourself to find one of the recognized resources (such as those above) and critically reflect on your leadership strengths. Once done, combine these with your self-reflections on Emotional Intelligence, The Connective Edge and The Leadership Practices Inventory presented earlier in this book. Reflecting on your Leadership, Learning Style, Emotional Competencies and Achievement Style within the context of your vision of success should begin to paint a picture of how your capstone may play out (and how enjoyable it will be!), as you encounter both challenges and opportunities over the next several weeks.

1. *Review the leadership models presented in this chapter and reflect on times when you have adopted the behaviors and competencies described. Alternatively, reflect on times when you have seen others exhibit excellent leadership of change.*
2. *Identify how your understanding of leading change can be used in your capstone experience as you approach the making of recommendations and, in some cases, even leading the implementation of your project.*

Transitioning to Research for Change

With your leadership models safely packed away into your toolkit, you have now arrived at the stage of your project in which you begin to apply what you know, and build a deep understanding of your topic while simultaneously redefining and refining your opportunity for positive change.

Talk, Talk and Talk (and Talk) Some More

The refinement and ongoing redefinition of your prospective change opportunity or topic begins with those broad conversations that you have had or are currently having with your expanding network. Be sensitive in your conversations for insights and emerging opportunities to add value as you increase your understanding. At this stage, for example, you might pay particular attention to unrecognized Customer Gains and Customer Pains (introduced earlier) that lead to a clear Customer Value Proposition. Remember that the act of talking, verbalizing and inquiry helps you to perceive the need for change, and construct a vision as you engage with your growing network. The greatest error to be avoided at this early stage of the process is to overcommit to a "solution" based only on anecdotal evidence, management bias and limited information. Keep talking!

Working the Complete Workplace

For any of us, it is natural that most of our time, interactions and relationships are within our own department or most immediate part of the organization. If you are not employed at the organization where you are doing your project, then your primary contact would then be where you would be most likely to be making inquiries and conducting research. Whether working at your capstone's location or not, begin immediately to look to other departments in your organization even if you don't consider it to be an area of your expertise or directly related to the immediate topic. This helps to ensure that you fulfill what was described as the greatest goal of any capstone: integration of all areas of business, as described by the Areas of Management Practice model.

Working across the organization is equally important when you are researching topics that exist both within a centralized function or those that tend to cut across functional areas such as Human Resources, Logistics or Customer Service. Remember that, given the integrative nature of your capstone, *any topic will impact or be impacted by multiple areas of the organization,* so taking on a Marketing project when your expertise is, for example, Accounting and Finance, is not only acceptable but critical to your project that undoubtedly has Accounting or Financial dimensions. Working across the organization has benefits for your own career development as well, since learning to "Lead the Learning" for a change project is never confined to one department or functional area.

Undergraduate Challenge

If you are a full-time undergraduate student, then you face the additional challenge of, first, finding an organization and then identifying a topic or potential change to explore. That said, you should know that you probably have more resources and a greater network than you think. Depending on your relationship to organizations where you have spent time, any part-time job, internship or previous summer employment may provide surprising opportunities when approached. Remember not to limit your request to that of your previous job with these organizations since you may now be ready to tackle something very different from your previous responsibilities. One recent undergraduate student, for example, had worked summers at a golf club doing what college students do (caddying, pro-shop sales, etc.) but he did a complete Digital and Social Media Communications Strategy for that club as his internship project. Like that student, if you have a personal relationship, and it can be used to build a new professional relationship based on your new role as an about-to-graduate business student, then do it!

Also, be sure not to dismiss a relationship due to geographical distance between your school and/or previous or summer employment back home even if separated by some distance. It is completely reasonable to begin the project early in the semester by phone, e-mail, Google Meets, Zoom and/or SKYPE and even to supplement those with one or two face-to-face meetings when returning home during the semester. This method has proven especially true when using a business that is owned by family or a close friend back home in which the level of transparency and trust quickly overcomes the miles between you.

The Bottom Lines

One of the most basic fundamentals of any organization is that people be aligned and pulling in a common direction. Getting such alignment is not easy and is built on a shared agreement about everything from the often lofty and long-term mission to shorter-term departmental and individual performance objectives. As you visit and talk to members of any organization, be thinking about the organization's stated values, as well as your own. Second, be sure to inquire and evaluate how they measure performance and success. Presumably, you have encountered the concept of "Triple Bottom Line," or "Balanced Scorecard" in at least one of your program's courses. This is extremely important, since the way your project's success is measured (economic

AND other) will drive both your design recommendation and the project's ultimate acceptance. If, like many students, you find yourself gravitating toward organizations that measure themselves by standards that get beyond financial metrics, then this is the time to dust off that thinking and put it to work!

Passion and Purpose

- Passion again?
  Yes, despite being treated in a previous chapter, I am compelled to mention it one more time here within the context of really drilling down into your topic. One of the most important paths to a successful capstone project is your level of interest in the subject matter. This is also one of the most difficult aspects for the instructor to assess. I have seen students dedicate their capstone to their passion for a previous course or subject, favorite sports, musical interests, religious affiliation, non-profit support, long-term career or employment goals and new business opportunities.

- Purpose again?
  In another chapter we go into more detail on this subject but I'm revisiting it here because it really does need to be kept "top of mind" as you engage in the process of learning, reframing your problem, understanding the organizational culture at a deeper level and assessing how much you identify with the purpose of your work. I am acting a bit "data-free" when I say that in my interactions with people young and old in a variety of venues the word "purpose" seems to be part of the zeitgeist. My feeling is that collective wisdom needs to be given attention!

- Passion and Purpose
  When students report on how they got through the inevitable difficult periods of workload, self-doubt, short timelines, long nights, writer's block and more, the single most important thing that helped them in these times of need was a "passion" for the subject and/or a belief in the purpose of their project and/or the organization's mission. If you haven't yet done so, then this is the time to clarify how your areas of interest, passion and purpose align with your project and organization. Use this alignment to consciously address what gets you excited about your topic.

Insight

At this point you might be wondering why there is such an emphasis on obtaining qualitative data through personal interviewing, direct observation and other person-to-person methods of inquiry. One of the greatest changes over the past few years in product development, business strategy, innovation, entrepreneurship, and organizational development is the recognition that *deeper understanding* and *insight* are increasingly important to these processes. This isn't meant to undermine the need for well-designed quantitative research when appropriate but does mean that a greater emphasis has been directed at the iterative design principles that have been advocated in this book.

In *Change by Design*, for example, Tim Brown says that from a design thinking perspective, insight "…does not usually come from reams of quantitative data that measure exactly what we already have and tell us what we already know. A better starting point is to go out in the world and observe the actual experiences of [others]" (Brown, 2009, p. 40). As the project owner of a proposed organizational change, your insight into a new customer value proposition will seldom be found in secondary research such as journal articles or government-generated statistics. While those have an important overall role in your literature review and baseline of research, insight is far more likely to come from making actual connections with customers and truly understanding their situation. For your work, it is highly probable that engaging with your network, including your own primary research, will provide you with fresh data as it "generates ideas and concepts that have not existed before" (Brown, 2009, p. 41).

The belief is that insight comes from asking what people's stories are and observing what they do, rather than how they describe what they want. As discussed earlier, Appreciative Inquiry, for example, begins with exploring our previous successes and probing how and why those outliers of success came to be. But this process of inquiring about strength-based experiences is not a quantitative exercise with a statistically-designed sample size. Instead, it reaches out to large numbers of stakeholders for their stories of success in an effort to glean the wisdom of the crowd. The emerging thinking in the areas of both Business Modeling and Design Thinking concur with this direct-to-customer approach of getting faster feedback on mock-up designs as a learning and growth methodology.

For the Design Thinking perspective, we turn again to Tim Brown, in *Change by Design*, in which he shares that "We watch what people do (and do not do) and listen to what they say (and do not say)...There is nothing simple about determining whom to observe, what research techniques to employ, how to draw useful inferences from the information gathered, or when to begin the process of synthesis that begins to point us toward a solution" (Brown, 2009, p. 43). A similar philosophy extended to business design comes from Eric Reis in his recent book, *The Startup Way* (2017), in which he applies this general approach to larger organizations when he writes, "Continuous transformation [comes from] an organization's ability to test and learn from experiments having to do with its own structure and processes, promoting the best proven techniques company-wide while limiting or discarding the rest-- is what will give that organization the ability to thrive in the modern era" (Reis, 2017, p. 317).

Risk and Uncertainty

Your initial discussions will have undoubtedly raised some red (or at least yellow) flags about your project. One of the most important lessons in managing change projects such as yours is that you be open to feedback and learning. Being open to learning isn't all about your ability to grasp information that supports your hypothesis of change. Learning is also being open to criticism, doubt, risks and uncertainties that will surface. Being open to risks and uncertainties is a good thing because understanding them, addressing them, and building them in at the front end, makes it more likely that you can pivot and adjust your desired future state as your project unfolds. Remember that your project may have an end game but at the same time needs to have some flexibility to account for risks and uncertainties that become known through your research process. What are the big risks? What are the greatest uncertainties? These become key questions to be explored and researched or, at least, held up as possible avenues of exploration and research.

"Doing by Learning" activity

Adjustments to Leading Change Self-Assessment

Based on the topics presented in the last part of this chapter, make any adjustments necessary to your Leadership Self-Assessment on how you might exercise change leadership given the identified changes.

Four Case Studies

CASE 1 – Inventory Management

Changes were identified in leadership style and employee empowerment to accommodate data that are more accurate, more accessible and more transparent. This also means that employees who have had minimal involvement with the warehouse and inventory management may now have that opportunity and this, itself, will require adjustments in leadership. All of this puts me in a position of advocating the change itself, change to the organization and to all levels of leadership.

CASE 2 – New Generation Target Market for Lending Institution

Most of my work up until this project was bounded by my role in the marketing department and didn't represent such a comprehensive effort in developing a new market. It wasn't too long into my research that I began to see emerging themes. Suddenly my inquiry seemed to be jumpstarting changes in my colleagues' responses before I had even finished my work. Upon reflection, what was happening was that colleagues were already seeing me as the expert and that my action research was initiating change just through the inquiry process. I found my role as a change leader emerging real time as I completed my research.

CASE 3 – Employee Training and Development for less turnover and better customer service

This change project gave me a significant "bump" in my interaction with and visibility to senior management that displayed my leadership ability. Because my approach to this project was so focused on making a positive impact and challenging the status quo in a positive way, it was warmly accepted. As this project unfolded, I was offered a new higher-level position in which I will be able to continue the ideas I developed here. In a way, the leadership mindset with which I approached this project became a self-fulfilling prophesy, and I became a company expert in something that I only embraced a few weeks earlier!

CASE 4 – Merging of multiple non-profits into one organization

While it is easy to say that I believe in my leadership ability, taking on a politically sensitive project with dramatic (even if positive) changes across multiple organizations really put my skills to the test. I kept reflecting back to my Emotional Competencies and, in particular, empathy, as the foundation of my ability to really understand what interview participants were saying and, most importantly, feeling about how a merger would affect them. My foundation of relationships also helped to provide a foundation of trust when discussions touched on sensitive issues. Probably more than anything, my thoughts kept coming back to Appreciative Inquiry's principle of simultaneity in which the change actually begins with the inquiry. I thought about this every step of the way because as I shared "draft" configurations for merging two or more organizations, I could see that, at least conceptually, change was making strides long before the adaptation of any formal plan.

CHAPTER 10
MAPPING YOUR POSITIVE CHANGE TO AREAS OF MANAGEMENT PRACTICE

The Change Mapping Process

Step-by-Step Guide

Perhaps the most important process of this book lies in your "mapping" of your project to all Areas of Management Practice and then creating a working document that outlines your project final report. But wait, you ask (very appropriately), how can we outline our project report while we are still so early in the research process? The short answer is that both the matrix and the outline are likely to change. The important consideration is that in doing this now, creating a road map for a solid path forward means that you always have a starting point, a direction, and boundaries and resources to make sense of any change you deem necessary. Without such a road map, it can be too easy to make changes that are whimsical, disconnected to any real plan and can, all too often, take you down rabbit holes.

1. **The Opportunity** – Develop a three-sentence summary of the proposed opportunity.
2. **Three Big Questions** – Identify the three biggest questions/uncertainties needing to be understood about your proposed opportunity and state them as questions.
3. **Areas of Practice - Top Three** – Look to see where your three big questions/uncertainties fit into the *Areas of Management Practice* matrix and reframe them as topics of study to be explained by each area of your capstone. These are likely to be the primary areas of your study to be researched.
4. **Areas of Practice-Remaining Seven** – Identify similar questions/uncertainties for all remaining Areas of Practice. While these may be secondary areas of study for your research, they are still extremely important in their supporting roles and, when you gain a better understanding of your topic, you may even want to elevate them to primary topics of study.
5. **Identify Resources (Courses and Big Ideas)** – Review the *Areas of Management Practice*, Courses and Big Ideas tables for each Area of Practice to identify likely resources that might help you to address the challenges of understanding and resolving your big uncertainties. Using these tables as a launching point, begin to assemble the names of both courses and specific frameworks that may be helpful in addressing the question you have for that specific Area of Practice.

6. **Build an Areas of Practice Matrix** – Build your own matrix consisting of the Areas of Practice, Subjects, Courses and Big Ideas (topics/models/frameworks) that may be connected to your project by addressing all your questions in your Areas of Practice Matrix.
7. **Build an Outline** – Using the Matrix described above as a basis for your topics, now build an outline of what can be your final "report" also called the Narrative.
8. **Reflect on your Road Map** – This becomes your road map for inclusion or exclusion of content.

Zeroing in on the Opportunity

Refining the Scale and Scope

Refining your project idea into something more concrete is putting a stake in the ground and the beginning of more active development of your project. While the conversations may continue with your whole network, this is the time to focus on the most important stakeholders in your chosen organization and to work with them to refine your topic and likely outcomes. Your starting point here is The Opportunity, Three Big Questions and Top Three Areas of Practice that you identified in an earlier chapter.

Validate the Positive Opportunity

The most important immediate question before you is: what is it that needs to change and why? Presumably your conversations either have taken you or will shortly lead you down the road of a real change possibly needed by the organization. It is important at this point to *adapt a mindset of positive change that supports innovation*. From the perspective of Appreciative Inquiry introduced earlier, we are interested in linking any possible change to identifying positive outliers or, in other words, examples of positive results around which we can begin to develop more formal positive change strategies. This concept is closely aligned with what Eric Ries describes in *The Start Up Way* (2017), in which he refers to innovation as "a form of positive variation" (p. 195) that moves the organization away from doing things as usual. This isn't easy. My own experiences confirm what Ries describes, however, that stakeholders will generally prefer to remain entrenched, at least initially, in their current practice and in making small incremental improvements. A more robust positive change will push on that tendency. It should be expected that just getting agreement on the *definition, scale and scope* of your positive change may take a substantial effort.

In this stage, you are really most interested in validating the magnitude of change being considered, what internal work pre-exists to build on, how well understood and documented the need for change is, and the level of support you would receive from the organization. Where just a few days (or hours) ago, you may have been triangulating a possible project, you are now tightening up the boundaries and limiting your conversations to a single positive change project with what will soon become a project with milestones and timelines for key deliverables.

Unless extensive research has already preceded your positive change project, your first job then is to understand, at a very deep level, the need for change. A classic mistake is to misinterpret the enthusiasm of a few stakeholders (or prospective customers) as a new idea without doing your own due diligence.

Clarify Three Big Questions

With some direct observation or input from the organization on the jobs to be done and a project having been selected, it is time to frame some fundamental questions that fall out of your project. While you may have your own questions or base them on the Areas of Management Practice questions from an earlier chapter, below are three generic questions that can also serve as a good starting point:

- How can we measure what we are currently doing?
- What would a perfect end point for this change look like?
- How would any positive change be measured?

Asking and beginning to answer just these three questions will help to define the rest of your project beginning with the most immediate change and working from there across other areas of management practice.

Areas of Management Practice – Reaffirm and Elaborate Top Three

In earlier chapters we applied the *Areas of Management Practice* model in identifying the primary, secondary and tertiary Areas of Practice for your capstone idea. This is now the moment when you will reaffirm and elaborate your chosen top three *Areas of Management Practice*. If there has been any time lag since you chose your top three *Areas of Management Practice* or if any new information is available, then you can reevaluate which are your top three. If there are no changes, then it is now time to elaborate on your top three.

Elaboration is done by going to the ten tables below and selecting the table for each of your three most important Areas of Practice. Within each of the three tables, you can identify the *Courses, Big Ideas and Topics* to use as resources for what needs to be understood in each area. You are encouraged to build a table similar to the one below in which all ten Areas of Practice are listed and in which you can now insert information for your top three Areas of Practice. For each of the three most significant Areas of Practice you may now craft one or more questions needing to be answered.

Quick Topic Description – This high-level description provides a snapshot of the change related to each Area of Management Practice. If for example, the project involves a new Customer Relationship Management System, then the Topic for the Information System might be "Design and Implementation of new Cloud-Based CRM Capability," while under Products, Services, Marketing and Sales, the topic could be "Design Customer Acquisition and Retention Processes." These should be short and very high level. If necessary, it is permissible to use more than one topic.

Key Questions of Inquiry – Generally, build from one to three questions that, if answered with reasonable thoroughness, would highlight the greatest opportunities or resolve most of the uncertainties associated with a particular Area of Management Practice.

Courses – In an earlier chapter you were asked to map out your own program in Business or Management along with the competencies you achieved and the Big Ideas you studied. This column is where you list your courses and map them to the Areas of Management Practice model. Note that any course can certainly be listed in more than one Area of Practice. One example might be a course in Operations Management that might be listed in "Processes Improved or Added" for its coverage of process management and "Project Implementation Plan" to the extent that project management may have been part of that course.

Big Ideas and Concepts – In the tables below, I have tried to include a comprehensive list of the "Big Ideas" that are most likely to have been included in your course(s) and that can be aligned with a particular Area of Management Practice. This list is not exhaustive but does provide you with a good starting point, especially if a long time has elapsed between your having taken it and now. Again, several "Big Ideas" are in multiple courses because, depending on your particular curriculum, it may have been taught in more than one course. What is important here is to take the time to identify the Big Idea, get it listed and, if needed, give yourself a quick refresher with an online search. A refresher does not need to be exhaustive and often just a short online description or video does the job nicely.

Questions – These can be considered your initial set of research questions to provide guidance in finding secondary research sources, developing interview questions, conducting surveys or any other research activity. It may be difficult to determine what order is best for building the matrix, so treating this as an iterative process is certainly appropriate. That said, I believe that, in general, it is easiest to work from the most concrete ideas to the most abstract. This would suggest an order of:

(1) **Quick Topic Description** – Many of these come easily and are based on conversations and experiences of colleagues and stakeholders. While you may need to change or adjust them, this is a solid place to begin.

(2) **Questions** – Begin with those that come the most easily directly out of the topics above and work forward from there. You may only have one key question to start with, leaving many cells to swing back to later for further elaboration.

(3) **Courses** – Plugging these in now helps to shape the relationship between what you know (your degree program) and the questions that sit before you. They also serve as an important bridge to the more specific concepts and big ideas in the next step.

(4) **Concepts and Big Ideas** – These are a critical step in your work because they ARE the link between your project in the field and your academic work in the classroom. Getting clarity on these will avert the temptation to just get on the project train and begin working through implementation with no disciplined approach. Remember that each course provided you with a disciplined approach to an area of Business and Management. This is the time to identify those resources that will be used to demonstrate your application of theory to practice.

Table 8 – Business Capstone Areas of Practice Matrix				
Business Capstone Areas of Practice Matrix (generic template)				
Area of Management Practice	Quick Topic Description	Key Questions of Inquiry	Courses	Big Ideas and Concepts
Alignment of Mission, Values and Strategy				
Products, Services, Marketing & Sales				
Processes Improved or Added				
Information Systems				
Organizational Impact and Change Management				
Leadership Capabilities and Requirements				
Economic Business Case (Financial & Economic Resources)				
Project Implementation Plan				
Economic Modeling				
Reflections on Learning				

Areas of Management Practice – Elaborating the Remaining Seven and Building a Matrix

In some of the first chapters of this book, it was pointed out that Integration of business disciplines was one of the most important goals of any business capstone. In having chosen three Areas of Practice (as opposed to just one) you have already begun that process. The next step is to stretch your thinking even further by imagining how your project will extend to the remaining seven Areas of Management Practice. This may not be immediately obvious and, at times, may really seem like a stretch -- and that's fine. Having as complete a roadmap as possible now will pay off numerous times as you negotiate your way through your project and complete your research. For now, I ask that you commit to all ten Areas and repeat the process of elaboration that you completed for the top three. It is important that you push yourself a bit and really work to identify specific big ideas, concepts and questions, and then continue to build your matrix. When you have finished, you will have a project guide that has every conceivable area of study accounted for in an easy-to-follow matrix format.

Areas of Management Practice: Tables

Alignment of Mission, Values and Strategy

Every capstone project is done within the context of an organization that, presumably, has aspirations to fulfill a mission and values to guide its direction. Those aspirations and values filter down to the smallest project and need to be addressed. These questions below are usable at any level in the organization.

- What is valued by the organization? What values seem to be driving the organization in this project?

- How large a gap exists between the espoused organizational core values and the actual values demonstrated by choices made?
- Will your change take on the tough ethical challenges or is there avoidance?
- Is decision making driven by a long-term perspective or is it consumed by short-term thinking?
- Are choices made consistent with organizational, personal and global values?

Table 9: Alignment of Mission, Values and Strategy - Courses & Topics		
Area of Practice (Generic Disciplines of Business, Management and Leadership)	**Courses** (Typical course titles)	**Big Ideas and Topics** (Frameworks, Models, Concepts, Tools and Techniques)
Alignment of Mission, Values and Strategy	• Business Policy and Strategy • Ethics • Value Driven Decision Model • Corporate Culture • Operations Management • Process Improvement • Action Planning and Decision Making • Human Resources • Sustainability • EthicsFinancial Decision Making • Business Law • Small Business Management	• Ethics and Decision Making • Strategic Planning • Values-Driven Leadership • Personal and Organizational Values congruency • The "WHY" of the Organization • Corporate Social Responsibility • Values and Authenticity • Innovation • Flourishing Organizations • Stakeholder Relationships • SOAR Analysis (Strengths, Opportunities, Aspirations and Results) • SWOT Analysis (Strengths, Weaknesses, Opportunities and Threats) • PESTLE Analysis (Political, Economic, Social, Technological, Legal and Environmental) • Global and Ethical Issues • Drivers of Change

Products, Services, Marketing and Sales

This *Area of Practice* has its obvious applications to anything that fits into the traditional definition of "Marketing" products and services externally to customers. It also has its application for most change projects internal to the organization in which employees and stakeholders require communication and "buy-in" strategies based on Marketing principles. For these, think of all stakeholders as customers!

- How are customer data used to support change or new products and services?
- Does an understanding of specific market segments provide guidance?
- To what extent are sales processes and feedback linked to the core business?
- How are new products and services truly innovative?

Table 10: Products, Services, Marketing and Sales: Courses and Topics		
Area of Practice (Generic Disciplines of Business, Management and Leadership)	**Courses** (Typical course titles)	**Big Ideas and Topics** (Frameworks, Models, Concepts, Tools and Techniques)
Products, Services, Marketing and Sales	• Customer Relationship Management • Sales • Retail Management • Marketing • Consumer Behavior • Innovation Management • Marketing Research • Business Research • Product Design • Digital Marketing • Marketing Analytics • E-Commerce	• Competitive Situation • Product Positioning and Strategy • Ethics of Research and Customer Interaction • Customer Gains and Pains • Target Market and Segmentation • Internal Marketing • Customer Value Proposition • Customer Development • Design Thinking • Entrepreneurial Management • New Product Development/R&D • Consumer & Marketing Research • Value Chain Analysis • Agile Product Development • SOAR Analysis (Strengths, Opportunities, Aspirations and Results) • SWOT Analysis (Strengths, Weaknesses, Opportunities and Threats) • Pricing Strategy • Promotion Strategy • Distribution and Logistics Strategy • Data Analytics • Social Networks Strategy

Processes Improved or Added

Changes in processes in the name of higher efficiency are a great source of capstone projects. Process Improvement is also a frequent secondary Area of Practice, since most changes will require some shift in work processes somewhere in the organization.

- How is success measured and communicated?
- How do metrics drive decisions, resource allocations and strategic choices?
- Are there feedback loops that generate improvements and are identified improvements implemented and measured?
- Is quality well understood?
- How are process improvement projects measured for performance?

Table 11: Processes Improved or Added – Courses and Topics		
Area of Practice (Generic Disciplines of Business, Management and Leadership)	**Courses** (Typical course titles)	**Big Ideas and Topics** (Frameworks, Models, Concepts, Tools and Techniques)
Processes Improved or Added	• Process Improvement • Operations Management • Coaching in the Workplace • Process Improvement Operations Management	• Six Sigma • Ethics of decision-making • Continuous Quality Improvement • Lean Methods/Thinking/ Manufacturing • Continuous Process Improvement • Value-Based Decision-Making • Innovation-Based Organization Design • Benchmarking and Balance Scorecards • Supply Chain Process Improvement • Capability Maturity Model • Problem-solving tools such as flow chart, brainstorming affinity diagram, cause and effect diagrams • New Product Development Processes • Innovation Processes • Value Stream Mapping • Design Thinking • Systems Thinking • Planning Capacity and Scheduling • Adaptive Project Management • Agile methodologies • Scrum methods, roles and responsibilities • Prototyping and Minimum Viable Product • Appreciative Inquiry • Action Research • Core Competencies of the Organization • Human Resource Development • Forecasting • Just-In-Time Inventory

Information Systems

Projects that are specifically Information Systems speak for themselves. Many other projects, however, despite being process oriented, immediately require support to capture and manage data. Finally, many changes reflect the increasing digitization of organizational activities of all kinds and as a result require a serious effort in this Area of Practice.

- How is information used strategically and for data-driven decisions?
- Is innovation based on a culture of widely shared information?
- What systems exist to capture, analyze and share information?
- Is there an upward and cross-organizational flow of information?

Table 12: Information Systems – Courses and Topics		
Area of Practice (Generic Disciplines of Business, Management and Leadership)	**Courses** (Typical course titles)	**Big Ideas and Topics** (Frameworks, Models, Concepts, Tools and Techniques)
Information Systems	• Process Improvement • Operations Management • Business Analytics • Managing Innovation • Management Information Systems • Strategic Information Systems • Database Management • Data Security	• Prototyping Testing • Technology Management • Ethics of decision-making • Enterprise Resource Planning (ERP) (pp. 273-274) • Capability Maturity Model • Risk Assessment • Digitization Strategies • Artificial Intelligence Application • Lean Thinking in IT Systems/Data • Agile Software Development • Integration of IT systems • Tools - The Ladder of Inference, Advocacy, and Inquiry; Unilateral Control method or Mutual Learning method • Data Management • Sources of Innovation/Innovation Networks • Ethical, technological, environmental forces that effect your company • Data Analytics • Design thinking

Organizational Impact and Change Management

A deliberate and thoughtful strategy is the backbone of almost every significant change effort so these questions focus on the organization's culture and its ability to be adaptive and embrace change.

- Are people and organizational units open to learning and change based on input from all parts of their respective systems?
- Is there a spirit of mentorship, coaching and facilitation?
- How are people communicating and are they really listening to each other?
- Are organizational members trusted and empowered?
- Do organizational members trust senior management to identify and facilitate changes?

Table 13: Organizational Impact and Change Management – Courses and Topics		
Area of Practice (Generic Disciplines of Business, Management and Leadership)	**Courses** (Typical course titles)	**Big Ideas and Topics** (Frameworks, Models, Concepts, Tools and Techniques)
Organizational Impact and Change Management	• Organizational Behavior • Organization Development • Human Resource Management • Performance Measurement • Change Management • Organization Leadership • Ethics and Management	• Leading organizational change • Ethics of leadership • Transformational Leadership • Authenticity in Leadership • Servant Leadership • Authority and Responsibility • Conflict Management • Assessing Change Context, Organizational Culture • Lewin's change model – 3 stages of change • Change Management Strategies • Action Learning Through Reframing • Organizational Structure and Design • Innovation Management • Entrepreneurial Management • Organizational Development Models • Appreciative Inquiry • Leadership Models for Change • Learning Styles and Employee Communication • Diversity and Inclusion • Values and Behaviors Driving Innovation • Organizational Readiness for Change • Multiple Perspectives

Leadership Capabilities and Requirements

This may seem to overlap with Organizational Change but it has its unique role.

- Is leadership capable of change consistent with new thinking?
- Is leadership development and mentorship part of the culture?
- Do organizational members trust senior management to identify and facilitate changes?

Table 14: Leadership Capabilities and Requirements – Courses and Topics		
Area of Practice (Generic Disciplines of Business, Management and Leadership)	**Courses** (Typical course titles)	**Big Ideas and Topics** (Frameworks, Models, Concepts, Tools and Techniques)
Leadership Capabilities and Requirements	• Organizational Leadership • Transformational Leadership • Communication • Leadership Development • Change Management • Positive Organizational Development	• Leading Change • Ethics of leadership and decision-making • Emotional Intelligence - Self-awareness, self-management, social awareness, and relationship management • Appreciative Inquiry • Communication and Dialogue • Leadership Style • Authenticity in Leadership • Organizational Culture • Mentoring and Leadership Development • Innovation Leadership • Communicating Workplace Change • Kotter's 8 Steps to Change/other change models • Managing Transitions of Change • Team Dynamics • Managing Conflict and Agreement • Small Group Facilitation

Economic Business Case

- What are the financial criteria used for measuring success?
- How are financial and economic resources allocated?
- Are resources sufficient to support the chosen strategy and growth?
- Are resources enough to meet short-term objectives?
- Does financial planning exist and, if so, does it have long term goals and how will the organization meet those goals?

Table 15: Economic Business Case – Courses and Topics		
Area of Practice (Generic Disciplines of Business, Management and Leadership)	**Courses** (Typical course titles)	**Big Ideas and Topics** (Frameworks, Models, Concepts, Tools and Techniques)
Economic Business Case	• Performance Measurement • Accounting and Budgeting • Entrepreneurial Ventures • Financial Decision Making • Performance Management • Managerial and Financial Accounting • Micro-Economics • Macro-Economics • Managerial Accounting • Financial Accounting • Financial Management • Investments • Process Improvement • Operations Management Multiple Perspectives	• Quantifying Value Added • Process Improvement Plan • Metrics and Key Performance Indicators • Ethics of measurement, reporting and financial reporting • Capital Investment and Expenses • Cost Savings • Time Value of Money/Net Present Value • Capital Budgeting • Risk and Return • Sunk Costs • Avoided Costs • Opportunity Costs • Breakeven • Payback Period • Return on Investment • Cost Management • Cost Behavior • Revenue Enhancing • Strategic and Non-Financial Benefits • Balanced Scorecard • Cost Management • Financial Analysis • Financial Considerations of the Supply Chain

Project Implementation

This area embodies a significant number of other areas.

- Does any plan take on the complexities of the project?
- Is planning consistent with other initiatives at the organization?
- Are best practices in Project Management applied to the greatest extent possible?

Table 16: Project Implementation – Courses and Topics		
Area of Practice (Generic Disciplines of Business, Management and Leadership)	**Courses** (Typical course titles)	**Big Ideas and Topics** (Frameworks, Models, Concepts, Tools and Techniques)
Project Implement	• Performance Management • Project Management • Process Improvement and Operations • Project Management • Operations Management • Procurement • Business Law	• Project Planning and Scheduling • Project Launch, Monitor and Control and Closing • Project Charter • Key Performance Metrics • Ethics of project viability and reporting • Technological Uncertainty • Novelty • Systems Thinking/Stages to Success • Project Management • Adaptive Project Management • Agile Project Management • Design Thinking • Scope Creep • Total Project Management (TPM) • Agile/Extreme Project Management • Milestones • Gant Chart (and project management displays) • Critical Path • Benchmarking • Variance Analysis • Supply Chain management • Lean Agile Project Management • Iterative Project Management Life Cycle • Project Team – Selection and Development • Project Kick-Off Meeting • Team Operating Rules • Team Communications • Assigning Resources • Inventory Management and Material Planning • Managing Conflict and Agreement • Small Group Facilitation • Implementing Innovation • Project Scope

Economic Modeling
- Does the model capture changes in revenues, costs and/or cost savings in all other areas of the organization?
- Are all benefits and positive changes quantified to the extent feasible?

- Are all costs and uses of resources accounted for to the extent feasible?
- Does the model express clearly the assumptions, benefits, costs and limitations of the analysis?
- Is the model transparent and honest in its assumptions and presentation of input and output?

Table 17: Economic Modeling: Courses and Topics		
Area of Practice (Generic Disciplines of Business, Management and Leadership)	**Courses** (Typical course titles)	**Big Ideas and Topics** (Frameworks, Models, Concepts, Tools and Techniques)
Economic Model	• Performance Measurement • Accounting Systems • Financial Management • Decision Making • Managerial Economics • Micro-Economics • Marketing • Marketing Research • Desktop Worksheet Applications such as MS Excel • Statistics	• Balanced Scorecard • SMART • Performance Measurement Matrix • Balance Sheets • Income Statements • Cash Flow • Time Value of Money/Net Present Value • Ethics of measurement and reporting • Capital Budgeting • Risk and Return • Sunk Costs • Avoided Costs • Opportunity Costs • Breakeven Analysis • Payback Period • Return on Investment • IRR • Financial Performance • Performance Prism • Profitability Analysis • Strategy Maps • Benchmarking • Efficiencies • Economies of Scale and Scope • Analysis of cost, volume and pricing • Performance management and cost management • Estimated vs. Actual Cost • Capital Rationing

Reflections on Learning

The ability to reflect on your learning is one of your most important qualifications.

- To what extent are all Areas of Management Practice represented and given time to learn?
- Is there adequate reflection and time for effective learning?
- Are all aspects of the project and the organization included?
- How have you changed as a result of this project?
- What new perspectives on ethical behavior have you derived from the project?

Table 18: Reflections on Learning – Courses and Topics		
Area of Practice (Generic Disciplines of Business, Management and Leadership)	**Courses** (Typical course titles)	**Big Ideas and Topics** (Frameworks, Models, Concepts, Tools and Techniques)
Reflections on Learning	• Leadership • Ethics • Workshops and Courses with self-assessments • Leadership Seminars • Critical Thinking • •Coaching/Mentoring related courses • Values clarifications related courses and workshops • Other personal journeys	• Adapt to Change • Ethics of research and positive change project's development and deployment • Competencies Developed • Emotional Intelligence • New Ways of Thinking • Self-reflection and awareness • Johari window assessment • Systems thinking • Appreciative Inquiry • Results-Based Leadership • Self-Assessment, Values and Self-Leadership (LSI, MBTI, EI, Strengths 2.0, Values clarification, etc.)

Road Maps for Four Case Studies

Since the earliest chapters of this book we have tracked four "case studies." The matrix that serves as the "Road Map" for each has been populated below to provide examples of how the matrix would be built with information specific to each capstone project.

Table 19: Case #1: Inventory Management System Upgrade				
Area of Management Practice	Quick Topic Description	Key Questions of Inquiry	Courses	Big Ideas and Concepts (Frameworks, Models, Concepts, Tools and Techniques)
Alignment with Mission/Strategy	• How the project reflects the changing corporate culture and values system, along with the shift towards automation	• Is this new management system consistent with our mission and values? • Is it fair to all stakeholders?	• Ethics • Business Policy and Strategy • Organization Development	• Value Driven Decision Models • Corporate Culture
Products, Services, Marketing and Sales	• How existing process and service mixes benefit from the project	• How does this positively impact our ability to serve customers?	• Marketing • Consumer Behavior • New Product Development	• Product Life Cycles • SWOT (Strengths, Weaknesses, Opportunities and Threats)
Processes Improved or Added	• Describing the specific systems that will be improved, added or removed due to this project	• How does this new system impact other processes? • Are future changes for further positive impact coming out of this effort?	• Operations Management • Process Improvement • Innovation Management • Management Information Systems	• Capturing the benefits of innovation Capturing the learning • Continuous Quality Improvement
Information Systems	• Development of the organization's innovation network	• What opportunities are there to leverage the enhanced data and reporting capabilities? • Will other IS changes be needed?	• Innovation Management • Management Information Systems	• Innovation Networks • Reorganization of resources • Application of new software

Area of Management Practice	Quick Topic Description	Key Questions of Inquiry	Courses	Big Ideas and Concepts (Frameworks, Models, Concepts, Tools and Techniques)
		Table 19: Case #1: Inventory Management System Upgrade		
Organizational Impact and Change Management	• Understanding this change within the context of other changes in managing assets	• How will the new system affect employees' need for training?	• Organizational Development • Change Management and Leadership	• Change Management
Leadership Capabilities and Requirements	• Managing expectations for the future	• Does this change the nature of leadership needs in this area?	• Leadership • Change Management	• Managing Conflict • Small Group facilitation • Breakthrough Business negotiation
Economic Business Case	• The importance of data integrity, quality and efficiency • Data accuracy drives all reporting and decision making.	• What are the benefits and costs?	• Managerial Accounting • Financial Management • Operations Management • Management Information Systems	• Quality Process Improvement, • Planning/schedule management
Project Implementation Plan	• The steps our organization should take to ensure proper application of project deliverables • Managing change requests and deliverables schedules is very important in competitive market	• What is the best case for merging timelines? • How would a project plan be managed before the merger?	• Project Management • Operations Management	• Adaptive Project Management Life Cycles (PMLC) models • Complexity and Uncertainty

Table 19: Case #1: Inventory Management System Upgrade				
Area of Management Practice	**Quick Topic Description**	**Key Questions of Inquiry**	**Courses**	**Big Ideas and Concepts** (Frameworks, Models, Concepts, Tools and Techniques)
Economic Model (Excel)	• The benefit of value-added processes on project success • Opportunity for value added processes to impact inventory management and implicit savings	• What are all the benefits and how do they accrue over time? • What is the revenue (donation) impact and cost?	• Financial Management • Operations Management	• Financial Statements • Cash flows • Valuation methods • Supply Chain Economics
Reflections on Learning	• What I learned through the MBA program and through this project	• Have we lost something special at each original organization? • Where does this end?	• Leadership • Self-Management and Leadership	• Action Learning through reflection

Table 20: Case #2: New Target Market for Lending Institution				
Area of Management Practice	**Quick Topic Description**	**Key Questions of Inquiry**	**Courses**	**Big Ideas and Concepts**
Alignment with Mission/Strategy	• Currently successful mortgage department • Need for additional loans in environment of rising interest rates	• How does this market segment fit our mission?	• Organizational ethics • Decision-making, finance • Business policy and strategy	• Balance values of customer focus vs. business growth • Ethics of business practices • Decisions needing to be made
Products, Services, Marketing and Sales	• Competitor offerings, industry trends and current customers • Regional market segments identified through research • How to work around an aging population • Need for new customers	• How does this product fit the larger changes in the external environment? • What are the dreams, values and desires of this market segment? • How will these new customers grow with us?	• Marketing • Innovation • Marketing Research	• How to identify and communicate with millennials as the next potential homebuyer • Ethical marketing to reach new customer segments • Understanding the Customer Value Proposition of millennials
Processes Improved or Added	• Practices in how we originate a mortgage that have proven difficult • Identify changes in our practice for efficiency without jeopardizing current products	• Will existing processes of sales customer on-boarding and customer retention work for this market segment?	• Process improvement • Operations Management	• Lean concepts and process improvement to reduce "work-arounds" and improve workflow efficiency • Identify linkage to information systems that leverage technology to improve both processes and products

Table 20: Case #2: New Target Market for Lending Institution				
Area of Management Practice	**Quick Topic Description**	**Key Questions of Inquiry**	**Courses**	**Big Ideas and Concepts**
Information Systems	• Look at "what's next" in the technology world of mortgage lending	• What analytic data need to be captured for this new market that is new to us? • What information transparency is needed by this new generation?	• Managing Innovation • Management Information Systems	• Focus on innovative sources and idea generation • Innovation teams • How to foster innovation and implement new technology • Group dynamics and avoid the negative group think • Change Models
Organizational Impact and Change Management	• Mortgage department importance to organization's profitability • New products and processes are a huge change needing careful orchestration	• Will any organizational changes be needed in product or customer segment management?	• Group communication and negotiation, leadership and change • Organizational Change	• Group dynamics and avoid the negative group think • Models of change management
Economic Business Case	• The economic business case is clear • Mortgage Department needs to find a way to maintain production volume in a rising rate environment.	• What is the customer value of this new market segment? • Is there an opportunity to leverage the costs of this new initiative to any other market segments?	• Financial decision making • Investments and financial markets • Performance management • Managerial and Financial Accounting • Micro-economics	• The information on financial markets and interest rates • Internal and historical mortgages with existing customers needed at varying levels of interest rates

Table 20: Case #2: New Target Market for Lending Institution				
Area of Management Practice	**Quick Topic Description**	**Key Questions of Inquiry**	**Courses**	**Big Ideas and Concepts**
Project Implementation Plan	• Review various project management models and find the best fit for this project. • Having a clear plan to follow that is balanced with flexibility due to unanticipated market changes	• How can the products designed for this market segment be tested?	• Project management • Process improvement and operations	• I anticipate all of the models used to be a part of agile project management, as the full solution is not yet known, and there are definite changes coming along the way, especially as there are a number of external factors at play.
Economic Model (Excel)	• Showing production during various rates and also with various loan products will be helpful. • I will also want to look at ROA and other financial measures.	• What is the long-term value of this market alone over five years?	• Financial decision making • Performance measurement • Managerial Accounting	• Financial Management calculations such as Breakeven, NPV and Payback • I will also be using internal reports. • Creating my own charts and models based on internal information
Reflections on Learning	• Review on the project as a whole to reflect on what I have learned • Focus on the assumptions going into the project versus what actually seems to be true after research and analysis	• Why are we playing "catch-up" with this market? • How can we be more adaptive and innovative in an ongoing way?	• Leadership • Leadership and Change • Self-Management and Leadership	• Leadership and dealing with ambiguity and uncertainty

Table 21: Case #3: Employee Training and Development to Decrease Employee Turnover and Increase Customer Satisfaction				
Area of Management Practice	**Quick Topic Description**	**Key Questions of Inquiry**	**Courses**	**Big Ideas and Concepts**
Alignment with Mission/Strategy	• This ensures the understanding of the mission, vision and goals that provide a path for the implementation of a newly redesigned training and development program.	• Is there a relationship between employee training and customer satisfaction that positively impacts our ability to meet our mission?	• Strategy/Policy • Ethics • Operations Management • Process improvement • Action planning and decision making • Human resources	• Action Learning Through Reflection • Process improvement • Leadership management • Effective decision-making Tools
Products, Services, Marketing and Sales	• Proper training of all employees involved with products, services, marketing and sales to benefit customer satisfaction	• What positive experiences in training and development have current employees had? • How should new programs be communicated?	• Performance measurement • Accounting systems • Marketing • Sales • Consumer Behavior	• Identifying, measuring, analyzing, interpreting and communicating information • Products and Their Competitive Positioning
Processes Improved or Added	• The processes requiring improvement include product knowledge, application techniques and confidence when selling.	• How does this training and leadership development fit into the overall processes of performance management?	• Process Improvement • Operations Management • Coaching in the workplace	• Process improvement • Continuous improvement • Leading, coaching, adjusting and feedback
Information Systems	• The new training program will produce multiple ways of learning and aids to assist in the process.	• What information systems are needed to track professional development in a way that allows self-directed learning?	• Process Improvement • Operations Management • Human resources and analytics	• Process Improvement • Digital platforms for teaching and learning • Effective decision-making Tools

Table 21: Case #3: Employee Training and Development to Decrease Employee Turnover and Increase Customer Satisfaction				
Area of Management Practice	**Quick Topic Description**	**Key Questions of Inquiry**	**Courses**	**Big Ideas and Concepts**
Organizational Impact and Change Management	• Leadership and all levels of management will need to stay on top of continuous improvements and adjustments to properly manage their employees.	• How does leadership development change the employees' expectations of both leadership and themselves?	• Performance Measurement • Managerial Accounting • Leadership seminar • Leadership and change	• Identifying, measuring, analyzing, interpreting and communicating information • Leading Organizational Change
Economic Business Case	• An analysis will be conducted displaying the expenses of the new training program, continuous expenses, materials and the benefits of these expenses.	• What benefits can be quantified? • What are the costs of a new leadership program?	• Performance Measurement • Managerial Accounting • Financial Management • Business Research	• Financial Analysis • Breakeven, payback, ROI, discounted cash flow • Strategic benefits
Project Implementation Plan	• This will define the exact measures necessary to create a new training program with a more effective approach and end goal.	• How can we test interest and program effect?	• Performance measurement • Process improvement • Operations Management • Project Management	• Performance Management • Process Management

Table 21: Case #3: Employee Training and Development to Decrease Employee Turnover and Increase Customer Satisfaction				
Area of Management Practice	**Quick Topic Description**	**Key Questions of Inquiry**	**Courses**	**Big Ideas and Concepts**
Economic Model (Excel)	• Income statement (or facsimile) highlighting the actual expenses, the benefits and all costs, also including the rate of employee retention and customer satisfaction through the increase of sales	• How do the benefits accrue over time? • What costs are being avoided through reduced turnover?	• Performance measurement • Managerial Accounting • Project Management • Strategic Marketing	• Analysis of all relatable costs, volume of products purchased, and retention of employees and customers • Products and their competitive positioning, customer and employee retention
Reflections on Learning	• The understanding of what a new generational training program can do to change and improve its current systems	• What does this program say about a changing workforce?	• Organizational Mission and Values • Leadership Seminar • Coaching in the workplace	• Reflective improvements • Leadership and personal change • Coaching, training, feedback and adjusting

Area of Management Practice	Quick Topic Description	Key Questions of Inquiry	Courses	Big Ideas and Concepts
Table 22: Case #4: Merging of Four Non-Profits into One Organization to Gain Economies of Scale				
Alignment with Mission/Strategy	• Why the organizations should merge and how this will contribute to their overall missions and strategies	• Can our three organizations successfully blend their values and agree on a unified mission?	• Business Strategy and Policy • Business ethics • Impact of globalization on business	• Stakeholders • Mission statement, values
Products, Services, Marketing and Sales	• How to re-brand the organization and analyze the impact a new brand might have on pilots, passengers, and donors	• How will our products and services change? • Are there new offerings possible?	• Marketing • Consumer Behavior • Managing innovation	• SWOT analysis • PESTLE analysis • Marketing plan • Innovation drivers • Regulatory constraints on markets
Processes Improved or Added	• Evaluate key processes that will be impacted by the merger. Identify redundancies that could be eliminated and new processes that might be added.	• What efficiencies are possible? • Can services actually be improved through consolidation?	• Process Improvement • Operations Management • Managing Innovation • Business Economics • Business Modeling	• Problem statement, analysis and rationale of process improvement, implications, risks • Reconcile operational differences and existing processes
Information Systems	• Explain how to ease the transition of the merger. • Identify systems used by the different organizations and how they can be merged.	• What Information system is needed to meet emerging requirements?	• Process Improvement • Operations Management • Managing Innovation	• Analysis of IT systems, proposed improvements, implications, risks • Customer management systems (i.e., Salesforce) • Accounting systems (QuickBooks)

Table 22: Case #4: Merging of Four Non-Profits into One Organization to Gain Economies of Scale				
Area of Management Practice	**Quick Topic Description**	**Key Questions of Inquiry**	**Courses**	**Big Ideas and Concepts**
Organizational Impact and Change Management	• Explain how a merger will impact ALL stakeholders associated with the organization: partners, clients, board members, employees, etc.	• What would the new organizational structure look like? • How would the transition to a new organization be managed?	• Self-management and leadership • Leadership and planned change	• SMART goals • Change and transition models • Vision of change, change strategy • Process of executive-level decisions later shared with employees
Leadership Capabilities and Requirements	• What will the leadership structure look like? • Three options – (1) everything moves to one location, (2) primary headquarters with satellite offices (volunteers?), (3) offices remain as they are. Big question…. Who maintains leadership?	• What differences in leadership will be needed?	• Leadership introduction • Leadership and planned change • Group dynamics, communication and negotiation	• Model for change leadership • Impact to stakeholders • Avoiding big assumptions • Managing conflict • Effective workplace interactions • Centralization and repurposing of existing operations that are smaller • Board-level changes and leadership changes

Table 22: Case #4: Merging of Four Non-Profits into One Organization to Gain Economies of Scale				
Area of Management Practice	Quick Topic Description	Key Questions of Inquiry	Courses	Big Ideas and Concepts
Economic Business Case	• Identify the value created by merging the organizations together. • Determine approximate annual income and estimated budgets and expenditures. • 3 scenarios – status quo (4 offices), move to one location, maintain minimal staff at 3 locations.	• What is the effect on current grants and benefactors? • Will efficiencies offset any lag in donations, etc.?	• Performance measurement • Accounting (Financial and Managerial) • Financial decision making for management • Process improvement and operations • Business economics and modeling value	• Statement of activities • Future scenarios • Accounting and legal principles across states • Risk and return dynamics • Internal information – expenses needed for each organization
Project Implementation Plan	• Outline a high-level plan and identify steps that will need to be taken to merge the organizations.	• What is the best case for merging timelines? • How would a project plan be managed before the merger?	• Project Management • Reflective Leadership and Planned Change	• Project scope, planning the project, project launch, monitor and control
Economic Model (Excel)	• Create an Excel spreadsheet of the proposed economic model.	• What are all of the benefits and how do they accrue over time? • What is the revenue (donation) impact and cost?	• Performance Measurement and Accounting Systems • Financial Decision Making for Management • Process Improvement and Operations • Business Economics and Modeling Value	• Present 3 scenarios for the economic business model and analyze different outcomes. • Different accounting principles across states (in-kind donations) • Risk and return dynamics

Table 22: Case #4: Merging of Four Non-Profits into One Organization to Gain Economies of Scale				
Area of Management Practice	Quick Topic Description	Key Questions of Inquiry	Courses	Big Ideas and Concepts
Reflections on Learning	• Provide insight on the learning experience of this project.	• Have we lost something special at each original organization? • Where does this end?	• Leadership 101	• Where does organizational leadership yield to the greater good? • How do cultures and values merge successfully?

"Doing by Learning" activity

Create an Areas of Management Practice Matrix

Following the examples provided in this chapter, build your own Areas of Management Practice matrix that links your project to all areas of your Business Studies. The outline from earlier in the chapter has been repeated below to aid you.

1. **The Opportunity** -- Develop a three-sentence summary of the proposed opportunity.
2. **Three Big Questions** -- Identify the three biggest questions/uncertainties needing to be understood about your proposed opportunity and state them as questions.
3. **Areas of Practice - Top Three** -- Look to see where your three big questions/uncertainties fit into the Areas of Practice matrix and reframe them as topics of study to be explained by each area of your capstone. These are likely to be the primary areas of your study to be researched.
4. **Areas of Practice – Remaining Seven** -- Identify similar questions/uncertainties for all remaining Areas of Practice. While these may be secondary areas of study for your research, they are still extremely important in their supporting roles and, with better understanding of your topic, may even be elevated to a primary topic of study.
5. **Identify Resources (Courses and Big Ideas)** -- Review the Areas of Practices, Courses and Big Ideas tables for each Area of Practice to identify likely resources that might help you to address understanding and resolving your big uncertainties. Using these tables as a launching point, begin to assemble the names of both courses and specific frameworks that may be helpful in addressing the question you have for that specific Area of Practice.
6. **Build an Areas of Practice Matrix** -- Build your own matrix consisting of the Areas

of Practice, Subjects, Courses and Big Ideas (topics/models/frameworks) that may be connected to your project by addressing all of your questions in your Areas of Practice Matrix.

7. **Build an Outline** – Using the Matrix, above -- as a basis for your topics, now build an outline of what can be your final "report" also called the Narrative.

8. **Reflect on your Road Map** -- This becomes your road map for inclusion or exclusion of content.

Outlining the Final Report

A Skeleton Starting Point

With the Matrix completed, the next step is to turn this into a skeleton of your final report. While the Matrix works well as either a table in a Word document or a worksheet, the outline really will need to be in a word format. This is the raw beginning to your final report that will essentially follow the Areas of Management Practice model, with adjustments for your unique project. You may also have requirements to meet for either your school's reporting format or the organization with which you have been working.

Here is a suggested approach in which the generic Capstone Project Outline shown above has been reordered three ways to follow the flow of some different "typical" capstone projects.

Project example #1: *A new product line extension* for an organization that is producing software and related support systems. The story begins with customers and then goes to the processes to make it happen. Information systems, organizational changes and leadership changes all follow. With those explained, the economics of how it works can be explained with references back to the earlier chapters. Finally, the nuts and bolts of the project plan contain the most granular level of detail.

1. Executive Summary
2. Proposed Opportunity
3. Research Conducted (Primary and Secondary)
4. Alignment with Mission/Strategy
5. Products, services, marketing and sales (product/competitive research here)
6. Processes improved or added (some research possible here, as well)
7. Information Systems (less impactful)
8. Organizational Impact and Change Management (strategic and outcomes)
9. Leadership capabilities and requirements
10. Economic Business Case (reference Economic Model in Excel)
11. Project Implementation Plan
12. Economic Model (Excel in separate file)
13. Reflections on Learning
14. Bibliography

Project example #2: *A major change in processes* of matriculating customer orders through the production cycle. Based on some internally created Lean Six Sigma data, it is apparent that the flow of work processes can be redesigned. A new process will first be tried in parallel to test assumptions of possible improvements with a goal of total redesign within one year.

1. Executive Summary
2. Proposed Opportunity
3. Research Conducted (Primary and Secondary)
4. Alignment with Mission/Strategy
5. Processes improved or added (quality improvement research here)
6. Organizational Impact and Change Management (research on the people side of change)
7. Project Implementation Plan (how it might actually work)
8. Information Systems (need to collect data)
9. Products, services, marketing and sales (little effect on customer)
10. Leadership capabilities and requirements
11. Economic Business Case (reference Economic Model in Excel)
12. Economic Model (Excel in separate file)
13. Reflections on Learning
14. Bibliography

Project example #3 – *A major restructuring* of the organization subsequent to a merger/acquisition. The restructuring will probably be, first, a bundle of organizational (people) issues in managing change. With that understood, the integration of Information Systems and Processes can be addressed.

1. Executive Summary
2. Proposed Opportunity
3. Research Conducted (Primary and Secondary)
4. Alignment with Mission/Strategy
5. Leadership capabilities and requirements
6. Organizational Impact and Change Management (research on the people side of change)
7. Information Systems (integration of systems will be key)
8. Processes improved or added (may be secondary to the organizational challenges)
9. Products, services, marketing and sales (presumably economies are possible)
10. Project Implementation Plan (best case)
11. Economic Business Case (reference Economic Model in Excel)
12. Economic Model (Excel in separate file)
13. Reflections on Learning
14. Bibliography

"Doing by Learning" activity

Create an Outline of your Final Report

Now that you have completed the Areas of Management Practice Matrix activity, create an outline of what will become your final report. This should reflect any unique characteristics to your matrix and will be adjusted further over the semester.

With an outline constructed, a skeleton of what will become your final report can then be built over time. For example, it could begin with inserting sub-topics under each chapter heading that mirror any questions or topics that you have in your Matrix. Reflect deeply on what you have created since you own it, and it drives your work from this point on. Remember that the Matrix was not done as busywork or as an academic exercise but to be a living document designed to guide your research. Taking it one step further by building out the outline into a somewhat populated skeleton outline gets you one step closer to completion. All you have ahead of you now is to do the research and connect the dots! Let's move on to the next steps!

CHAPTER 11
RESEARCH FOR POSITIVE CHANGE

Before Beginning Research

Why Research?

In this chapter we get serious about the research that you will be doing, both within your organization and with stakeholders closely associated with your organization. I have chosen to give you some context about the research process and what it means and how best to meet the needs of your capstone.

Build on Strengths and Principles

Before moving on, it might be helpful to do a personal check-in on the strengths that you have built so far for your capstone.

- A **network of support and guidance**, including at least one "mentor" who can provide professional guidance on the topic, your process or both
- A **well-chosen and articulated positive change** in which you have a deep personal interest and organizational support
- A **clear vision of success** for both you and the project itself
- A **roadmap of your change** project that in the suggested matrix form maps to your program competencies and/or the provided Areas of Management Practice but also provides key research questions, areas needing to be explored, and resources from your entire program needing to be revisited, taken off the shelf and "dusted off" to use, as appropriate

Build a Plan

On this foundation you will now build a plan that will enable you to answer the biggest questions. To begin, let's see how our five principles provide some guidance in the development of your plan.

1. **Question and listen carefully** -- As you continue to engage with your present network and as it expands to new materials, people and concepts.
2. **Look for strengths** and know that your questions ARE the beginning of change. Avoid the pitfall of negative thinking and endless problem revelation.
3. **Be prepared to pivot** – to modify your research approach and to alter the need for additional data. The capstone is grounded in the strengths of Action Research, Appreciative

Inquiry, Managerial Research, Adaptive Project Management, Design Thinking and Lean Entrepreneurism – all of which make use of the strength of inquiry.

4. **Engage others** in a process of iterative change. Remember that your inquiry is the beginning of a change (Appreciative Inquiry principle of Simultaneity). While you do want to stick to your research plan, remember the importance of others.

5. **Be the leader of learning and positive change** – your role as a leader begins with leadership in learning and is quickly followed by leadership in positive change. You are the leader!

Research Anxiety

Doing research for a project of this magnitude can be intimidating to many students. In your previous courses you were undoubtedly asked repeatedly to "research" a given topic for a paper, explore an organization's strategy or financial statements, understand customer data, or simply identify resources to supplement a class discussion. An experiential capstone may have many of those as well but is still VERY different. It diverges from your previous research because you are "alone" (either individually or as a team) in defining a change, working with an organization and managing a self-directed learning process to provide a recommendation or at least some well-organized information that can then be used as a basis for continued work.

The foundation for your final deliverable is your data, which probably won't be found online or in your library's resources but instead will come from a greater diversity of locations such as internal reports, personal interviews, vendor proposals, employee surveys, focus groups, or direct observation at your selected organization. If this produces a sense of anxiety, then you should know that you are not alone.

Yes, undertaking such a large and self-directed project such as this *is* different. Be assured that by going through the process of building your final deliverable following our recommended process will help to ensure that you will be successful with less stress! Next to the Matrix and Outline created earlier, your research plan is the next most important work product because it has such a positive effect on your outcome.

Doing this kind of research is generally not following a linear path, and it is good to realize that now, early in your research process, that there will be "moments" of both clarity and confusion that are all completely normal. The reason is simple. For most of you, this may be the first time when you have had to take in such a disparate set of data, some of which is very informal, even casual. For example, how do you reconcile a casual interview over lunch with tables of demographic data from the U.S. Bureau of Labor Statistics, along with a two-year-old marketing research report? As Tim Brown describes in *Change by Design*, "every design process cycles through foggy periods of seemingly unstructured experimentation and bursts of intense clarity, periods of grappling with the Big Idea and long stretches during which all attention focuses on the details. Each of these phases is different, and it's important -- if only for the morale of the team -- to recognize that each *feels* different and calls for different strategies" (Brown, 2009, p. 64).

Practitioner-Researcher Role

Your role as a student leading the exploration of a positive change requires a unique mindset and perspective. As a student, you are being asked to meet the requirements of your capstone course and to integrate your program competencies that stand behind your degree. As a researcher, you are accountable for meeting research standards and following methodological protocols. If you are employed or an intern, then you are also potentially working close to or even intimately involved in your proposed change. These multiple roles have implications for your approach to the opportunity and how you will manage bias in your research. More importantly you should recognize that your role is also more integrative than that of a simple researcher responsible for doing a "study." Instead, your role is closest to that of an *Action Researcher* but with the need to integrate any pre-existing knowledge into your specific research to better understand your opportunity for a proposed change.

Action Research Overview

As an Action Researcher, you will not be confined to the screen of your laptop or tablet while you download statistics, journal articles and reports. In all likelihood you will also not be bound to the rules of sampling size and statistical database analytics. Instead, you will be using multiple methods and, all the while, taking good notes. This may also be a new role for you as you collect "data" from every observation and conversation that needs to be entered into some form. For fieldwork, handwritten note-taking is still a viable method because it allows a conversation (or interview) to flow more easily than if you are keying in information. If keying data into a laptop or tablet works for you, however, so be it. If handwritten field notes have been taken, however, best practice is certainly to key in a transcript of any interviews or other interpersonal data. Along with interview data, it will also be important to save your own observations, reflections and connections that you've made in the analysis of your data. How you structure, save, back up and protect those files is your choice but I personally favor triple redundant backup (hard drive, external drive and cloud at a minimum) to ensure that months of work don't vanish unexpectedly.

Ethical Considerations

Any research always has ethical considerations as you enter into relationships, receive data and reports that are proprietary and learn things about your organization that are not widely known (and shouldn't be). In a nutshell, your role as a researcher places you in a position of trust with those in the workplace. Given the nature of your project (proposing a change), this presents some immediate risks and ethical considerations as you move forward. *In Designing and Managing a Research Project*, Polonsky and Waller (2011, pp. 69--72) provide an excellent resource for Business students in which they highlight the following areas as ethical issues to consider:

- *Voluntary Participation* (including confidentiality and anonymity) for employees is important to protect against any bias. What if, for example, senior management hand-picked participants to survey?
- *Informed Consent* – Ensure that people understand what you are asking them to do and the need to communicate ahead of time about what your research is and what their role is in it.
- *Confidentiality and Anonymity* – Different ideas. Anonymity means participant information is not identified, and confidentiality implies knowledge of who participants are but that their information has been withheld.
- *Potential for Harm* – It is possible to harm participants through your work whether it be physical, emotional, psychological, or any number of other ways. It is your responsibility to maintain control over your data, not share it in any way that could be harmful, and to understand the possible effects of your study.
- *Communication* – Issues such as plagiarism, academic fraud, and misrepresentation of results can all come out of the misuse of information as both inputs and outputs to your research process. This is avoided by paying close attention to your sources of information, giving appropriate credit through citations, and being careful to manage what your data truly says.
- *Deceit* – When interviewing participants, they need to be told with complete transparency what you are researching and how the results will be used. Unless testing participants' reactions

to some stimulus, for example, deceit about the study itself, their role, or the use of their reactions should, in general, avoid deceit.

The World of Research for Business and Management

"Business Research"

While many business curricula may have a single course titled, "Business Research," it is seldom a required course. As a result, and if you are like most students, your research has been limited to the use of the Internet and online databases of "literature" along with any books available in your school's library. This is supplemented, of course, by a broad collection of resources available on the Internet, such as blogs and videos. "Business Research" is an area of study that includes a wide range of inquiry methods and many of them, because they originate in the research disciplines of math and science, are highly structured in their approach to both data collection and analysis. While a full explanation is outside the scope of this publication, the chart below provides a brief overview of the most widely used topics that might be found in a typical Business Research course. (Source: Zikmund, W., *Business Research Methods,* 7th edition, 2003)

Table 23: Business Research Topics	
Business Research Topics	**Explanation**
Exploratory Research and Qualitative Methods	Generally used as a starting point to larger research. Initial research conducted through interviews, group interviews, focus groups and small-scale surveys. Studies to provide guidance on topics, survey design and other more statistical techniques.
Secondary Data	The use of pre-existing data or studies that can be applied to one or more of your research questions. This is useful as a starting point to understand the scope of the problem.
Experimental Research	Larger studies conducted to test and measure variables, typically independent and dependent in nature.
Survey Research	Surveys are usually "designed" to meet statistical standards in order to control bias, obtain an appropriate sampling and be based on response rates that ensure that a specific target is met.
Measurement Concepts	Rules of measurement as applied to various types of scales used in survey questions, structured data collection and data analysis.
Sampling and Statistical Theory	The use of standard population parameters and sampling techniques to ensure appropriate sampling of a target population.
Data Analysis	Statistically driven analysis of univariate, bivariate and multivariate data using numerous standard techniques such as hypothesis testing, t-Distribution, Correlation Coefficients, Regression and more.

Topics adapted from: ***Business Research Methods*** by William Zikmund (2003)

Two things about the above topics should be observed. The first is the emphasis on creating *statistically valid* numbers through well-documented methods of data collection, measurement and analysis. The second is the flow of research that typically presumes qualitative research used in an exploratory manner in order to serve as a precedent to more structured and "scientific" statistical analysis. For a handful of students who are doing a formal research study this methodology and mindset are highly appropriate. For most students engaged in a more experiential approach in the workplace, however, such as the experiential capstone projects that are the subject of this book, it is less likely that you will be doing a study large enough in design and data collection to meet such stringent quantitative standards.

"Management Research"

Another approach to research in the areas of Business and Management may be more appropriate for experiential capstone work. Given the topics of traditional "Business Research" as described above, you may be asking yourself where to even begin researching a small change to your organization. Other questions that might come to mind include: "What type of research is most appropriate for a workplace change project such as mine?" or, "How would I ever design and launch a formal study, collect data and analyze the results within the constraints of my course that may be as short as six weeks long?"

While a more formal and statistically significant study based on "Business Research Methods" standards of sample size, experimental design, and data analysis may be the focus for those business students engaged in a full "Research" project, most capstone projects need to rely on a derivation of the "Business Research" techniques called "Managerial Research." My favorite source for information on this topic, and one that I use as a textbook in my own Business Capstone courses is called *Research Methods for Managers* (2010) by John Gill and Phil Johnson. If there is one book that I would recommend (other than this book) to support your capstone work, it is that one. A quick review of the topics that they include takes us into methods that are less reliant on large samples and more stringent statistical techniques.

Table 24: Management Research Topics	
Management Research Topics	**Explanation**
Diversity of Management Research	The topic itself says it all -- that a diversity of approaches is needed when "researching" from the management perspective. This suggests an openness to the blending of methods that are less dependent on statistical sampling methods.
Choosing a Research Topic	The more open research agenda (above) makes allowances for topics that are more "project"-oriented than experimental.
Quasi-Experiments	This form of research moves research out of the laboratory and into the field. While this makes the manipulation of variables more difficult, it does provide data in a more natural environment.
Experimental Design	Classic experiments and the use of control groups are included.
Action Research	Action Research is a more process-oriented approach to defining a problem, making inquiry as to possible solutions, taking action to test hypothesis, learning and adapting and then repeating the process.
Inductive vs. Deductive	The use of data that is deductive (theory to be tested, driven by testing a hypothesis through research design) and inductive (driven by observation to build a theory).

Table 24: Management Research Topics	
Management Research Topics	**Explanation**
Survey Design	Managerial Research still includes statistically driven samples for surveying but does so within the context of other methods supporting the research.
Qualitative Research	One of the greatest departures from classic Business Research is the use of Ethnography and other qualitative methods that treat "field notes" and observations as usable data.
Mixed Methods	The concept of mixing methods makes allowances for the triangulation of a problem with multiple types of data (surveys, qualitative, action research, etc.).
Case Study Research	Case studies make no pretense of sampling but instead rely on a deep understanding of a single case study as an example of practice.

Topics adapted from: *Research Methods for Managers*, (2010), John Gill and Phil Johnson

While the differences between these two outlines may not be obvious initially, the approach, design constraints and inclusiveness of more varied "data" are significant. The topic of "Deduction vs. Induction" speaks to the recognition of learning from data that is more experiential and less constrained by statistical techniques. Last, and perhaps most important, is the recognition of mixed methods and case study research as managerial tools. While Management Research is still structured and, where appropriate, uses statistical sampling and experimental design, it is simultaneously accepting of less stringent but highly usable qualitative and mixed methods that reflect the realities of doing research for management where decisions need to be made with the best information available. The field of "Management Research" is saying, essentially, that research is not an "all or nothing" approach that requires scientifically-based quantitative methods but that it allows for a more diverse set of approaches that fit today's dynamic business environment.

Before moving on, it may be important to point out how managerial research will serve your capstone project. Greater use of both inductive and deductive methods is highly significant. Explain further the difference and how this type of research uses both.

Focus, Focus, Focus

If at this point you haven't yet developed a succinct research focus, then now is the time! Actually, you really can't do any research without it because any research needs a focus. From the wide boundaries of opportunity that your "project" provides, you should now bring your topic down to a few sentences. But this shouldn't happen in thin air. Use your resources! Review your Capstone Matrix where you have already invested significant time and energy in defining the big questions in each Area of Management Practice. Reviewing these and any other work products you may have done up until this point will help to ensure that your topic sentences don't become too esoteric. I suggest beginning with focus-producing phrases such as:

- *"The opportunity that this project will explore and/or develop is to* (insert your proposed change) and the organization" and
- *"The research to support this project will include...* (list all at a very high level)" and

- "*The report will seek to...* (any other specifics that help to explain what you are proposing and why)" and
- "*The success of this proposal will be measured by ...* (insert metrics, scorecard, performance changes, etc.)"

In a research process such as this it is particularly important that you establish, to the extent feasible, a *clear understanding of what exactly will change*. While this may not be evident to you initially, it is important to begin with what you envision changing and then update that as your research unfolds. This becomes especially useful at the time when you need to establish the value of your proposed change when you will be comparing your change to the status quo. This is explained more in the following chapter on Economic Value.

Putting Positivity into your Change Project

For a number of reasons presented earlier, I strongly advocate a "strength-based" approach to designing your capstone change project. Also evident, especially in the "Inquiry" chapter as well as the last few chapters, is the value of inquiry and the emphasis on developing key questions as the most important pathway to a successful project. In addition, most well-documented and useful tools to support a strength-based approach and thoughtful inquiry, are introduced in earlier chapters is the field of Appreciative Inquiry. As you work forward with your topic, *Area of Management Practice* questions and key research questions, this is an appropriate time to reframe questions to give your research a more positive outcome. If you haven't done so until now, it is time to put a bit of positivity in your change project.

Developing positive questions can be done any time in the process but now, with your fundamental questions having been developed, you really need to begin using questions in doing your research. To design and define a positive change it takes positive (or Appreciative Inquiry based) questions to get things going in the right direction. Diana Whitney et al, in their book, *Appreciative Leadership* (2010), outlines a three-part process for designing Appreciative questions (p. 42).

1. **Value-based affirmative topic** – Two to four-word phrase that says what you value and want more of in your organization
2. **Rapport-building lead-in** – A three to four sentence paragraph that explains what the topic means and why it is important
3. **A string of empowering probes** – Questions that probe into the specifics of the high-point story and causes of its success

Positive Questions

As discussed earlier, the Appreciative Inquiry *Principle of Simultaneity* and *Principle of Positivity* tells us that change begins with the important first question(s) asked and that, positively framed, encourage generative and positive responses. Some examples might be in order. Below are sets of positive questions on two different project examples: *Career Development* and *Technology*. While the two topics may seem a bit broad, they are appropriate for many students' capstone projects, which often touch on the use of technology or the development of human resources. These two examples are from the book, *The Encyclopedia of Positive Questions* (Whitney et al., 2013, pp. 59 & 75).

Topic: Career Development
1. Tell me about the most challenging and exciting career development opportunity you

have experienced. What was it? Why did you decide on it? What made it challenging and exciting? How did you benefit? How did the organization benefit?

2. How do you learn best? Tell me about the time you learned something challenging. What contributed to your learning?

3. Tell me about the work experience in which you learned the most. Tell me about the situation. Who else was involved, and what did they do? What did you do to foster your own development? What made this a high point learning experience?

Topic: Technology (Usage and Application)

1. Describe the single most significant contribution that technology currently makes to you, our organization, and our customers. In what ways are your work and your quality of life enhanced by having access to this technology?

2. What are the three most important enhancements you would wish for in our current technology so that it could be of more service to you and our customers?

3. Imagine an organization in which technology only exists in the service of the people who are within and outside the organization.
   a. What types of technology are employed?
   b. What kind of training and development precedes people's use of the technology?
   c. How is the technology maintained, updated, and enhanced over time?

"Doing by Learning" activity

Positive Questions

1. *Stop and reflect on the two topics above and the tone of the questions.*
2. *Imagine yourself being interviewed and being asked these questions.*
3. *What would your response be?*
4. *Reflect on how your response differs from what it would have been if the questions had been less strength-based and positive?*

Finding Data and Information

Useful Data Sources

So where to begin? Based upon hundreds of successful student projects at both the undergraduate and graduate levels done by students in a variety of organizations, I find that Action Research methods that fall within the "Managerial Research" approach fits the scale and scope of business capstones. Action Research, by definition, embraces traditional research as appropriate but is more flexible in its ability to mix research types and even reframe the "problem" as new information becomes available.

In reviewing the years of the best examples of countless students' capstone research, I find that students' use of *Action Research* is almost universally supported by three general sources of data: *Internal Data (*Primary and

Secondary), *Student Conducted Primary Research* and *Secondary Research* in various forms. As you might expect, due to time constraints, student capstone research is only infrequently done based on a single "designed" experiment with a large sample size. Instead, it tends to be done somewhat iteratively, with small sample sizes (for surveys) and a great dependency on person-to-person interaction across the organization and its stakeholders. Let's look briefly at each of these types.

Internal Data -- Primary and Secondary

Unless your project is to design a new business, it is likely that some very useful preexisting data, commissioned studies or topic-specific reports can be used to help you in understanding the basic opportunities and constraints you are facing. As you develop your project, you will inevitably be looking for ways to measure success, and you will need a starting point -- benchmark data for comparison purposes. Internal data will provide a basis for understanding not only the change itself but the economics of the change. It begins by asking, "What is measured?" and "What data is available?".

As you engage with the organization on your project, you may also discover that current routine (weekly/monthly/annual) reports already exist that help to inform your project. If not, then you may be requesting that a new report be generated but be sure to do so as early as possible, since there is often a backlog in workload for new reports to be developed. For any process changes especially, this information can be vital.

Internal data can also take on a variety of non-quantitative forms and may include "minutes of meetings, official correspondence, policy directives, outlines of procedures, statements from management, rule books, job descriptions, and so on." (Jarvis, *The Practitioner Researcher*, 1999, p.113). Remember, however, that these documents have been produced within a unique context at some place and time different from yours. While they may inform your research questions in a general way, they seldom provide a direct response to your specific research question(s). Remember, too, that they were written by organization members who, themselves, carry the influences of political and social phenomena and so their research needs to be interpreted accordingly to account for any bias.

As you can see, internal data can be either primary or secondary in nature. Often, internal routine reports, white papers, consultants' reports, and memos to file exist and just need to be located as a starting point. Reports may also be designed to meet a specific data request as a first step in researching your topic and considered to be a primary source because it is so specific to your research question(s). Regardless of how internal data are categorized, it is an extremely important part of the research process because, if for no other reason, it includes many stakeholders who may understand or need to understand your project either now or in the future. Getting their input now, early in your research process, shows excellent change leadership skills on your part!

Student Conducted Primary #1 -- Interviews and Group Interviews

One of the most important learning opportunities coming out of a field-based (experiential) capstone project is conducting primary research in the form of interviews, surveys and other similar methods. Very few traditional academic courses offer the opportunity to create and ask questions directly of stakeholders. Artfully blending your primary data with that of internal reports and secondary research provides lessons in the realism of actual decision making using the "mixed methods" of management and action research.

Think of your interview participants as resident Subject Matter Experts, as they are, who are willing to share with you a lifetime of knowledge and experience – what an opportunity for you! Finding people to talk to begins with those close to the most obvious part of your project but then, as you extend into other Areas of Management Practice, is open to any area of changes associated with your project. In one of our case study examples, for example, the drive to increase a specific customer segment moved quickly beyond marketing research and into all other Areas of Management Practice.

Interviews are, undoubtedly, the backbone of primary data collection for most students. One reason, of course, is the ability to "scale" interviews up or down depending on your situation. Early in the process, when building your network and exploring possible topics, you are already beginning your "research" with interviews that may be semi-structured and may provide information that can aid in constantly reframing your final research topic and questions. Following up later with these same participants but using a more structured interview guide is not unusual.

Interviews are also able to be combined with other routinely scheduled face-to-face meetings by simply extending the meeting time. This is a good example of how the logistics of performing any research in the workplace always needs to be cognizant of people's time and to be as efficient as possible. This can be a delicate balance if your mentor is someone with whom you are working on other projects. It is easy, for example, to carve out small chunks of time weekly in which to focus on your project as part of other regular meetings. Some of the most successful projects were done using this structure of frequent short meetings with the student's mentor!

Interviews also allow for deeper exploration of a subject based on either previous responses or recently gathered information from other sources. Tacit knowledge that might otherwise lie dormant can be released through interviews. One of the reasons for this is that people love to tell their stories. Contrary to what you may believe before actually doing interviews, getting interviewees to stick to a schedule and wind down is often the most difficult part of interviewing. Frequently an interviewee will be able to provide additional leads for other people to interview who may be able to further enlighten you on a subject.

Appreciative Interviewing, for example, to understand and build upon organizational strengths, is easier to manage for positive input than by distributing a more detailed survey asking for text-based explanations. One thing regarding strengths-based research that almost goes without saying is the need to *avoid interviews becoming a complaint session* about what is wrong, what's broken, and what changes won't work. Instead, taking a more appreciative and strengths-based perspective puts participants in the role of imagining what would work and leads to a very different place.

Relationships built through interviewing are also excellent resources for additional research questions later in the process. Students frequently swing back to those interviewed early at various stages to get additional input or clarification. Because of the relationship built through one or more interviews, follow-up can be done with less of a time commitment through e-mail or by telephone.

Interviewing Techniques will vary depending on the nature of your project, where you are in your process (early vs. late), and how open or tight the boundaries are in your exploration. If, for example, your project is relatively loosely defined and you are interviewing a wide set of stakeholders on their perspective on possible changes, then your questions will tend to be more open ended and exploratory. Later in your work, when your project is well defined, you may be asking questions that have discreet choices on which you may probe to further refine your proposed change. Such an interview may approximate a survey at times in order to collect quantifiable data but provides the flexibility of also engaging in a dialogue about the assumptions behind a participant's responses. In all cases, you will want to be sure that your questions are as objective as possible and not leading to any unintentional inherent bias.

Interview Types

In the earlier chapter on Inquiry some attention was given to *types of questions* and much of that material is highly usable in the context of designing your interviews. In his work, *Action Research and Organizational Development* (1993), J. Barton Cunningham provides a typology of Open-Ended Interview Types that may be helpful as you consider who you will interview and what questions to ask. They include:

- **Behavioral** – Asking about past behaviors and the details supporting that behavior as a predictor to future behavior
- **Problem Solving** – This is guided by the statement, "let's solve the problem," and the goal is to help the person being interviewed in their process of identifying ways to change or improve.
- **Discovery** -- The emphasis is on the development of ideas, suggestions, information or theories. It is characterized by, "we're looking for ideas." The interviewee is given the opportunity to explore ideas and thoughts in response to general questions.
- **Helping** -- Driven by the need to allow people to express frustration, anger, and deep dissatisfaction that need to be expressed before people can be changed. The open expression allows the interviewee to look more openly and honestly at their own perceptual field.

One note is that everything presented here (and earlier on Inquiry, Question Development, Appreciative Inquiry (and more) can be applied to group interviews as well.

Student Conducted Primary #2 – Surveys

Surveys are wonderful sources of data for almost any capstone project, and there is good reason. Ever since the introduction of online survey tools like Survey Monkey, the use of surveys has been liberated from the researchers and information technology departments to the entire organization. As with any such change, there is good and bad news. The good news is that for those willing to think carefully about the questions asked, the target audience, the use of the data, and the impact on change, having access to these tools is an amazing opportunity. The bad news, if there is any, is that surveys can be overused and, if poorly designed, provide little useable data.

Generally, I have found that organizations, themselves, are good at self-regulating against the overuse of surveys. Most have at least some sort of required approval process to guard against employees being overwhelmed with information requests. This puts the burden of proof squarely on you as the capstone student to provide both a solid rationale and a well-designed survey before it is launched.

If you are a student with a strong enthusiasm for surveys, then you should simply be prepared to be thoughtful and deliberate in your design and to not expect automatic approval. Be aware that this approval process can take time. My advice is to begin probing on the approval process immediately if you have any inclination to conduct a survey. Because the approvals may be based on a "committee" of some type, it isn't unusual that such committees only meet monthly and may not be easily fit into your semester schedule! Be warned!

While there are other resources that better explain survey and questionnaire design, I will touch on a couple of the most important points. In any research, and especially in an Action Research capstone project in which you, the researcher, may be very close to the proposed change, *bias* is always a concern. Building a survey that results in unbiased and actionable information will take some time, so be prepared to work aggressively.

Surveys generally assume a designated target population and this by itself can easily be the most difficult part of doing them. Imagine wanting to assess a new product, or a new process in your supply chain, or even a new policy to improve employee retention. All three scenarios presume access to a population that is willing and able to provide unbiased responses to your survey. In today's busy work environment in which people are overwhelmed with e-mail and other online requests it is becoming increasingly difficult to capture their attention. Here, organizational support is a must, and that may include some support in the way of pre-conditioning the target audience with an advance notice request from senior management for participation, an incentive, or even individual follow-up by some means.

So why use them? Surveys are a highly useful tool that can provide quantitative data from large numbers of a population in a very short period of time. For student capstone projects they are seldom the only source of data but when used well can provide extremely important data that serve as a follow-up to interviews and focus - groups. In some circumstances, surveys may be used early in the process to set the stage for more in-depth interviews and internal research. I have known both these sequences to be extremely successful. Two broad pieces of advice in General Questionnaire Design, provided in *Research Methods for Managers* by Gill and Johnson (2010), can be extremely helpful and include:

- **Questionnaire Focus** -- The survey is intended to cover various aspects of the research problem and all the variables that you have identified. This allows you to analyze not only the impact of the independent variables but also the relationship of independent variables to one another. Also, be sure to avoid asking too many questions that don't really inform the primary research problem.
- **Questionnaire Phraseology** -- Questions need to make sense to the participants. This is why a pilot survey is a good idea; sometimes questions that seem clear to you as the writer may be baffling to the survey participant! My advice is to begin with some close friends and work out from there!

Student Conducted Primary #3 – Direct Observation

While often underplayed, there is a role of directly observing people, processes and your organization that deserves to be mentioned separately. Direct observation has always been included as a method of documenting and structuring your own experience, for example. For obvious reasons, this type of research is highly subject to being strongly biased, especially if not done using some structured process and data collection techniques.

Secondary Research and Literature Review

The use of all available secondary data is a must and reviewing "what is known" through the literature (including books), published studies, external consulting group publications, etc., is something to be done early (when exploring a subject) and on a continual basis as your subject becomes better defined. Early in the capstone project it is the literature that provides you with a mind-map of the major concepts and, as described earlier, the language of your topic. Remember, you are becoming the expert on your topic more quickly than you may realize, and the chances are excellent that no one has asked the *exact questions* and especially *within the same context*. That said, any research process begins with what is known, and the speed and ease of today's databases make finding appropriate information an extremely smooth process.

In thinking about the value of reviewing literature, a helpful perspective is that you are really telling a story and managing a process of building a case for some new idea. The value of a Literature Review and rationale provided by Dorothy Craig (2009) in *Action Research Essentials* (p. 59) includes:

- Making Connections
- Themes
- Context
- Gaps
- Method and Data
- Relevancy

Craig also goes on to identify what the lit review should also accomplish (Craig, p. 59) (adapted):

- Provide an overview to related, previous research.
- Help provide boundaries to the action research vs. the more general topic.
- Explore contradictory findings.
- Connect Action Research to previous studies.
- Identify gaps in previous studies and ways in which this action research will fill a gap.
- Provide a basis and rationale for action research.
- Clarify the direction of the study, methods, data required and analysis.

The literature review may be handled in, basically, two ways, depending on your particular capstone requirements. For many courses with a more academic focus, the "Literature Review" is a distinct "chapter" in the final research report based entirely on *previous research*. Doing it this way clarifies the purpose of your research project as a continuation of one or more "lines of research" in your field of inquiry.

Another less formal approach is to use the literature in a similar way but to provide insights, based on existing literature and studies in a separate area of the paper but also "sprinkled" throughout the paper, as appropriate. For business capstones that are accountable for demonstrating the relevance to multiple Areas of Management Practice this often seems to be a better fit.

Some combination of the two is also a good approach. Including some of the most important lessons learned from the literature in a separate chapter provides a foundation and context for the topic, while using sources as appropriate in other chapters provides theoretical support for your own findings and recommendations.

Regardless of your specific use of literature, it always has value as, at least, a starting point to building a fundamental concept map of the area of study. This landscape, even in the absence of any specific material relevant to your context, provides a sense of perspective that will be invaluable as you march into the weeds of your project landscape. Doing this LONG before your research is highly recommended because, if nothing else, it will sensitize you to the issues and topics for reflection and your own process of creativity and innovation.

Dr. Don Haggerty, M.A.T., M.B.A., Ed.D.

"Doing by Learning" activity

Create a Research Plan

*Provide a description of what you have begun or intend to do for research in support of your Capstone. It should describe any and all research you intend to do such as your **Literature Review**, **Secondary Research** and **Action Research**. A suggested format is below, and it should include, as a minimum:*

1. ***Project Overview*** *-- One to three-sentence summary of your project, including the organization and proposed change.*
2. ***Questions and Information Needed*** *-- Your key questions to be addressed or information needing to be identified through your research.*
3. ***Literature Review and Secondary Research*** *-- Short description (2-3 paragraphs) of what you intend to research through any secondary sources such as the library, white papers, reports, government and demographic data, etc.*
4. ***Action Research and Primary Research*** *-- Short description (2-3 paragraphs) of research that you intend to do to discover new information. This could be through personal interviews, focus groups, or employee/stakeholder surveys.*

Four Case Studies

CASE 1 – Inventory Management
My research included numerous internal colleagues, as well as reports that were developed internally as well as outside the organization.

CASE 2 – New Generation Target Market for Lending Institution
My research consisted of both primary and secondary resources. My primary research consisted of a survey that included approximately 50 young adults who had a history of savings or lending but were not yet homeowners. The data was able to be compared to responses to identical or similar questions for a more senior demographic group to discern some specifics with regard to both the mortgage process and the use of technology as part of that process. A second source of primary data was the interviewing of numerous senior leaders on their perspectives regarding the younger generation as potential mortgagees. Secondary research included a wide range of journal articles on lending practices and, in particular, loan practices of younger generations.

CASE 3 – Employee Training and Development for less turnover and better customer service
My secondary research consisted of numerous articles and other resources on corporate training programs and processes. I was also able to examine all our current and past employee training materials. For the design of a new training program I was able to interview employees (both past and current), trainers and management. While not direct primary research, my many years of experience in working with customers provides a basis

for analysis by my understanding of customer requirements for technical support.

CASE 4 -- Merging of multiple non-profits into one organization

My research consisted of both secondary and primary sources. For the literature review I was able to find numerous studies on the benefits and challenges of doing a merger. The blending of organizational cultures, for example, is a topic for which there is an abundance of literature. Earlier coursework provided content that was highly useful when used at the right level of detail and when adjusted to the particular context. My most relevant data came from interviews directly with multiple stakeholders at all potentially merged organizations and that addressed multiple areas of the organization (Finance, Marketing, Information Systems, Human Resources, etc.).

CHAPTER 12
ONGOING DATA COLLECTION AND ANALYSIS

Your Research Process

The purpose of this chapter is to briefly touch on some of the key actions and behaviors you need to *address simultaneously while engaged in your project*. This is when the work gets hard, and the rubber really meets the road. It is in the heat of battle when time is short, scheduling seems impossible and fear of failure looms on the horizon that you may all too easily forget some important ingredient of success!

While your project may seem to have a beginning and end that corresponds to your course, the reality of any experiential capstone project is very different. As discussed in numerous chapters, your project began long before your actual research and will continue long after you submit a "final" report. It is important to keep this in mind as you engage in the reflective process of researching, understanding, building new theories, experimenting, and learning. If you have followed the process laid out in this book, then you began months ago with informal yet focused initial conversations, and these have continued as you have developed your thinking. The whole point of experiential capstones is that you have entered into and are now immersed in an endless cycle of learning.

Field Notebook and Reflective Learning

Whether done in a spiral-bound notebook or on a mobile device, keeping "notes to self" and reflective thoughts in one location is good business. These notes only need to be understood by you so they needn't be too formal. That said, if they are too cryptic, even you may not understand them in two months when you are writing your final report. How many times have you found a few words in a note to yourself that generate a "What was I thinking?" response? The more reflective your journal is, the better. Remember our original set of competencies for Business and Management? Demonstrating reflective thinking with thoughts about what you learned and the learning process itself will, in all likelihood, be a part of your final "report." Reflections are difficult to capture from memory over several months and really do need to be documented along the way. This topic will be discussed in more detail in the final chapter.

Organize Areas of Management Practice

This book has been quite clear about the need to be systematic about the "Integration" of multiple business disciplines that we have named Areas of Management Practice. In an earlier chapter you chose approximately three primary Areas of Management Practice that most closely describe your project. As you do your research, you will also want to address all the other areas, as well. This may mean talking to others in areas of the organization not directly related to your project but which may influence/be influenced by your project. This is the time to be asking those questions!

Strengths Based and Appreciative Inquiry

At this point in your project, with a clear topic, research underway and data being collected, it is easy to feel overwhelmed. When that happens, it is important now, more than ever, to stay focused on building from strengths rather than pursuing a "problem fixing" mindset. As you set about reframing your topics, making final tweaks in questions for interviews, or building your surveys, remember some key principles of taking a *strengths perspective in looking for opportunity*:

- **Begin with respect for what is being done currently** – This is done by taking the time EARLY in the research process to seek out specific information and data on what current practices are in place and why. It is frequently the case that many parts of a process are highly successful and need to be built upon rather than replaced.

- **Build an understanding of how and why we do what we do** – Understanding the entire picture is extremely important. Two parts to this are, first, your early secondary research about the organization and the industry and, second, early conversations that were broad in their scope to help you see the entire landscape. Hopefully, this second part was part of your early networking.

- **Know why previous work has been successful** – Drilling down to the reasons for success is useful but may involve understanding other parts of the organization or even other industries, as well.

- **Know any limitations that are known** – You will inevitably run into negative and "problem" mindsets when you begin your research. Because you are working hard to adopt a "strengths-based" perspective, it doesn't mean ignoring constraints. These need to be understood and balanced against opportunities in order to resolve them.

- **Be open to possibilities that don't currently exist** – One of the beauties of Action Research is the releasing of tacit knowledge as well as making new connections along the way. It isn't unusual to discover alternatives that haven't been explored. Remember that you are the expert, so trust yourself and your instincts as you see new possibilities that build on strengths!

Scheduling

Time is not the friend of capstone projects needing to be completed in short timeframes. For one thing, as important as your project may be in your eyes or even your department, it competes with numerous other projects for time and resources. Given the need for access to people, reports, data and other resources, you really need to begin scheduling meetings as soon as you are comfortable with the scope of your project, even in the absence of any well-developed interview guides or surveys. For most semester-long (or shorter) courses you need to get comfortable with multiple balls in the air and laying out a schedule of meetings and other requests for information. This is your first big uncomfortable step.

Metrics of Change

For any project it is necessary to collect data in order to understand and explore the problem but it is also important to agree on metrics needing to be measured for learning. Eric Ries, in his book, *The Startup*

Way (2017), captures the importance of using metrics that *contribute to your learning* about a project but that are often not financial at all. He refers to such metrics as "validated learning: scientifically gathered information based on frequent experiments" (Ries, 2017, p. 176). Given the timeline of most capstones, time may not allow you to perform multiple iterations of a change. Despite this time constraint, you can adapt the mindset of establishing metrics to use immediately in your project's initial stages and then in the future development of your project as it goes through cycles of learning and adjustments. The fundamental point is that in building your capstone project, remember to maintain a mindset of inquiry into *what data is needed to support the assumptions* built into your project and that measurements taken now will be one of many tests to quantify your project's financial impact later. The metrics you choose will, presumably, be those that can point to positive change and are consistent with the Appreciative Inquiry perspective. By focusing on the positive attributes, using positive outliers and benchmarks of success, you are creating the world that you seek.

Document and Quantify

The Action Research process is iterative and consists of tests and measurements to learn and to revise your theory, how it might work, and any key assumptions. As you engage in understanding your proposed change, you will want to *document changes in necessary costs, financial benefits and strategic benefits*. Carefully documenting anything possible NOW while engaged with your stakeholders in meetings, interviews, and focus groups, will save time and anxiety later.

Your data begins with documenting both your current situation and your prospective change along with what both the drivers and outcomes of your proposed change will be. Some drivers and outcomes will be very closely associated with your change and extremely obvious, while others may be less directly connected to your change and may even be unlikely to occur under normal circumstances. It is important for you to be thinking of data collection immediately so that you may introduce your needs into your conversations as early as possible. Data is often not easily accessible or may require new reports or analysis on behalf of you or your sources. It is also never too early to begin thinking about the relationships of any potential benefits to costs. While it is premature to be jumping ahead to more formal analyses (Breakeven, Return on Investment or Discounted Cash Flow, etc.), it is always appropriate to begin thinking about what you are seeing in your data and where things might land!

Hard Data and Strategic (Soft) Data

As your project begins to take shape and you begin to identify the assumptions, changes, metrics, and benefits to the organization you will inevitably run into a roadblock in quantifying some changes. I refer to these as "strategic" changes that have well understood value but are nearly impossible to quantify. We will treat this phenomena in more detail in the chapter on Economic Modeling. For now, while you are collecting data, it is important to realize that some benefits will be problematic. While you may be comfortable with the paradox, you may find interview participants who are not and who need to be enlightened about the distinction. Philips and Philips, in their work *Show Me the Money* (2007) refer to these as Hard and Soft Data. Some examples from their analysis are shown in the charts below.

Table 25: Hard Data			
Hard Data*			
Output	**Quality**	**Costs**	**Time**
• Units produced • New accounts generated • Applications processed • Output per hour • Shipments	• Failure rates • Waste • Shortages • Inventory adjustments • Compliance discrepancies	• Treatment costs • Budget variances • Fixed costs • Program costs • Sales expense	• Cycle time • On-time shipments • Repair time • Efficiency • Lost-time delays

*Adapted from: *Show Me the Money* by Philips & Philips (2007), p. 43

Table 26: Soft (Strategic) Data					
Soft (Strategic) Data*					
Work Habits	**Work Climate/ Satisfaction**	**Initiative/ Innovation**	**Customer Service**	**Employee Development/ Advancement**	**Image**
• Tardiness • Violations • Communications	• Employee complaints • Employee engagement • Stress • Employee loyalty	• Creativity • New Ideas • Process improvements • Suggestions	• Customer complaints • •Customer satisfaction • Customer loyalty • •Lost customers	• Capability • Readiness • Networking • Performance appraisal ratings	• Brand awareness • Leadership • Reputation • Social responsibility

*Adapted from: *Show Me the Money* by Philips & Philips (2007), pp. 44 & 45

As you engage in collecting information, simply be as specific as possible in defining what data exists to describe the current situation and what data would best describe any potential change or innovation in the future state. Remember that is always easier to collapse data into like categories or eliminate a variable than it is to create one that you initially forgot to include.

The Organizational Landscape
Because you are investigating a prospective change, there are some immediate consequences about organizational boundaries that will need to be understood. Depending on the nature of your change and the degree to which it crosses organizational boundaries, you will need to show some sensitivity about how to initiate your research. Sensitivity doesn't mean avoidance, however, and it is important to begin conversations early to get leadership's support. I have occasionally had students who ignored this piece of advice and found themselves late in the semester, blocked from crossing organizational boundaries to the extent they needed and unable to obtain some key data.

Looking across your organization may have begun in your early discussions to build a network and, if so, you probably have the full support of your organization. If not, then you need to think about how your project fits into the organizational landscape, who would be affected, and how to engage those affected to ensure that their input is included. If you are having difficulty imagining where your project fits across the organization, then simply go to your original matrix built on the Areas of Management Practice. For each area in which you have research questions, ask yourself, "Who owns this area and/or the data?" or "Where should I go to answer these questions?"

Shifting Sands of Research

As you begin to gather data, it is not unusual to feel that the sands are shifting beneath your feet. As described earlier, doing this type of "research" isn't as well defined as scientific research in which variables are more controlled. At the end of the day (or the semester) you will be making judgments about your Positive Change Project based on some combination of hard data, soft data, emerging trends, strategic value and external analysis. A high level of ambiguity may develop in many of your decisions about your recommendations. This is quite normal when researching a change that has, by its applied nature, so many dimensions. As employees or business owners, we need to embrace change and with that comes uncertainties and risks. These shouldn't be thought of as something that needs to be wished away but as a part of your emerging landscape that needs to be documented and shared with others, from the early data collection through your final presentation!

Stakeholder Landscape

If you have built a network leading up to this project, then this is the time to remember them and continue to include them in your work! If there are stakeholders who haven't been part of your research or network then, bring them in now, while your ideas haven't yet crystallized and some fresh perspectives might help you to resolve some contradictions and paradoxical phenomena that you are struggling with. If you are deeply involved in your project and haven't been connecting with your mentor regularly, then this is the time to do so. In a nutshell, an experiential capstone project is not a solo endeavor and is all about stakeholder relationships. Are you connected to your stakeholders?

Ethical Landscape

In an earlier chapter the topic of Ethics was addressed. As you go through the research process, you will be challenged on many fronts to uphold confidentiality, to divulge research information outside of your project, to be objective or to introduce bias into your interviews, to look clearly at the data, and to make recommendations based on what you see rather than what management is expecting. And the list goes on. It could easily be said that the number one job in doing such a project is to maintain your integrity and uphold a high standard of ethics and excellence. How is it going?

Your Social - Emotional - Leadership Landscape

Leadership was introduced at two different levels, leading learning and leading in change. While they are somewhat artificially separated, it can be said that both depend on your own social/emotional competencies to put forth a successful capstone effort. It is widely said that 75% of the difference between highly successful and less successful leaders lies in the domain of Emotional Competencies which were addressed in an earlier chapter. You may remember that self-awareness, self-management, social awareness and relationship management are the building blocks of these skills at both levels of leadership. These are things that are not just "nice to know" but CRITICAL skills to learning experientially with and through others. How are you consciously managing your development of these skills, and how are they playing out as you conduct your research in the workplace?

Ongoing Data Collection and Analysis

If your project follows a path that is at all typical, then you probably have an abundance of notes from interviews and other metrics. This material is best managed in an "as you go" manner rather than waiting until you have completed all your research.

Interviews -- While it may seem like extra work, you should strongly consider building Word/document files of each interview and keying in the transcript as soon as possible after each interview. This is especially true if you are only taking notes by hand or keyboard (as opposed to recording them). Most students do not feel comfortable using recording devices but do take notes in some way. Cleaning up these data and putting them into electronic form will help in your learning process and are also more likely to result in insights that are useful in subsequent analysis. If you have data from multiple interviews, then go back regularly and look for connections between participants, emerging themes, and key ideas.

Focus Groups and Group Interviews – Holding a dialogue with a group always brings issues to the surface that wouldn't have emerged in individual interviews. Because the conversation moves quickly and often in unexpected directions, it is even more important that you attend to your field notes as soon as possible. While it is best to key in a transcript, even going back through your hand-written notes, adding words to turn shorthand into complete sentences or filling in the blanks, is all done best immediately following each session. Again, going back to these and reflecting on what participants were REALLY saying is the most important use of your sessions.

Small Scale Surveys are now routinely used by students with approval of the sponsoring organization. Aside from the importance of doing fundamental statistical analysis on the response data, surveys are also an important resource for any follow-up needing to be done through interviews, whether face-to-face or by phone. If there are responses to specific questions, for example, that can be tracked to specific segments of your survey group, then a follow-up may lead to some new insights. I raise this possibility specifically because it seems counterintuitive to the normal research process of qualitative research such as interviews preceding the development of a quantitative survey based on what's learned from the interviews. When working within a very finite population, the survey can act as a means of gathering input on core issues, along with an opportunity through text responses to solicit other data before investing the time in interviews.

Visual Data Analysis
Whether on a room-sized whiteboard or on the back of a napkin, using visual methods may help to unlock and unfreeze your thinking when looking for insights. While there are numerous tools and methods to capture or classify data in order to make new connections, I will mention two here as my personal favorites.

- **Mind-Map** – These are also called "Bubble Diagrams" and use association between ideas either written (white board) or using any writing surface. The logic behind them is that information is set out in hierarchical order but with independent pieces of information in each "bubble." Mind-Maps can be used in an exploratory way, especially with small groups to generate both information and relationships. According to Burnett and Evans, in their book, *Designing Your Life* (2016), the "graphical nature of the method allows ideas and their associations to be captured automatically. This technique teaches you to generate lots of ideas and because it is a visual method, it bypasses your inner logical/verbal censor" (p. 70). Mind-Maps also work nicely when documenting your research because they provide a visual tool to organize your results while simultaneously looking for new connections that perhaps you hadn't been able to make in the absence of a more visual representation. An example of a Mind-Map is seen below:

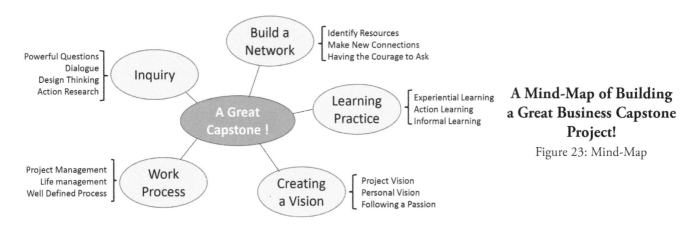

A Mind-Map of Building a Great Business Capstone Project!

Figure 23: Mind-Map

• **Affinity Diagram**

Another favorite technique, both for generating information and organizing it, is called an Affinity Diagram. The concept is simple. Independent pieces of information are generated (written) on separate pieces of paper (traditionally "Post-It" notes). While it may seem like a small detail, using large "Post-It" notes and felt-tipped pens (Sharpie fine to medium point), creates information that is easier for groups to see when they are posted on the wall or whiteboard. The process for grouping, or seeing affinity among similar ideas, is to put independent ideas on separate papers and post them at random on the wall (left side of diagram below). Once all ideas have been generated, they can be moved and clustered by themes that emerge. New large "Post-it" notes are then written to provide "Headings" for the new themes (right side of diagram below).

While this technique is used primarily in group settings, it is also an excellent tool for you as a researcher to use for your capstone project. I have personally done this with major writing projects using an entire wall of a room. This can be begun at any time in your research process and left to be constantly reworked as new information is identified. One application, for example, might be to create headings that correspond to all Areas of Management Practice, under which you could post ideas for how each area contributes to your project.

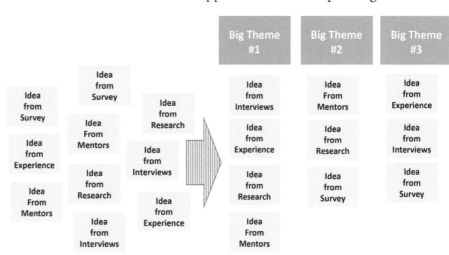

Affinity Diagramming on the wall

Figure 24: Affinity Diagram

Building the Narrative

At some point in the not too distant future you will need to submit a final report on your capstone project. The Matrix and Outline, described in an earlier chapter, provided you with a good starting point that you have begun. As you engage in doing research, connecting with stakeholders, conducting interviews or creating an Affinity Diagram, you should now begin to put "nuggets" of information into this document. The process of building this raw set of bullets, based on the Areas of Management Practice, into a final document will be described in more detail in a later chapter. For now, just taking the time to pull insights, observations and any data into a single document does great things for how you will feel about your project!

At this point you are well on your way by collecting data and building your case for positive change. This is an excellent time to connect with fellow students and share your experiences. This is likely to give you some perspective about what adjustments you may need to be making to your research processes. It is time to assess the realities of doing an experiential capstone project with others.

Four Case Studies

CASE 1 – Inventory Management

My data was relatively easy to manage, digest and synthesize. Most of my interviews with employees were on my site so access was relatively easy. Also, and more importantly, the support from senior management was amazing, and this translated into incredible response times from employees to whom I needed access.

CASE 2 – New Generation Target Market for Lending Institution

The survey data was very clean and useful for analysis. It was possible to create both descriptive statistics and cross-tabulations that characterized the younger generations' interest in mortgages and in our organization as a lending source. The interview data provided an excellent backdrop of our organization's best thinking by senior leaders. Less formal discussions with community members also provided some valuable context to my work.

CASE 3 – Employee Training and Development for less turnover and better customer service

My secondary data provided a strong direction in terms of program design, current methods and best practices for employee engagement and program costs. My primary data, which was much more grounded in the realities of our particular business, provided excellent material for the specifics on an initial program design. Other data included internal information on any metrics involving lowering employee turnover, increasing customer satisfaction, improvements to training and continuous development, and confidence of sales personnel as it impacted sales.

CASE 4 -- Merging of multiple non-profits into one organization

My data was primarily qualitative in nature and more focused on the organizational change issues than technical issues. While the data on technical systems needing compatibility was important, the potential cost savings from eliminating redundancies more than offset any short-term pain caused by changes.

CHAPTER 13
ECONOMIC AND STRATEGIC VALUE

Creating Value

The value of your project is always the first and last question needing to be answered, and yet it is often the most difficult to address. There are several reasons for this. First, the organization itself needs to have clarity about how it measures success both financially and in other ways. While many organizations espouse commitment to employees, responsiveness to all stakeholders, and other admirable performance measurements, the reality may be that financial/accounting metrics still rule. Performance measurements such as those seen in The Balanced Scorecard (Learning and Growth, Customer Relationships, etc.) can be difficult to calculate and, more importantly, to quantify in their financial impact. Finally, many of the things that are most important to organizational success such as "strategic value" or building a "culture of innovation" are extremely challenging to measure. Despite these challenges, new projects, new products, and improvements in processes are all held accountable to *adding economic value,* however difficult it may be to quantify in financial terms.

Goal = Economic Value

The ultimate goal of this chapter is to help you to create an "economic model" of how your proposed change will positively impact the organization in quantitative terms. This is generally done in a worksheet such as Excel in a format that uses the power of an electronic worksheet to easily allow for easy changes and to permit the development of scenarios. While this does require a basic knowledge of worksheets, it is not necessary to use sophisticated modeling or forecasting techniques. What is important is that you carefully articulate any measurable change and then translate that into financial impact.

Mapping the Change

The next step is to look hard at your data and ask yourself: What's changing? What are the variables? How are they measured? If they are not currently being measured, how can they be estimated and measured in the future? This, too, will probably result in some stress-producing moments. This is a big moment in which you are asking yourself to really understand and articulate your proposed change in financial terms. The work you have done, both in developing questions and identifying changes across all Areas of Management Practice, will make this process more manageable. For example, begin with the top three *Areas of Management Practice* identified earlier, and begin to list the changes needed in order to make them happen.

The challenge here is to take a deep breath and realize that, like the current costs model done above, this, too, is really a set of simple calculations but, like the previous model, needs several non-financial values in order to estimate the economic impact. One way to begin is by building a small Mind - Map (described in Chapter 12) that begins with your proposed change in soft financial terms and to clarify what needs to be known or estimated in order to get there. In doing this, you will need to highlight any values that require additional research and where you may need to swing back to your network or, based on what information you have available, estimate their value. Remember that this step in the process is also interactive and iterative, so be prepared to revisit some fundamental assumptions as you review your research data.

Current State Benefits and Costs

Activities and Costs
The first step in this process, of course, is to go back to your initial research questions and to ***analyze your data*** to understand what your current costs are for your situation, if appropriate. If you are proposing a completely new product, of course, this may not be needed. If, on the other hand, you are proposing a change in a business process, then quantifying what your current costs are is important to any decision making. Doing this as early as possible is an important step in your overall research because it will force you to recognize any gaps in your understanding that may need to be addressed in subsequent research. Doing this while there is still time to make adjustments is also important because the process of creating the worksheet allows you to see more clearly how you will express the economic value of your proposed change. Begin by creating a small worksheet that shows these costs.

Typically, you will have data on activity levels through *metrics* or performance indicators, costs through budgets or financial reports or, in some cases, both. Generally, students find that they have one or the other and must "back into" the numbers for the other. As an example, you may have a process that consists of multiple steps and employees' activities that are known (time required, the speed of activities and so forth) but for which no one has ever looked at the cost.

On the other hand, you may have a budget number showing how much is spent within an area of an organization performing some part of the value chain but have little understanding of the activities required to get the work done. To move forward, you will want to understand, to the extent feasible, both the activities *and* the costs behind the work as it is currently being done. Said another way, costs don't exist in a vacuum but are caused by activity. It is the *activities* of the organization that are the drivers of both *benefits and costs,* and you will need to quantify what you can. As mentioned in an earlier chapter, impacts may be caused by both hard data and more strategic (or soft) data. Some activities provide value in less obvious ways but they still need to be identified and measured to the extent feasible.

Guesstimates in Current Activities and Costs
Be ready to find yourself in a situation where you may see the need for a measurement that you don't have and cannot calculate based on real data so it may need to be *estimated*. I predict that this will feel very uncomfortable because in most of your financially oriented courses (Finance, Accounting, Economics, Statistics, and Operations Management) the data was generally provided, and its existence was never (or infrequently) in doubt. Unfortunately, in practice, many values needed for even the simplest of calculations may not be available and may need to be estimated. Students' questions at this point are invariably some derivation of "Do I just make this up?", and the answer is a qualified "Yes, but carefully and with documentation." The challenge of working through the economics of any innovation and change is that there are unknowns. Despite these

unknowns, there may be enough known to estimate one or more values, bootstrap a "model" and approximate a chain of calculations.

Estimated values aren't built on particularly difficult math or forecasting, although those tools can be applied. The difficulty lies in simply defining, understanding, and articulating the value of something that may not be well documented because it never needed to be. If you are doing something new, there is simply no history on which to base your numbers. Since you are proposing a change, it is now important to set a benchmark for your improvement, and this is the first step in that process. Because the nature of your research is more interactive and iterative, it is highly appropriate that this initial "first cut" be shared with your mentor and colleagues for their input.

So, what sources do you use when you don't have a real number? Learning to triangulate any problem or data point is an important skill in doing financial analysis. For many of your change measurements, you will be artfully combining sources that may include, for example: historic data, expert opinion, trade information, survey data, interview data, and more. The use of multiple sources such as these is a key skill in doing managerial and action research.

Financial Model of Current Situation

Students struggle with this more than any other part of the capstone because there are so much missing data, estimation and uncertainty. Secondly, there are very few courses in either undergraduate or graduate curricula that focus on the skills for building simple financial models from scratch. Courses in Finance, Economics and Accounting, for example, work within well-known templates and paradigms with known data. To the extent that benefits parallel revenues and costs equate with expenses, the starting point is generally something that resembles an "income statement." While this is a great start, the format often deviates from this to more clearly demonstrate a very particular activity or sequence of activities, each with its own unique set of costs. Benefits, for example, are more often reductions in costs or processes eliminated than they are a new revenue stream, per se. Modeling the current situation is often the spark that ignites some exciting and fresh modeling for the future state.

Typical Capstone Project Activities, Benefits and Costs

The table below provides some examples of the types of activities and costs that would need to be tracked for various types of projects. The benchmarking on current activities and costs is particularly important and needs to be done early in the research process since it sets the stage for change design and implementation.

Table 27: Typical Capstone Project Activities, Benefits and Costs			
Typical Capstone Project Activities, Benefits and Costs			
Project Focus	**Current Activities' Costs**	**Future Activities' Benefits**	**Future Activities' Costs**
More secure customer transactions and payment methods in healthcare environment	• Cost of reputation loss • Lost customers • Litigation • Financial costs (with credit card vendors)	• Higher customer retention • Avoided cost of reputation repair • Avoided cost of litigation • Lower credit card cost per transaction	• Internal security changes to software and systems • Full time director of payment security • Ongoing annual testing and maintenance of security systems
Improved methods of recruiting, onboarding and training employees	• Marketing Media • Interviewing • Employee Turnover • Employee Training	• Reduced or eliminated media • Reduced employee turnover costs • Reduced employee training in volume	• Social network marketing • Development of new systems and processes • Creation of new employee development program • Tracking systems • Leadership training
Agile Product Development	• Long product development cycles • Lost revenue from products not being in the market	• Quicker to market = more product success and revenues • Lower overall product development costs • Lower product return rate • Change to agile thinking affecting other areas of company with $$ benefits	• Higher per-product development costs • Cost of product failure from premature entry into market • Team and Leadership development in accepting agile methods
Improved Inventory Counting System	• Inventory shrinkage • Lost customers • Lost sales	• Reduced lost inventory • Higher customer retention • Higher sales revenue • Reduced errors	• Ongoing cost of inventory counts • Higher inventory management costs

Table 27: Typical Capstone Project Activities, Benefits and Costs			
Typical Capstone Project Activities, Benefits and Costs			
Project Focus	**Current Activities' Costs**	**Future Activities' Benefits**	**Future Activities' Costs**
Total Remake of Business Office Practices and Procedures	• Paper processing and management • Records storage and tracking	• Reduced processing costs • Reduced storage costs • Increased decision-making ability	• Investment in various software (desktop, network and cloud) • Training personnel • Information systems upgrade

Future State Benefits and Costs

Measuring Change in Activities

The next step is to build a small financial model showing the impact of your proposed change project going forward in the "Future State." Go back to your modeling of the Current Situation and using any of your variables that you've identified as current costs, pull together data (or estimates) to show both what changes in activities will occur as well as the financial impact of those changes. Measuring the change activities, themselves, is an important step. Generally, the impact of your change will fall into one of several categories:

- Direct increase in activity or process
- Direct decrease in activity or process
- Indirect increase in or new activity or process
- Indirect decrease in or elimination of activity or process
- Avoided activity and/or costs
- Budget changes -- increases and decreases in costs
- Strategic benefits that might be quantifiable in the future

This is an important time to bring up the Areas of Management Practice model as a tool to look across the organization for changes. For example, a change in quality control and waste reduction might also have the effects of fewer returned products, higher customer satisfaction ratings leading to lower customer acquisition costs, fewer legal settlements (depending on the product), and lower call center costs, to name just a few. This is the type of activity assessment and cost analysis that makes a capstone truly integrative. The Areas of Management Practice model is just a tool to structure your thinking, research, data collection and analysis in a truly integrative way!

For each of your identified activities you now need to create an input into your economic model that begins with its starting (current state) and ending value (estimated) based on your proposed change. This can be difficult because you will often need to make broad assumptions based on little information other than estimated values combined with qualitative information from your research. Relax and breathe! My perspective on this is that you need to ask yourself whether you are better off to estimate based on the best information and judgment available or to avoid doing so because of your discomfort with estimated values.

The more detailed answer is in two parts, the short and long run. In the short run, you are better off because just by going through this process you are building a deep understanding of the change. Even with estimated values you have defined what the impact will be, even if only conceptually. In the long run, your model provides a template and structure for you and the organization to use going forward as better data isq collected and more is known. Without such modeling you will be flying blind, at least at the outset, and unable to measure the success of your project. With the economic model you have a very rational method of decision making, even if currently based on what you consider to be very "fuzzy" numbers.

Remember also that we no longer live in a world in which product life (and product development) cycles are decreasing exponentially. Few organizations are in an industry in which they can wait for perfect information, and yours is no exception. As good as it may be, your analysis will probably not be the final word on this change. The sooner you feel comfortable with the fact that any of our work products are an iteration providing the best possible solution and forecast available at this point in time, the happier you will be. Building a model, being clear about your assumptions, and documenting the level of confidence in those assumptions is the best you can do. It isn't a compromise in quality, it's just the way life is.

Errors of Omission vs. Commission

As you gather your change project's activities and costs, you will be faced with numerous decisions about the level of detail to include. If, for example, you were including a cost of transportation for a small business, you might just estimate this cost as a percentage of revenues based on standard industry ratios. My fundamental rule of thumb on what to build into your model (or not) is that "if you can measure it, then include it!" Include any separate activities and costs that you can reasonably identify and, just as important, disaggregate any activities and costs as much as possible.

In general, by documenting things to the finest level of detail possible and building those estimates into your financial model, you only make the model more accurate. The reasoning is pretty simple. If you include the breakdown of a cost and the value is even in the ballpark, you will probably have a small percentage error of commission. In doing so, however, you are generally so much better off than disregarding the detail (with a gross assumption) because the implied and unknown percentage error of omission is inevitably higher! Further, by building in the ability to "tweak" the assumptions you can even refine it and squeeze the error rate to insignificant levels with more data!

Hopefully you can see that the "economic model" isn't as scary as it sounds. The basis is an understanding of the **current** costs behind one primary designated activity and its effects in other activities in multiple Areas of Management Practice. The structure of this model provides a starting point for measuring the costs of activities in the **future**. This is a perfect beginning for any subsequent analysis.

Defining the Investment

For most projects of the magnitude used for student projects (even graduate/MBA level), the typical investment model of discounted cash flow based on a capital investment, depreciation, tax shields, etc., is not required. The rationale is, first and foremost, that there is often a very small "investment" initially. Projects involving changes in process or even business models more frequently require a small investment followed by ongoing costs for development or support. Some projects, of course, do require such analysis, and for them I would refer you to any of the standard Financial Management textbooks' section on Discounted Cash Flow and Net Present Value (or whatever financial model preferred by your organization). Second, from an economic perspective, many of the costs are reflected in reduced budget line items or projected reductions in the costs of some activity's cost or profit center(s). Third, smaller projects tend to have a much shorter timeline associated with them than used with DCF models, something that is consistent with management routinely looking for a shorter payback and more immediate ROI.

That said, it is important to identify any "investment" required and to treat that as such, if necessary. In general, organizations have a preference for the type and level of analysis, so the best practice is to be consistent with that.

Budget and Multi Year Models

Budgets aren't often the focus of courses in Accounting, Finance and Economics. That said, for student projects providing measurable benefits with little investment, you can be sure that organization members are thinking about budget impacts as you describe any change. Budgets simply can't be overestimated in their importance to the mindset of your participants, your data, and the outcome/projections of your proposed change because the questions are always "Whose budget will pay?" and "How will my budget see the savings?" These are important questions that need to be top of mind for you as you set out to research a change to the organization.

While not part of your incremental analysis, any cost will need to be expressed at least on a one-year basis and, if possible, aligned with budget impacts and changes. Moving from an annual budget to a multi-year model is the next step and is important because it recognizes the benefits and costs that accrue over time. If there is a significant resource requirement then of course this leads you back to doing some formal investment analysis. Multi-year does present some choices about how to spread any initial costs (cash flow vs. accrual) and, to some extent, what you do again depends on your organization's preference for the level of investment you are proposing.

Investment Analysis

As stated above, most capstone projects require at least some economic analysis based on sound principles of Investment Analysis. While descriptions of these technical analyses are available in virtually any Financial Management textbook, their usefulness will be addressed below.

When capstone students present their findings to management, it is actually unusual that the "investment" is significant enough to fall under the capital budgeting process. When that happens, it is important to follow not only standard textbook analysis but to adjust that process for each particular organization's particular standards.

It is more typical that the presentation of recommendations should typically be more detailed than a single Net Present Value, Return on Investment, or Internal Rate of Return. The table above gives some insights into the types of costs that go into an economic model for some typical projects. Notice, for instance, that these examples do not bury the project within the financial statement of the organization or even the division or profit center. Instead, the analysis is based on the incremental economics that answer the question of "What changes?" Hence, these models really needn't be overly complex in the number of line items (Benefits and Costs) but should be detailed in the assumptions behind those line items, to the extent feasible. It goes without saying that standard worksheet process should be followed so that all cells are appropriately linked to ensure easy changes and scenario analysis.

So, what analysis is typically called for? In order of usage:

- **Annual Cash Flow** – This takes us back to the discussion about budgets and the need to be concerned about short term (up to three year) impacts on the budgets affected. It is generally relatively easy to describe the benefits and costs separately over a three-year period showing the likelihood of any expected variance. I might also add that while graphs may be helpful for some audiences, the use of numerical figures that clearly express the incremental benefits and costs of your particular project is the single most important thing to communicate.

- **Breakeven** – While not used as an "investment criterion" to compare projects, a "breakeven" either expressed in time or units, whichever is most appropriate, is the next most logical and useful to small and relatively short-term projects. It is also a nice extension of the "Annual Cash Flow" described above.

- **Benefit/Cost Ratio** – With the Benefits and Costs having been articulated in the Annual Cash Flow and a Breakeven provided, it can be helpful to express the benefits and costs as a ratio. While protocols may vary by organization, it probably makes sense to do cumulative benefits and costs over the time period. This is particularly useful when there is no large single investment at the project's outset.

- **Payback** – While lacking in the sophistication and accuracy of some models, this can be used in the same way that the breakeven analysis is described above. Its use is really a matter of organizational or managerial preference.

- **Return on Investment (ROI)** – This technique is deceptively simple and tends to be either misused, miscalculated, or overused without adequate documentation. The trickiness here is that it doesn't take the time value of money into account like Discounted Cash Flow models (below) but does attempt to bundle multiple years into a single ROI value that can be misleading, if nothing else. Again, be sure that your calculations are consistent with your organization's and management's preference before tossing out an ROI to make an impression.

- **Discounted Cash Flow (DCF)/Net Present Value (NPV)** – Assuming that you have taken at least one course in Financial Management, then you should be well aware of the strengths of using DCF/NPV techniques. If your project has any significant initial investment, I highly recommend doing an NPV analysis. Because you have begun with Annual Cash Flows (above), taking the next step to DCF/NPV is really quite straightforward. That said, like all the techniques described here, there are always nuances to their use in any organization. One that comes to mind, for example, is the use of a terminal value in the final year to account for ongoing cash flows in some number of years beyond the five to ten-year period of detailed analysis. This single number can have a dramatic impact on the NPV, so be careful to be respectful of any protocols used for investment decisions at your organization.

- **Internal Rate of Return (IRR)** – As you are undoubtedly aware, the IRR is a tricky calculation due to the assumption of cash flows being reinvested into the project over time. For this reason, I have seen few organizations use this, especially for projects of the scale and scope of student capstone projects.

- **Profitability Index (PI)** – This is used less frequently than all other techniques described here and, if you have done a DCF/NPV analysis, this is actually a relatively uncomplicated calculation and doesn't have the warning signs of IRR calculations.

Moving Numbers and Shaky Ground

Hopefully, this chapter has provided some comfort to accompany your need to truly "bootstrap" an economic model that will be unique to your project. Additionally, given the scale and scope of your project, it is likely that you will need to develop or refresh your abilities in:

- Using MSExcel or a comparable worksheet program to develop a model from scratch
- Building a flexible model, even if conceptually, with the goal of revisiting assumptions
- Blending qualitative and quantitative data into an economic model
- Daring to guess and doing the best you can with the hand you are dealt
- Giving rough justice to assumptions and measurements
- Realizing that in today's business environment "Perfect is the enemy of good"

It is now time to develop the "Economic Model" for your project. This doesn't need to be as intimidating as many students fear it to be. Whatever your project may be, there is a change of some kind that provides an economic benefit. Your job is to capture and quantify what those benefits (and costs) would be. The struggle for many students is the uncertainty of quantifying changes for which there is no firm data.

There is no magic bullet -- the goal is to find a way to quantify your change somehow. If, for example, you were proposing a change in "on-boarding" new employees with your organization, then the quantified saving might be both reduced training costs and lower employee turnover, for which you may have limited information.

My key message to you is to do the best you can but know that you are not alone in feeling the ground shake a little when the assumptions seem "made up." Trust me, you will be OK, so make some reasonable assumptions, begin building a small worksheet (in Excel or other), and take it from there.

Four Case Studies

CASE 1 – Inventory Management

The model focused on both project costs and the most quantifiable benefits from reductions in shrink. The project costs included the new software, employee training and additional employees needed. The economic benefits were derived from reduced shrink in both the main warehouse and several satellite locations under assumptions that were drawn from experts in that field.

CASE 2 – New Generation Target Market for Lending Institution

The economic model provided a glimpse into the possible benefits from a new and more focused technology-driven strategy using more social media. Some of the metrics driving the economics were: technology interaction, responsiveness to social media content relevant to mortgage/home purchasing, online loan application behaviors, days to loan completion, loan size and interest rates/risk.

CASE 3 – Employee Training and Development for less turnover and better customer service

My economic model provides a net economic benefit to the organization. The economic gains include higher sales, more repeat customers and higher customer satisfaction (which adds value in both economic and strategic ways). Other economic gains include the reduced costs of recruiting, onboarding and training new employees. The costs of the new training include program development, curriculum continual upgrades, additional instructors and program management.

CASE 4 -- Merging of multiple non-profits into one organization

The economics of this project are somewhat predictable. Most of the savings come from the efficiencies of consolidation in everything from strategic planning to accounting to marketing and fundraising. That said, the implementation isn't without its challenges as donors often have allegiance to their "local" agency and, once combined with others into a more national presence, may not continue their financial support. There is also a dip in overall cash flow as all merging agencies incur the cost of continuing operations while developing new systems or redeploying an expanded system based on one organization's existing infrastructure. Cost estimates for the "new" organization were easily estimated because of actual and historical costs.

CHAPTER 14
CREATING A REPORT

Pre-Work

If you have followed the Capstone Project Plan chapter as well as all the "***Doing by Learning***" activities throughout this book, then this chapter should be your easiest part of the semester. Hopefully, you are entering this phase of your capstone with all of the heavy lifting behind you, your research completed, sensible economic model carved out and, in a Word document destined to be your final report, a "skeleton" outline based on the *Areas of Management Practice*. Within that outline, you should have identified approximately three "primary" areas that best fit the focus of your project. Also, in all areas you should have a few questions needing to be addressed. Finally, by now you should have completed or nearly completed both your secondary and primary research and have nicely compiled any "data" into usable electronic form. The net result of this work is that you are not "beginning" a writing exercise but instead are stepping on a moving train and "all" you have to do is write without the anxieties caused by incomplete research, lack of clear direction or a vision of your end point for a final deliverable.

Phase 1 – Mentor Review Draft Report

To facilitate the report writing process, I've described it in phases that can serve as a "quasi" plan for the details of taking all of your work to the finish line with as little anxiety and stress as possible while still ensuring that you have all areas of business well covered. In the general recommended order, below are some suggestions for developing your final report:

Establish Format

In writing up a major project such as this there are few things as painful as realizing late in the game that you have not followed a format protocol or that your entire bibliography now needs to be built. So, before anything else, clarify whether you will be using APA Format (typically for Business and Management) or some other format. If using APA, be sure to chase down some APA Style Guides, either through their publications or online resources. Also, be sure to begin building your bibliography "as you go" so it is there to refine when you are done with your major writing. Building an entire bibliography from scratch may mean locating resources for the second time and identifying the specific pages in a book from which quotes came. This is not a pain that you want to endure!

Identify Changes

The past few weeks of your capstone were probably spent scrambling. There are so many things to read, stakeholders and employees to interview, ideas and "leads" on which to follow-up and conceptual models (from your curriculum) to use creatively. While you are putting your head down and "getting it done," it is difficult to simultaneously reflect on what's changed at the same time. This is the moment to review everything and be sure that there are no new uncertainties about the value of your project and the assumptions behind it. If something needs additional research or thought, this is the time to address it -- before seriously engaging in the writing process.

Modifying your Outline

In the chapter on building your Project Matrix and Outline you were provided with some "typical" outlines that are built upon the Areas of Management Practice model. Review your selection now, and begin to think about whether any areas need to be combined. For example, if your project is to develop a new Leadership Training Program and a big part of the program is to "market" the program to employees, then the "Customers, Sales, Marketing" section might be rolled into the Leadership Program itself. A word of warning, however, is that it is very easy to lose sight of an "*Area of Management Practice*" when it is bundled into another area, so you will want to be sure to maintain separate analysis and treatment of, in this example, the communication and selling of the program to employees based on best practices in customer value proposition and communications.

Elevator Pitch

While not a step in writing, this is an important step in preparation for any further writing without those time wasting "second thoughts" about where you are going. If you haven't done so, try writing a short (few sentences) "Elevator Pitch" about your project. This might include what opportunity exists, what possibilities for solutions were explored, what your recommendation is, and why and how this adds value to the organization.

Write *Proposed Opportunity*

Write the section on your Proposed Opportunity next, because this should be unwavering at this point, and the Elevator Pitch provides a great stepping-stone to writing this in a more detailed narrative form. This might also include how this opportunity came to be, how it fits with your organization's direction, how it will provide other opportunities, and the level of organizational support. This section is the perfect launching pad for all other sections of your report.

Write *Research Completed*

While it is frequently the case that there is "one more interview" or "additional survey responses coming in," you should, by now, know enough to write this section. While you will be referring to research throughout the report, it is important to document your overall research process by describing your primary and secondary research. This needs to be done at the right level of detail so that you give the reader a solid understanding of your information and processes. It needn't mention every author or include, for example, survey or interview questions.

Write Executive Summary (first half+/-)

With the " Research" and "Opportunity" sections written, it is now possible to write the opening sections of the Executive Summary that include at least those topics. I generally recommend waiting on other sections (recommendations and why) but it depends on your level of completion. If your research is done and recommendations finalized, then it is, of course, fine to complete as much as possible at this juncture.

Write Primary Sections

This book has been built on the use of the Areas of Management Practice model and, more specifically, the selection of approximately three Areas of Management Practice that are most relevant to your project. It is important to write these primary areas now with all (or nearly all) of your work completed. You may, for example, want to pull these forward in your outline to be ahead of other areas of practice. If, for example, you were implementing a new Customer Service software system, you might want to write up the "Customers, Sales, Marketing," "Information Systems," and "Economic Value" sections. Again, if your work is at a level of completion allowing you to write more, then, certainly, don't hold back!

Begin ALL Sections

With your primary sections written, it is now in your best interest to bring some clarity to the rest of your report. If you have followed our process of building an initial outline made up of Areas of Management Practice, then all other sections should include (a) a few key questions, and (b) some relevant thoughts regarding the relationship of each area to your project. In the previous example of Customer Service System, you may have inserted information on "Organizational Changes" or "Strategy." Your objective now is to write the purpose and relevance to your project for each section of your report. As you do this (and trigger your own thought process), add bullets in each section on what you anticipate writing about, what "models" of theory provide frameworks, what research will inform that section, what needs to be researched (if anything), and any relevant thoughts you have regarding that section of the report. For the final reflections section, following the outline provided (or one of your own), you should begin the process of documenting your learning process. If you have, as suggested earlier, a field journal, then this is the time to look for some big lessons and insert them as bullets for now (see Final Reflections chapter for additional details).

Write Recommendations

Assuming that you are far enough along in your thinking, you should now write the section on "Recommendations." This can be as detailed as necessary to convey the complexity of the project but should stop short of being the "Implementation Plan" for project management purposes, which is a separate section.

Complete Economic Model (Worksheet)

This step is outside of the Word document but is necessary in order to write the following section. If you have not completed your Economic Model that generally stands alone as a "worksheet" such as MS Excel, then this is the time to complete that step. Additional details can be found in the Economic Modeling chapter.

Write Economic Value Section (Report Section)

This section is a narrative version of what you have demonstrated in your Economic Model (above). One rule of thumb is that this written section should "stand alone" and explain with some level of detail the economic business case for your project. It should answer the question, "How does this project provide economic benefit to the organization?" The answer should include a short narrative, as well as key tables showing benefits, costs, or any other relevant data regarding, for example, the costs of activities used to implement your project.

Schedule your Mentor Review and/or Input

I include this because, assuming that you are using a "field mentor" who will evaluate your work, you may want to get this draft to them as a first step in the review process. I find that students' levels of completion vary considerably at this point, and your report may even be in very finished form, ready for final mentor review. Even if not ready for review, this is the appropriate time to connect with your mentor and schedule a review time when you have a document that is ready to share. The challenge is that you may be writing and editing up until late in the semester but your mentor may need some lead time for review, pushing the mentor evaluation right into the end of the semester. Do everything you can to avoid this crunch and the inevitable tension as you push for a review from a mentor who, like all of us, leads a busy life with multiple balls in the air!

"Doing by Learning" activity

Write Mentor Review Draft Report

Following the guidelines and process outlined in the first section of this chapter, build a first draft of your final report. This will feel like a real turning point in your capstone experience because you are creating a draft final report! You will use the outline built earlier as a starting point.

"Draft Report" needs some elaboration. In a draft it is assumed that there will be some messy written descriptions, bulleted ideas, sentence fragments and "notes to self" that are all part of your work-in-progress narrative. My goal is to get it out of your head (and notes) and into some semblance of order. The level of completeness and readability should be something that you can share, however, with your mentor.

Phase 2 – "Serious" Final Draft

The "Serious Draft" is your final report in finished form, ready for sharing with management. While anything here could be done earlier (again, depending on your level of completion), I have held back on these in order to facilitate the completion of Phase 1 being done in a timely way. Below are some final steps in getting your project to the finish line.

Integration's Last Word

With your outline now configured to best match your project (combining Areas of Practice as needed) and some sections written, it is time to finish the job. Continue to build out any Areas of Practice needing to be developed further, expand and add detail to your research results, develop your final "Implementation" section, and conclude your recommendations. Also, be sure to explain your use of any frameworks and models from your curriculum. All these loose ends can now be addressed.

Tables, Charts, Appendices – What, Where and When?

By now you have probably found it necessary to express some of your material through the use of tables, charts and graphs. With virtually all sections written, this is an excellent time to rethink their use. Read through your entire report, and decide where additional charts, tables or graphs might have the most impact and add them. That said, don't overuse them, especially graphs, because they can actually inhibit the reader from focusing on the text.

Write, Write, Write

Your writing at this point should be "finish work" but new discoveries have been known to happen during the final writing process! Continue to refine the flow, and be sure that, above all, you are "telling a story" and "making a business case." Your story should clearly convey answers to the basic topics seen in your elevator pitch, the opportunity section or the executive summary. When this draft is done, you are certainly at a point where you should share this "Draft" with your mentor.

Take Time Off and Share
If you have planned well, you should have allowed a few days toward the end of the semester when this "draft" is out for review with your mentor or any others in your network willing to provide feedback. It is important, too, for you to step away from writing for at least a couple of days to give yourself some processing and reflection time before doing a final report.

If you have been following the advice above, this draft is pretty much as good as it will get, with the exception of tiny edits and tweaks. This draft could be shared with members of your collaborative network, mentor (if not shared previously) and colleagues – all for feedback.

Phase 3 – Final Draft(s)

With your feedback from your mentor and others in your network, it is time for the final tweaking and making those small but important changes such as light editing, pagination, table of contents, etc. This may happen once or even a few times depending on your level of feedback. When done, you are ready for submission. Congratulations -- you've just written up an Experiential Business Capstone!

This is it…a final draft that can be submitted for grading to your organization's leadership and others.

Presentation

Regardless of whether it is used or not, I strongly recommend developing a short (5-10 slides) presentation of your project. Go back to the elevator pitch for general guidelines and build out from there to meet the needs of your audience. The process of stepping back, moving from the complexity of the topic to its simplicity, is an important part of your learning and will be a critical bridge to your final reflections (described in the upcoming chapter).

"Doing by Learning" activity

Create a Presentation

Just the act of creating a presentation takes you from the "world of complexity" that you have been immersed in to "the other side" of simplicity. It allows you to step back and tell your story and may actually add a new dimension to your understanding!

CHAPTER 15
REFLECT ON YOUR EXPERIENCE

Reflective Practice*
*portions adapted from *Becoming a Reflective Practitioner*. Haggerty, D. (2013i).

Throughout this book, we have emphasized the role of learning and, specifically, reflection as a pathway to taking a strengths-based approach to your experiential capstone project. Chapters on both learning and leadership, as well as others, emphasize the need to approach work in a reflective manner that opens the door to better communication, relationships, innovation, and ethical excellence. Helping you to become a *Reflective Practitioner* is the focus of this chapter. After all, reflection is not an end in and of itself -- it needs to be linked to how the world can be changed for the better. That's your charge.

This chapter serves as an opportunity to both support your current experiential capstone and to also pull things together as you prepare to graduate and carry them with you in your future work. While we used the *Areas of Management Practice* model to integrate the application of your business curriculum, the most long-lasting competencies coming out of your capstone experience are more likely to be your learning and growth as a reflective practitioner. Reflective practice is really more a process than an event. What I provide here is a broad brush but it is up to you to pick up the brush and fill in the details.

What are the Skills of Reflective Practice?
Let's begin by turning to Joe Raelin, one of the world's most authoritative authors on workplace learning and management development, for his list in his book, *Work-Based Learning* (2008). This includes:

- ***Being*** -- Being open to experiences without immediate interpretation, not defending, not blocking ourselves against our own experiences, real listening, commitment to the group, using deep listening, pausing – reflecting and contemplating, seeking out assumptions, observing judgments, understanding your framework that you use to think individually.
- ***Speaking*** -- To express meaning, express group norms, bring out uncertainties, or review unfounded assumptions.
- ***Disclosing*** -- Sharing our doubts or voicing our passion, revealing feelings, disclosing something about yourself.
- ***Testing*** -- As part of a group, going back and testing your own process.
- ***Probing*** -- Directing inquiry to one person at a time in order to tease out the facts, reasons,

assumptions, inferences, and possible consequences of a suggestion or action.

Hopefully, these practices are somewhat familiar to you. They are the backbone of the numerous models of leading learning and leading positively presented earlier. All, for example, are grounded in the spirit of True Dialogue. As we said back in the earlier chapters, these are not complicated models. The difficulty is in the implementation. Let's now review some other aspects of becoming a reflective practitioner.

Application of Reflective Practice

Reflective practice is not meant to be a theoretical construct for merely academic interest -- it is meant to be applied to the world of work. We all need to challenge ourselves to become reflective practitioners for ongoing improvement of our own careers, our work processes and our organizations. In other words, reflection is a tool to facilitate a positive change. This integrates nicely with our strengths-based approach and an Appreciative Inquiry perspective. That said, unfortunately, there is no magic formula for *reflective practice*. Learning reflectively, or engaging in reflective practice, can still take on a wide range of meanings, depending on the individual and the context. Said another way, *the precise method of learning from experience depends on the nature of that experience, no two of which are identical.* Despite that, we can apply several models to our experience and choose methods that seem to make sense as a starting point in developing our own methods. The most important point is this: *learning from experience is most effective when it is deliberate.* Like implementing any personal change, it begins with establishing simple systems, measuring success, and then building from there.

Your Toolbox for Reflective Practice

In many ways, each chapter of this book provides a slightly different perspective or set of tools for the development of your skills as a *reflective practitioner*. Each reading (or activity) looks at a specific aspect of *reflective learning* in an attempt to provide a robust definition for your future work. To be sure, there is a certain degree of the "chicken and egg" phenomenon in breaking out each of these topics. Let's look back at some key topics and how each (I hope) will contribute to your own reflective practice.

Workplace Learning

A long history of theory and practice is centered around the concept of organizational learning. A significant part of that rich history teaches us that *learning begins with the individual* in the workplace and that an individual's learning is more than cognitive learning alone and that it is connected in a very meaningful way to both the social and emotional aspects of the work experience. This explains the importance of Emotional Intelligence and its usefulness in connecting and working with others as being so foundational.

Our workplace learning experience, then, has the capacity to be reflective or not, depending on the skills of the individual and, just as importantly, the context, or the workplace itself. It is extremely difficult, for example, to think and act reflectively in a work situation that works overwhelmingly against it. Conversely, an organization that provides support for reflective behavior will facilitate reflective behavior.

Dialogue

Dialogue, as a topic and method of inquiry, is the strong silent type. While other topics and models in this book may have more "panache" and communities of practice, dialogue is a cornerstone to effective learning in all of them. Rather than attempting to distill the dialogue lesson here, I recommend that you flip back to the section on Dialogue in chapter four and review Isaac's model. Issacs captures the essence of what dialogue is and what it is not and reminds us that the problem with introducing true dialogue into the workplace is that people often think they are doing it already. In a nutshell, discussion is fine but dialogue takes your communication and learning to another whole level of Reflective Practice.

Experiential Learning

The process of *deliberately* (key word!) learning from our work experiences is grounded in a theoretical basis of its own. As in any area of study, there are several "models" that have been developed to explain this phenomenon. Our work is grounded, first, in the research and learning theory of David Kolb, whose work links directly to some leading learning theorists. The key concept introduced earlier is Kolb's "cycle of learning" that we all inevitably follow in learning from any new experience. Kolb's model provides a foundation for much of our work in this book since reflective observation is the cornerstone of learning from experience and is what tends to be the most overlooked in today's busy workplaces. It is this notion of *reflection* that has been extended to the two terms *Reflective Learning* and *Reflective Practice*. The Learning Style Inventory, which was described in the chapter two, is built from Kolb's model and provides great insights into the relationship between learning, career development, leadership and organizational behavior.

A second learning "cycle" model, based on Action Learning teams, provides an expanded version of the Kolb model. This was supplemented by the process for problem solving. Both these models included steps for reframing or reflection.

A third model, by Ikujuro Nonaka in *The Knowledge Creating Company* (Nonaka, I. and Takeuchi, H. 1995) provides a different "cycle of learning" that helps us to understand more clearly the social aspects of learning in the workplace. Nonaka's model is useful because it helps to explain the link between learning at the individual and organizational levels. The most important concept we learned is his explanation of how "knowledge" moves from being tacit (hidden) to explicit (open and shared). The reverse is also true, of course, as explicit organizational knowledge becomes adopted by individuals (tacit). It is another "simple" model that in practice becomes a bundle of complexity in practice but is clear enough to keep in our mind's eye as we go about our work.

Action Learning

Action Learning provides a framework that pulls from a variety of disciplines to build a *process and mindset* for effective and collaborative teamwork. It is built around four attributes that, taken together, create a model that is powerful and distinguishable from the simpler concept of "teamwork."

- First, the deliberate ***reframing and reflection*** *of problems* is extremely important because it forces us to slow down the decision process and "get it right" by examining the problem thoroughly.
- Second, there is a *strong **focus on learning*** that, for most problem-solving processes, too often gets swept under the rug in the haste of moving on to the next problem.
- Third, the *process is built around **taking action*** and gaining empowerment by allowing those closest to the problem the freedom to solve the problem together and learn by implementing a solution.
- Fourth, which is the foundation for the first three, is the *high level of **communication*** required through conversations that are based on the principles of ***dialogue*** rather than debate.

Appreciative Inquiry

Appreciative Inquiry embraces all the above work-based learning models but takes the skills of reflection and inquiry and asks us to apply them in a more direct way. By taking an "Appreciative" or "Strength-Based" approach to change, we look at our best practices, share them, build a positive vision of the future and then work towards that vision. This is particularly useful as an intellectual umbrella or guiding philosophy to organizational change. Because of our emphasis on the "Positive Change Project" Appreciative Inquiry has been sprinkled throughout this book at multiple levels. Appreciative Inquiry is grounded in the belief that we inquire about and generatively build a shared vision that grows from strengths and that doing so yields very different results than, alternatively, dwelling on problems.

Design Thinking

Design Thinking is one of the most recently developed models in which many of the behavioral attributes of Reflective Practice sit squarely in support of the process. This is especially true of the experiential learning cycles described above and the need for transparency and trust in both Appreciative Inquiry and Dialogue. The shortened learning cycles that are characteristic of Design Thinking make all the behaviors even more relevant.

Reflective Learning

And so we finally come to Reflective Learning. What is it exactly? Our definition of reflective learning is constructed from a variety of sources and is designed to be comprehensive and inclusive. It is grounded in experiential learning theory, as well as the most highly respected research on workplace and organizational learning. The critical concept to keep in mind is the complexity of the definition. Our working definition is presented here with key concepts in bold.

> *"Reflective learning is a **change** in **understanding** or **social-emotional** development that results from a deliberate act of **sincere inquiry** that includes some combination of: **problem solving**, introducing **change**, posing challenging **questions, and**/or making **implicit knowledge explicit**. That act may be performed **alone**, through **participation** with or by the inclusion of **others** either in **preparation for, during**, or **after** a work experience and is likely to be **transformative** in nature."*

Haggerty, D. (2001)

The "thumbnail" explanation is that reflective learning, by definition, means a ***personal change*** that is facilitated by a ***deliberate*** learning effort on behalf of the learner. This definition moves us from reflective learning, as defined in the Kolb model at the individual level, to its application in our respective workplaces. It begins (but only begins!) to answer the question of how we can apply the theory of workplace, experiential and reflective learning to our own practice. The attempt is to broaden our interpretation of what constitutes "reflective" and reinterprets the learning theory in a more applied basis. Suggestions for "bootstrapping" one's own reflective practice are made with the caveat and the deep belief that reflection needs to be "baked into" the work experience and work products. Like dialogue, it needs to be woven in. Here, a delicate balance needs to be made by each of us in our own workplace to design each of our own "reflective acts" that make sense for our unique situation.

Nine Dimensions of Reflective Practice

The Nine Dimensions of Reflective Practice (Haggerty, 2001) model provides a framework by which you can assess and develop your reflective practice in your own workplace and, in particular, your capstone project. The dimensions look broadly at what impacts reflective practice at the individual, group, and organizational level.

They can be used as one resource by which to measure and build your own reflective practice. The work of Joe Raelin is particularly helpful here because he has looked so carefully at the social dimensions of reflection that are so key to the workplace. The concepts of *public reflection* and *dialogue* are critical because we are all part of an "organization" (however small) and need to *communicate openly* in order that our collective thinking can be moved forward. These concepts link directly to the work of Nonaka, but provide more detail on how our practice can help to build organizational knowledge. The acid test for whether or not these efforts are successful, of course, is in the quality of thinking and decision making that comes from them. Reflection is not suggested as an activity in and of itself. Instead, it is simply a means to an end and is as accountable for results as any other work process that we adopt.

Applying the Nine Dimensions of Reflective Practice

The model presented below provides nine dimensions of reflective practice in the workplace (Haggerty, D., 2001). Each of these nine can be used individually, or in combination to assess and build reflective practice. They can be applied to your capstone by asking yourself how you or your organization exhibited these attributes.

- *Reflective Acts* – This encompasses a wide variety of written, diagrammatic, or verbal activities undertaken by the individual as a tool for reflective learning. The writing of journals is the most obvious and widely used tool.
- *Time and Resources* -- These two resource constraints are most likely to impact our ability as workers to make space for reflection in our lives and/or workspaces.
- *Learning through Others* -- The learning practices of working closely with other employees in dyads, small groups or even teams are frequently the important first step to reflectivity.
- *Access and Role* -- The ability to access others outside one's immediate learning circle (learning through others) and to assume a role that is valued by the organization by sharing and testing ideas and concepts that impact the organization.
- *Self-Disclosure* -- The process of taking the personal risk of reflecting publicly and engaging in a process of self-disclosure as a means to expression, self-evaluation, and further reflection.
- *Leadership* -- For the individual, the type of leadership skills employed in leading others to learn; for the organization, the degree to which leadership affects the learning environment for reflective practice.
- *Confidence in Action Learning* -- The confidence and manner with which the employee carries out learning that is linked to the individual's work-based or experiential learning history, learning style and research skills.
- *Culture* -- The degree to which the organizational culture supports a learning environment that allows for reflectivity.
- *Process Management* -- Process, project and quality management take on a more structured, almost mechanical aspect to learning but can play an important role as a catalyst for reflection while institutionalizing a learning process.

Each dimension, for example, could be turned into a question or series of questions for the assessment of an individual, team, organization, project, or process.

The key to making reflection work, especially online, is to have a consistent method for stitching things together and to have multiple processes throughout your project that fit the context of your own learning and leadership styles, your project, and the organizational context. In addition, it is important that you increasingly take on the role of the *facilitator of reflective practice* in order to develop self-confidence and the ability to see reflectively (or not) and to initiate actions that help that process. Your capstone should have been a good first step in doing that.

Topics of Reflection

As you have progressed through your project, each chapter in this book has hopefully provided guidance on some phase of your work. Just as importantly, I hope that you have also been supported in building the competencies needed to be successful in an experientially-based project. Some form of reflection is undoubtedly required for your capstone final report. While the first part of this chapter should get you grounded in the rationale for reflective practice, you may be wondering "Reflect on what?". Fair enough. I've listed below some of the topics that might be most appropriate for reflection. These are offered as a starting point in your reflections on your capstone learning experience, and I'm sure that you have identified others.

- **Product or Project's Value** – At some point you needed to take a leap of faith and dive down into your project, on the assumption that it would create a positive change to your organization. How did that feel at the time? How did your faith in the project's value ebb and flow over the course of the semester? Did you feel that the true value was captured? Is there anything that you would have done differently?
- **Leadership** – It may have come as a surprise to you that leadership was such a large component of a "project" designed to fulfill the requirements of a single class. How did you accept that? Did leadership awareness and skills help you to navigate your project to the finish line? Could you have used more leadership earlier? In hindsight, what leadership competencies were the most valuable? When did you feel a "breakthrough" and begin to recognize that you were really using leadership competencies that were unexpected?
- **Ethical Choices** – Any project has numerous "moments of truth" in which ethically-based choices and decisions were made. What were those moments for your project? What choices were made at those times when you felt best about doing the "right thing" when some alternative would have been less ethical?
- **Job Skills** – A large part of a capstone is "technical" in the sense that you are really applying models and frameworks from your academic program. How did your application of your training work for you? What were the highlights when you felt, "Yes, I really now see how this all applies!"?
- **Relationships** – It probably came as a surprise to you that relationships and building a network were such important parts of a capstone project, especially if you did yours alone (not team-based). How did it feel to be building this network? As you went through the semester, did the need for relationships become more or less evident? Did you manage those relationships well? How does your management of those relationships fit with your Emotional Intelligence competencies? How did your use of relational styles of achievement develop over the semester?
- **Project Management** – Did the management of this project go smoothly? How did the project management inform you about your own strengths and opportunities for improvement? Was your project management style agile enough?... too agile?... other?

- **Systems Thinking** – The *Areas of Management Practice* model provided a very structured approach to including all areas of your Business Program in an integrated way. How successful were you in tying together multiple areas of practice and in addressing your problem from a more holistic systems perspective? What were the highlights when you saw connections between areas of study that previously seemed very separate?

- **Reflective learning** – Is "Reflective Learning" something that comes easily to you? Why is that? What about the study of reflective learning (to include all experiential learning models) was the most transformative for you? How did your self-assessments of your learning style inform your self-awareness about how you learn in the workplace?

- **Career management** – How did this capstone affect your career ambitions? As a result of this capstone are you more or less interested in your specific areas of study? What new opportunities do you see coming out of this experience?

- **How have you changed** – One of the most important things to be asking yourself after having completed any learning experience is to assess and reflect on how you have changed. This may refer back to any of the topics above, of course. As an example, you may have been deeply impacted by the leadership role you assumed or about how your learning style affects your career choice. The sky is the limit!

- **Expectations vs. Reality of Experience** – Finally, we come to the capstone experience itself. I am guessing that your instructor will want to understand how this experience met your expectations. This isn't a yes/no or good/bad answer but one that deserves some reflection back to your vision of the capstone before the semester, your field notes taken during the project, and your reflections about the course's expectations of you. Thinking big picture..."How did it go?"

"Doing by Learning" activity

Final Reflection

The Final reflection may stand alone or be embedded in your final report at the discretion of your instructor. Regardless of the format, your job is to think deeply about the project, your learning and growth, and your discoveries in self-awareness. This chapter is designed to bring under one umbrella many of the tools and frameworks that are the most likely to help spark your reflections.

BIBLIOGRAPHY

Ambrose, S. & Bridges, M. & Lovett, M. & DiPietro, M., & Norman, M. (2010). <u>How Learning Works: Seven research-based principles for smart teaching</u>, San Francisco, Jossey-Bass

<u>The Change Leader's Roadmap: How to Navigate Your Organization's Transformation</u>, Linda S. Ackerman Anderson and Dean Anderson, Reading Summary retrieved from: http://catdir.loc.gov/catdir/samples/wiley031/00011969.pdf (6/13/18)

Anderson, L. & Anderson, D. (2001). <u>A Change Leader's Roadmap: How to Navigate Your Organization's Transformation</u>, San Francisco, Pfeiffer/Jossey-Bass

Andersen, L. and Andersen, D. (2001). <u>Beyond Change Management: How to Achieve Breakthrough Results Through Conscious Change Leadership</u>, San Francisco, Pfeiffer/Jossey-Bass

Berger, W. (2014). <u>A More Beautiful Question: The power of inquiry to spark breakthrough ideas</u>, New York, Bloomsbury Books

Boaz, N. & Fox, E. (2014, March). <u>Change leader, change thyself</u>. Retrieved from https://www.mckinsey.com/global-themes/leadership/change-leader-change-thyself

Boyatzis, R. and McKee, A. (2005). <u>Resonant Leadership</u>, Boston, Harvard Business School Publishing

Bransford, J. & Brown, A. & Cocking R., (2000). <u>How People Learn: Brain, Mind, Experience, and School</u>, Washington, D.C., National Academy Press

Brown, T. (2009). <u>Change by Design: how design thinking changes organizations</u>, New York, Harper Collins

Burnett, W. & Evans, D. (2016). <u>Designing your life: How to build a well-lived, joyful life</u>, New York, Borzoi/Alfred Knopf/Penguin Random House

Building Learning Power – Sorting out Resilience, Perseverance and Grit, Retrieved from: https://www.buildinglearningpower.com/2015/11/sorting-out-resilience-perseverance-and-grit/

California State University – Fullerton, Capstone description, January 2018, Retrieved from: http://catalog.fullerton.edu/preview_program.php?catoid=3&poid=992#tt4657

California State University – Monterey, Capstone description, January 2018, Retrieved from: https://csumb.edu/business/capstone

Calvin College, Capstone description. January, 2018, Retrieved from: https://calvin.edu/academics/departments-programs/business/academics/courses/

Champlain College, May 2018, Specific Examples of Good Questions, Retrieved from: file:///C:/haggerty/Business%20Capstone%20Book/Resources/Lesson_6_Module_2-Facilitating_Learning_and%20Integrated_Practices%20(1).pdf

Champlain College, May 2018, Developing Questions, Retrieved from: https://champlain.instructure.com/courses/181364/files/18701063?module_item_id=4936139

Coghlan, D. & Brannick, T. (2005). Doing Action Research in Your Own Organization, 2nd Edition, London, Sage Publications

Coghlan, D. & Droomgoole, T. & Joynt, P. & Sorensen, P. (2004). Managers Learning in Action, Routledge, New York

Colorado State University, Capstone Description, January 2018, Retrieved from: http://csuglobalhelp.knowledgeowl.com/help/what-is-the-capstone-course

Cunningham, J. (1993). Action Research and Organizational Development, Westport, CT, Praeger

Craig, D. (2009). Action Research Essentials, San Francisco, Jossey-Bass/John Wiley & Sons

Eligibility Procedures and Accreditation Standards for Business Accreditation, AACSB International – The Association to Advance Collegiate Schools of Business http://www.aacsb.edu/-/media/aacsb/docs/accreditation/standards/business-accreditation-2017-update.ashx?la=en

Duckworth, A., (2016). Grit: the power of passion and perseverance, New York, Scribner

Elizabethtown College, Capstone description, January 2018, Retrieved from: http://users.etown.edu/m/moorerc/capstone.html

Fink, D., (2003). Creating Significant Learning Experiences: an integrated approach to designing college courses, San Francisco, Jossey-Bass

Forrester, D.R. (2011). Consider: Harnessing the Power of Reflective Thinking in Your Organization, New York, Palgrave McMillan, St. Martin's Press

George, B., (2015). Discover your true north, Hoboken, NJ, John Wiley & Sons

George Mason University, Capstone description, January 2018, Retrieved from: http://business.gmu.edu/

bus498/

Gill, D. (2008). It's About Excellence: Building Ethically Health Organizations, Provo, Utah, Executive Excellence Publishing

Gill, J. & Johnson, P. (2010). Research Methods for Managers, 4th Edition, London & Thousand Oaks, CA, Sage

Haggerty, D. (2001). Doing by Learning: How reflective practice builds learning for members of work-based learning teams. Unpublished doctoral dissertation, University of Vermont

Haggerty, D. (2013a). Workplace and Reflective Learning. Champlain College. MBA 500 - Integrated Reflective Practice. Retrieved 6/4/18 from:

https://champlain.instructure.com/courses/181364/files/16156840?module_item_id=4446632

Haggerty, D. (2013b). Learning Style Inventory. Champlain College. MBA 500 - Integrated Reflective Practice. Retrieved 6/4/18 from:

https://champlain.instructure.com/courses/181364/files/16156842?module_item_id=4446633

Haggerty, D. (2013c). Emotional Intelligence I. Champlain College. MBA 500 Integrated Reflective Practice. Retrieved 6/4/18 from:

https://champlain.instructure.com/courses/181364/files/16156844?module_item_id=4446634

Haggerty, D. (2013d). An Overview of Action Learning. Champlain College, MBA 500 - Integrated Reflective Practice. Retrieved 6/4/18 from:

https://champlain.instructure.com/courses/181364/files/16156839?module_item_id=4446647

Haggerty, D. (2013e). Understanding Dialogue. Champlain College, MBA 500 - Integrated Reflective Practice. Retrieved from:

https://champlain.instructure.com/courses/181364/files/16156846?module_item_id=4446665

Haggerty, D. (2013f). Problem Solving in Action Learning. Champlain College, MBA 500 - Integrated Reflective Practice. Retrieved 6/4/18 from:

https://champlain.instructure.com/courses/181364/files/16156853?module_item_id=4446666

Haggerty, D. (2013g). Action Research Cycle. Champlain College, MBA 500 - Integrated Reflective Practice. Retrieved 6/4/18 from:

https://champlain.instructure.com/courses/181364/files/16156837?module_item_id=4446681

Haggerty, D. (2013h). Emotional Intelligence II. Champlain College, MBA 500 - Integrated Reflective Practice. Retrieved 6/4/18 from:

https://champlain.instructure.com/courses/181364/files/16156843?module_item_id=4446694

Haggerty, D. (2013i). Becoming a Reflective Practitioner. Champlain College, MBA 500 - Integrated Reflective Practice. Retrieved 6/4/18 from:

https://champlain.instructure.com/courses/181364/files/16156897?module_item_id=4446706

Haggerty, D. (2013j). <u>Heart of Change Summary</u>. Champlain College, MIT 550 – Reflective Leadership and Planned Change, Retrieved 6/4/18 from: link to be identified

Haggerty, D. (2013k). <u>Leadership Models for Change - Practices and Commitments of Exemplary Leadership</u>. Champlain College, MIT 550 – Reflective Leadership and Planned Change, Retrieved 6/4/18 from: https://champlain.instructure.com/courses/111009/pages/week-2-reading-leadership-models-for-change-by-don-haggerty?module_item_id=1460830

Haggerty, D. (2013k). <u>Leadership Models for Change – American Leadership</u>. Champlain College, MIT 550 – Reflective Leadership and Planned Change, Retrieved 6/4/18 from: https://champlain.instructure.com/courses/111009/pages/week-2-reading-leadership-models-for-change-by-don-haggerty?module_item_id=1460830

Haggerty, D. & Stone, V. (2011). <u>Champlain MBA: Development of an MBA Program Based on Integrated Reflective Practice</u> in <u>Building Learning Experiences in a Changing World</u>, New York, Springer

Hauhart, R. & Grahe, J. (2015). <u>Designing and Teaching Undergraduate Capstone Courses</u>, San Francisco, Jossey-Bass

Henscheid, J.M. & Breitmeyer, J.E. & Mercer, J.L. (2000). <u>Professing the disciplines: An analysis of senior seminars and capstone courses</u>. Columbia, S.C., National Resource Center for the First-Year Experience and Students in Transition, University of South Carolina

Hoffman, R. & Casnocha, B. (2012). <u>The Start-Up of You: Adapt to the future, invest in yourself, and transform your career</u>, New York, N.Y., Crown Publishing

Isaacs, W. (1999). <u>Dialogue and the art of thinking together: A pioneering approach to communicating in business and life</u>, New York, N.Y., Doubleday

Jarvis, P. (1999). <u>The Practitioner-Researcher: Developing Theory from Practice</u>, San Francisco, Jossey-Bass

Juntilla, H. (2013). <u>Find Your Passion: 25 Questions you Must Ask Yourself</u>, Amazon Digital Services LLC

Kahneman, D. (2011). <u>Thinking, fast and slow</u>, New York, Farrar, Straus and Giroux

Kaplan, R. & Norton, D. (1996). <u>The Balanced Scorecard: Translating Strategy into Action</u>, Boston, Harvard Business Review Press

Kelley, T. & Kelley, D. (2014). <u>Creative Confidence: Unleashing the creative potential within us all</u>, London, William Collins Books/Harper Collins

Kerka, S. (2001). <u>Capstone experiences in career and technical education</u>. Practice Application Brief No. 16, ERIC Publications

Kolb, D. (1984). <u>Experiential Learning: Experience as the Source of Learning and Development</u>, _____, FT Press

Kolb's Experiential Model Best Fit Self-Assessment (May, 2018), Wentworth Institute of Technology, Retrieved from:
https://wit.edu/lit/engage/kolb-learning-styles

Kouzes, J. & Posner, B. (2002). <u>The Leadership Challenge: How to Make Extraordinary Things Happen in Organizations,</u> San Francisco, Jossey-Bass

Kotter, J. & Cohen, D. (2002). <u>The Heart of Change: Real-Life Stories of How People Change Their Organizations,</u> Boston, Harvard Business Review Press

Lave, J., & Wenger, E. (1990). <u>Situated Learning: Legitimate Peripheral Participation.</u> Cambridge, UK: Cambridge University Press

Learned Optimism Test (Based on Seligman, M. book *Learned Optimism*) from Stanford University, https://web.stanford.edu/class/msande271/onlinetools/LearnedOpt.html

Lipman-Blumen, J. (1996). <u>Connective Leadership: managing in a connected world,</u> Oxford and New York, Oxford University Press

Marquardt, M. (1999). <u>Action Learning in Action: Transforming problems and people for world-class organizational learning,</u> Mountain View, CA, Davies-Black

Marquardt, M. (2005). <u>Leading with Questions: How leaders find the right solutions by knowing what to ask,</u> San Francisco, Jossey-Bass

Mintzberg, H. (2004), Managers not MBAs, a hard look at the soft practice of managing and management development, San Francisco, Berrett-Koehler

Mohr, B., & Cox, R. (2004, October 27). Effecting positive change through appreciative inquiry. Retrieved from
https://www.theglasers.com/uploads/2/0/3/4/20348443/ai_article.pdf

Moore, R.C., CAPSTONE COURSES, Elizabethtown College, Retrieved from:
http://users.etown.edu/m/moorerc/capstone.html

Nadella, S. (2017). <u>Hit Refresh: The Quest to Rediscover Microsoft's Soul and Imagine a Better Future for Everyone,</u> New York, HarperCollins

New England College of Business, Capstone Course Description, January 2018, retrieved from:
http://learn.necb.edu/programs/bachelor-of-science-in-business-administration/?utm_source=google&utm_medium=cpc&utm_campaign=NECB+-+BS+Business+Adminstration+-+Regional&utm_content=Business+-+Course&utm_term=%2Bbusiness%20%2Bcourse

Nonaka, I. & Takeuchi, H. (1995). The Knowledge Creating Companies: How Japanese Companies Create the Dynamics of Innovation, New York, Oxford University Press

Osterwalder, A. & Pigneur, Y. & Bernarda, G. & Smith, A. (2014). Value Proposition Design: How to create products and services customers want, Hoboken, New Jersey, John Wiley & Sons

Padget, R. & Kilgo, C. (2012). 2011 National Survey of Senior Capstone Experiences: Institutional-level data on the culminating experience. Columbia: National Resource Center for the First-Year Experience and Students in Transition, University of South Carolina

Polonsky, M. and Waller, D. (2011). Designing and Managing a Research Project: A Business Student's Guide, Los Angeles, Sage

Purdue University - Capstone description for CERTIFICATE IN ENTREPRENUERSHIP AND INNOVATION PROGRAM, January 2018, Retrieved from
https://www.purdue.edu/entr/capstone-courses/

Porter, M. (1998). Competitive Advantage: Creating and Sustaining Superior Performance, New York, Free Press

Portland State University, Capstone description, January, 2018, Retrieved from:
https://www.pdx.edu/sba/senior-capstone

Raelin, J. (2008). Work-Based Learning: Bridging knowledge and action in the workplace, San Francisco, Jossey-Bass

Raelin, J. (2003). Creating Leaderful Organizations: how to bring out leadership in everyone, San Francisco, Berrett-Koehler

Rath, Tom (2007). Strengthsfinder 2.0: Discover Your Clifton Strengths, New York, Gallup Press

Razaki, K. & Collier, E., (2011??). Ethics: the soul of a business capstone course, Journal of Academic and Business Ethics, Retrieved from:
http://www.aabri.com/manuscripts/11848.pdf , January 2018

Robson, C. (1993). Real World Research: a resource for social scientists and practitioner-researchers, Oxford, Blackwell

Ries, E. (2017). The Startup Way: How Modern Companies Use Entrepreneurial Management to Transform Culture and Drive Long-Term Growth, N.Y., Currency Publishing Group

Rothwell, W. (1999). The Action Learning Guidebook: A Real-Time Strategy for Problem Solving Training Design, and Employee Development, _____, Pfeiffer

Rotman School of Business -- Capstone description, January 2018, Retrieved from:

https://inside.rotman.utoronto.ca/admissions/2014/07/07/capstone-course-rotman/

Schein, E. (2011). Helping, how to offer, give and receive help, San Francisco, Berrett-Koehler

Schein, E. (2018). THE PROCESS OF DIALOGUE: CREATING EFFECTIVE COMMUNICATION, Retrieved from:
https://thesystemsthinker.com/the-process-of-dialogue-creating-effective-communication/ (June 2018)

Schon, D.A. (1983). The Reflective Practitioner, How Professionals Think in Action, United States of America, Basic Books, Harper Collins

Seligman, M. (2006). Learned Optimism, How to Change your Mind and your Life, _____, Vintage Paperback

Southern University, Capstone description, January 2018
https://inside.sou.edu/business/mim/core-courses/capstone-guidelines.html

Standards and Criteria for Demonstrating Excellence in BACCALAUREATE/GRADUATE DEGREE PROGRAMS, Accreditation Council for Business Schools and Programs (ACBSP)
https://c.ymcdn.com/sites/www.acbsp.org/resource/collection/EB5F486D-441E-4156-9991-00D6C3A44ED1/ACBSP_Standards_and_Criteria_-_Bacc-Grad.pdf

Stratton-Berkessel, R. (2010). Appreciative Inquiry for Collaborative Solutions: 21 Strength-Based Workshops, San Francisco, Wiley

University of Montana (Montana Tech), Capstone description, January 2018, Retrieved from:
https://www.mtech.edu/academics/clsps/bit/faculty/gordon-flanders/capstone-class-student-perspective.pdf

University of Richmond, Capstone course description, January 2018

University of Scranton, Capstone description, January, 2018, Retrieved from:
http://www.scranton.edu/academics/ksom/mba/cornerstone-capstone.shtml

University of Washington, Capstone description, January 2018, Retrieved from:
https://www.uwb.edu/babusiness/bothellcampus/program

Vogt, E. & Brown, J. & Isaacs, D. (2003). THE ART OF POWERFUL QUESTIONS: Catalyzing Insight, Innovation, and Action, San Francisco, Whole Systems Publishing, Mill Valley, CA

Watkins, J. & Mohr, B. & Kelly R. (2011). Appreciative Inquiry: change at the speed of imagination, San Francisco, Pfeiffer/Wiley

Watkins, K. and Marsick, V. Informal and Incidental Learning, Manufacturing Leadership Certificate Program: Coaching and Developing People, (May 2018), Retrieved from:
https://niagaracollegemlcp.files.wordpress.com/2008/10/cdp-article-informal-incidental-learning.pdf

Marsick, V. & Watkins, K. (1990). <u>Informal and Incidental Learning in the Workplace</u>. London and New York: Routledge

Whitney, D., Trosten-Bloom, A., Cooperrider, D. & Kaplin, B. (2013). <u>Encyclopedia of Positive Questions 2<u>nd</u> Edition</u>, Brunswick, OH, Crown Custom Publishing,

Whitney, D., Trosten-Bloom, A., & Rader, K., (2010). <u>Appreciative Leadership, focus on what works to drive winning performance and build a thriving organization</u>, New York, Corporation for Positive Change, McGraw-Hill

Zikmund, W. (2003). <u>Business Research Methods</u>, Mason, Ohio, South-Western/Cengage Learning

INDEX

ABOUT THE AUTHOR

Don Haggerty is a leading educator in the field of experiential learning. With decades of experience as both a business professional and professor, he has spent his life bridging the worlds of business and education.

Don was educated at Providence College (B.A., Economics) and the University of Vermont where he received his Masters of Arts in Teaching (MAT), Masters in Business Administration (MBA) and Doctorate in Educational Leadership (Ed.D.). Previous to joining higher education, Don enjoyed a highly successful and decades-long career in corporate business development, entrepreneurial ventures and consulting. His expertise includes economic modeling, business strategy and new business creation. For the past twenty years he has served as a professor, program developer and administrative leader in experientially-based business education at both the undergraduate and graduate levels.

At Champlain College where he currently teaches, Don created and launched an experientially-based MBA and then oversaw the development of ten graduate programs built around his own project-based and Action Learning inspired model, called *Integrated-Reflective-Practice*. His most recent work has been teaching the areas of Business Strategy, Managing Innovation and Technology, Leadership and Business Capstone projects (undergraduate and MBA). He is also working with the college's online programs to include greater use of experiential learning models.

He is the co-author of *Leading My Department*, republished as *Leadership's Broken Link* that connects employees at all levels with their organization's strategy through collaborative learning.

Contact him at drdon@mydoingbylearning.com

CPSIA information can be obtained
at www.ICGtesting.com
Printed in the USA
LVHW070907291222
736051LV00008B/270

9 781735 769028